# The Roof of [illegible]

***Wether Fell, Dodd Fell, Gr[illegible] Knoutberry Hill, Lunds Fell, Great Shunner Fell, Lovely Seat***

## A portrait of Wensleydale's Two Thousand Foot Fells

**Stuart Lennie**

HAYLOFT

First published 2005

Hayloft Publishing Ltd, Kirkby Stephen,
Cumbria, CA17 4DJ

tel: (017683) 42300
fax. (017683) 41568
e-mail: books@hayloft.org.uk
web: www.hayloft.org.uk



ISBN 1 904524 30 3

A catalogue record for this book is available
from the British Library



Produced, printed and bound in the EU
Photographs by Peter Koronka

*For Pamela*

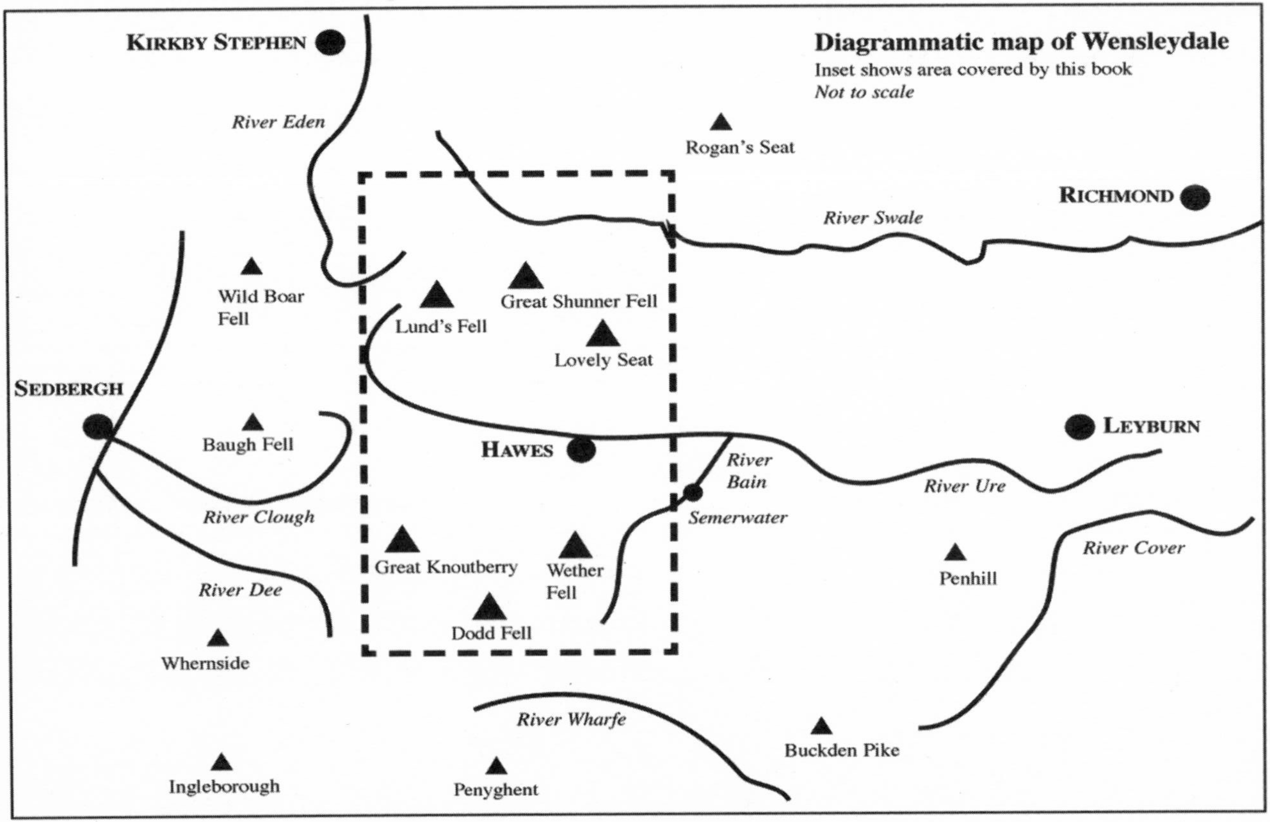
Diagrammatic map of Wensleydale
Inset shows area covered by this book
Not to scale
KIRKBY STEPHEN
River Eden
Rogan's Seat
RICHMOND
River Swale
Wild Boar Fell
Lund's Fell
Great Shunner Fell
Lovely Seat
SEDBERGH
Baugh Fell
HAWES
River Bain
LEYBURN
River Ure
Semerwater
River Clough
River Cover
Great Knoutberry
Wether Fell
Penhill
River Dee
Dodd Fell
Whernside
River Wharfe
Buckden Pike
Ingleborough
Penyghent

*Dalesfolk live in the valleys but look to the hills - the hills that are always there, symbols of stability and permanence, not changing noticeably within a long human life. On the hills, quiet and healing solitude can be found after the exertion of the climb.*

Arthur Raistrick

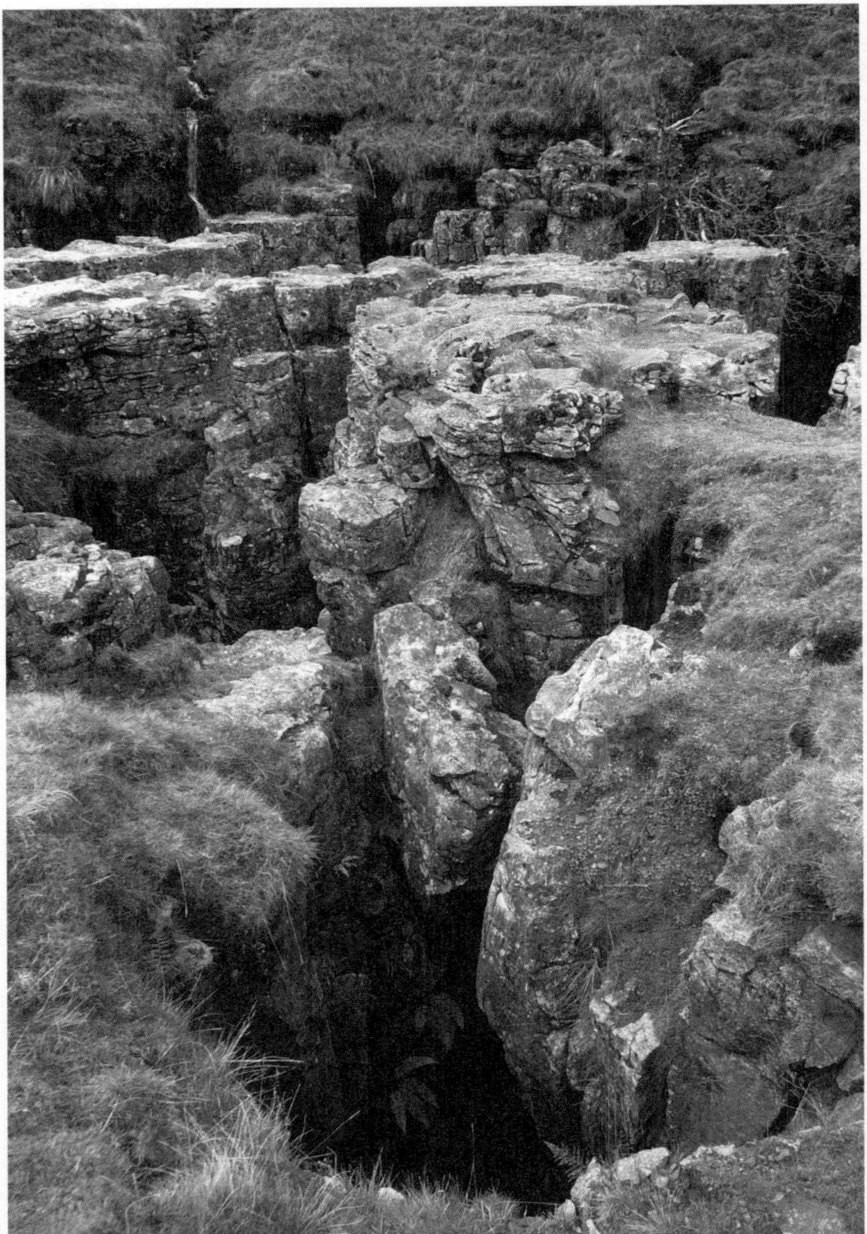

*These potholes can be seen on either side of the Buttertubs pass linking Wensleydale with Swaledale.*

## CONTENTS

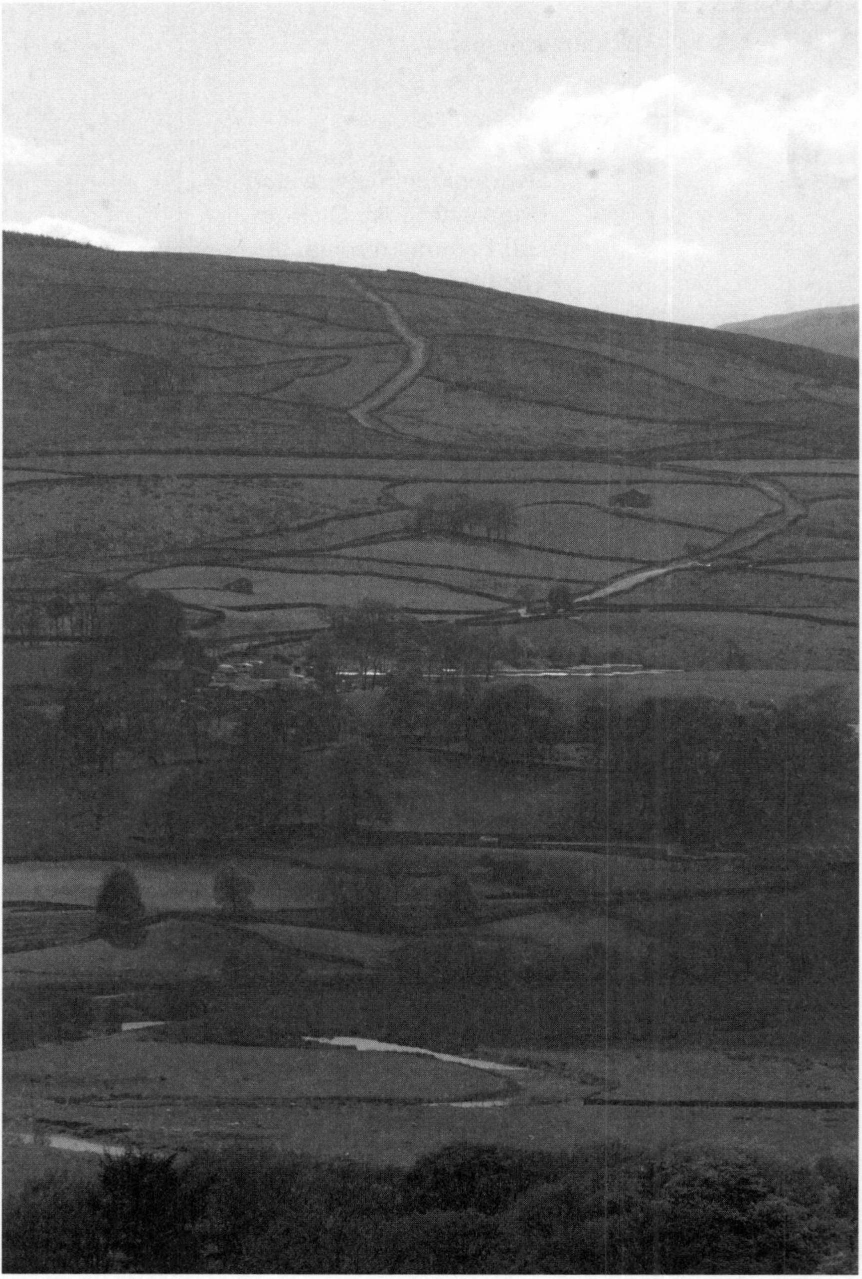

*The Cam Road coming down off Ten End to join the B6255. It is often used as an alternative Pennine Way in severe weather.*

## Acknowledgments

First of all I would like to record my most sincere thanks to my wife Pam for her constructive advice, unfailing support and encouragement when enthusiasm started to flag; above all for her energy and patience in word processing the seemingly endless re-drafts of the manuscript.

Secondly I wish to acknowledge two books which were instrumental in germinating the seeds of my own effort; to Phil Clayton's *On High Yorkshire Hills, Exploring the Two Thousand Footers*; to Harry Rée and Carolyn Forbes's *The Three Peaks of Yorkshire*; between them these two works encouraged me in the belief that the six 2,000 foot fells of upper Wensleydale deserved their own full length portraits.

Grateful thanks go to Ron Stirk of the Yorkshire and Humberside Brass Band Association (YHBBA) for answering my questions and providing me with much useful historical information on the Hardraw Scar Brass Band (and Choral) Contest. Thanks also to Mark Thompson, innkeeper of the Green Dragon Inn at Hardraw, who put me in touch with Colin Wormald, my first contact at the YHBBA - to Colin thanks for undertaking to forward my enquiries to Ron Stirk.

Thanks also go to Brian Peacock for reading the section on hill farming in the Yorkshire Dales and offering helpful advice; to Mark Owens, landlord of the Moorcock Inn, Garsdale Head, for bringing to my attention the role of the Moorcock in the 1910 accident on the Settle-Carlisle railway line and for providing me with a copy of a poem written in 1911 in which the Moorcock's role in the aftermath of the accident is set out in verse; to Mason Scarr for clarifying the nature of the Maize Holes near Sedbusk.

I would also like to express my thanks to Geoff Garrett of the Yorkshire Dales National Park Authority for supplying me with information on the National Park Authority's woodland policy and strategy and to Matt Neale also of the Yorkshire Dales National Park Authority for explaining the Environmentally Sensitive Area Scheme (ESA) and the Countryside Stewardship Scheme (CSS).

Finally I wish to extend my thanks to the Friends of the Dales Countryside Museum in Hawes for allowing me to use the Local Studies room at the museum on a regular basis and to the staff at the museum for dealing with all my enquiries; thanks also go to the staff at Darlington and Northallerton Public Libraries for answering my questions and providing specific books on request.

# PREFACE

It may come as something of a surprise to many people to find that there are some 25 fells over 2,000 feet within the current boundaries of Yorkshire. Of these, six are shared with Cumbria and one with Lancashire. Of the remaining eighteen, which are totally in Yorkshire, Wensleydale has six - Great Shunner Fell 2,349 feet, Lovely Seat 2,215, Great Knoutberry Hill 2,205, Dodd Fell 2,192, Lunds Fell (Sails) 2,185, and Wether Fell (Drumaldrace) 2,014. Collectively these six Pennine giants make up the greater part of the landscape at the head of Wensleydale effectively creating impressive, but not impenetrable, mountain barriers to the north and south of the River Ure. Hawes, the major settlement of the upper dale, and its satellite villages - Gayle, Burtersett, Appersett, Hardraw and Sedbusk - are virtually cradled by these majestic fells. There is no question that, individually, these fells are an impressive size. They are even more commanding, when taken collectively, with their combined bulk covering an immense area of approximately seventy square miles of meadows, rough pasture, rocky escarpments and high rolling moors. Colin Speakman (*Walking in the Yorkshire Dales*, Robert Hale, 1982) speaks affectionately of the area's '...epic landscapes, the brooding northern wilderness with more than a hint of Scandinavia, a Sibelius landscape where human influence and the softer aspects of human experience seem at best, only momentary.'

I first gazed on upper Wensleydale's fells some 28 years ago whilst staying in the village of Askrigg. From that day to this their impressive height, bulk and intriguing names have left an indelible impression on me. Tramping hundreds of miles across them, over the years, has brought me immeasurable pleasure. Their landscape features, the use to which their land has been put, the vagaries of the weather to be encountered on them, their radiant light and their strong sense of history, have never failed to interest and attract me. To walk their extensive summits, to view their stark beauty under a mantle of snow, or to feel the mystery that pervades them when wrapped in low cloud, are experiences not easily erased from the memory. Having lived for the past eight years surrounded by these hills, this circle of grandeur with their ever changing seasonal colours and moods, my affection for them remains undimmed more than a quarter of a century later.

The idea for this book arose out of the desire to do for Wensleydale's 2,000 foot fells what Harry Rée and Caroline Forbes did for Penyghent, Ingleborough and Whernside some 22 years ago, (*The Three Peaks of Yorkshire*, Wildwood House Ltd., 1983); that is to compile individual portraits of all six of Wensleydale's 2,000 foot fells and by so doing create a feeling for the landscape of the dale head. Following an introductory chapter, which describes Wensleydale in its Yorkshire Dales setting, each successive chapter deals with one of the fells. Within each chapter there are a number of subsections covering a wide range of features such as Hardraw Force, the Cam High Road, the Galloway Gate, the Settle-Carlisle railway, Lady Anne Clifford's Way and the Buttertubs. Topics such as the geology of the area, the weather, quarrying, farming, dry stone walls, woodlands, lime kilns, flora and fauna are also covered. Running through the book, underlying these features and topics, are a number of salient themes namely: the natural landscape, land use, man-made features, communications, history and the scenic or picturesque.

Let us explore these themes a little more beginning with landscape. Whilst geological movements of the rocks beneath the earth's surface have shaped the Wensleydale landscape over millions of years, changes to its surface features have been wrought, in relatively more recent times, through glacial erosion, frost, wind and rain. You should never underestimate the scale of changes in the landscape brought about by severe weather in the high Pennines. Many natural topographical and geological features on these hills will engage our interest such as the waterfalls at Hardraw Force with its single, almost 100 foot drop, the fascinating potholes called the Buttertubs, not to mention becks, tarns, escarpments and the rocks beneath our feet.

Farming has been the major use of the land in these hills for thousands of years. The evidence of its activities is to be seen all around us with cattle grazing the lower pastures, the high fells dotted with sheep and the lush green meadows of early summer turned golden after the hay has been cut. For hundreds of years the farmer has shared the land with the miner and the quarryman - the legacy of their activities highlighted in the scores of old mine workings and abandoned stone quarries. Other man-made features which are to be found across this landscape are lime kilns, barns too many to count, miles of dry stone walls and the tunnels and viaducts of the Settle-Carlisle railway.

In the natural world various plants and flowers have colonised the fells by their ability to adapt to the variety of microclimates found there, such as peat bogs, heather moorlands and rough pasture. Out on the fells you encounter the wildlife of the area. Here you are in the habitat of such birds as the golden plover one of several waders now frequenting the area. A buzzard will not be an uncommon sight, along with many other birds of prey. On the heather moors you are in the company of the grouse. On the hillsides and in the meadowland you may see a fox or a deer, the latter having strayed from its cover in the mixed woodland and conifer plantations which, today, spread across the fellsides in a number of dales.

Communications across these fells have been, and still are, many and varied. One of the routes you can follow is that of the Roman soldiers who marched along the Cam High Road over Wether Fell to and from their fort at Bainbridge. Then there are the tracks and pathways used by the packmen and their horses as they wended their way across the fells hoping to sell their household goods and trinkets in the villages and outlying farms. You can either walk the Galloway Gate over Great Knoutberry Hill, a track once used by drovers to drive cattle from Scotland to English markets, or travel by train along the fell's flanks on the Settle-Carlisle railway. You may marvel at the fortitude of Lady Anne Clifford and her retinue who, in the seventeenth century, travelled from Skipton along the slopes of Lunds Fell to her castles in the Eden Valley. You can follow in the footsteps of thousands of Pennine Way walkers as this long distance footpath reaches its highest point, since leaving Edale, on Great Shunner Fell. If you wish, you can motor over the famous Buttertubs pass which links Wensleydale with Swaledale.

Amongst these hills, with the evidence scattered all around us across the landscape, it is impossible to escape a sense of history. I try to conjure up images of Roman surveyors measuring the routes of their roads and of Norsemen, the forerunners of today's hill farmers, settling on the bleak uplands. I reflect upon the ruins of a former inn which once served to slake the thirst of weary travellers whilst not forgetting, in more recent times, those whose vision led to the creation of the Pennine Way in the years following the Second World War. I try to imagine miners and quarrymen trudging across the moors in appalling weather to work in the most difficult conditions imaginable. I look at crumbling farmhouses, disused lime kilns and broken down walls and try to picture the people who lived in, worked and built them.

Wensleydale's high hills provide many examples of great beauty. Perhaps one of the most stunning is the incredible clarity of the light which floods the landscape on certain days of the year. In such light everything from a single rock, a lone tree on an escarpment, to an isolated barn in a field is sharply etched. In such light wander up on to any of these fell summits and experience the magnificence of the distant vistas. In this vast landscape clouds cast their individual shadows on the sunny slopes creating contrasting patterns of light and dark. In early spring the dying snowdrifts behind the dry stone walls create a speckled white, green and brown canvas of great beauty. The walls themselves produce rectangular patterns on the hillsides and more irregular patterns in meadows, near farms and close to villages. Many famous painters and poets, such as Turner and Wordsworth, who visited the area in the nineteenth century, were inspired by the beauty and dramatic nature of the landscape.

Where a particular topic is common to all the six fells a note in the text will draw the reader's attention to this fact. For example farming is covered under Wether Fell but applies equally to the other five fells. As this book is exclusively concerned with the high fells of upper Wensleydale, villages are excluded from the narrative except for geographical orientation. The reader who requires further information on the villages referred to in the text will be able to draw on the numerous books available on Wensleydale.

As a postscript I have included the basic details of the route for a walk over each of the six 2,000 foot fells described in this book. In addition I have included a comprehensive motor tour which goes through the heart of upper Wensleydale enabling the motorist to identify the six fells and appreciate the grandeur of the landscape in which they are located.

Finally, to those who aspire to their summits, go horse-riding along their flanks, hang-glide above them on the thermals, motor over them to enjoy the scenery or just take pleasure in looking up at them, I hope my portraits of these six 2,000 foot fells will, whilst being informative, convey my affection and enthusiasm for the magnificent landscape of upper Wensleydale.

## 1
## WENSLEYDALE

Wensleydale lies in the Yorkshire Dales which are part of the Pennine chain of hills that form the backbone of England. Before discussing the Dales, in particular Wensleydale, it is worth relating the curious way in which the name Pennines came about. As Tom Stephenson has so interestingly related Charles Bertram, a young Danish professor of English, claimed in 1747 that he had discovered a fourteenth century chronicle which described Britain in Roman times[1]. Britain, it stated, was divided into two equal parts by a mountain chain called the Penine Alps (Alps Penina). This 'information' then led two geologists, Coneybeare and Phillips, to adopt the name 'Pennine' in 1822. Although the chronicle was later proved to be a forgery on Bertram's part, many of his invented names of Roman sites, such as Pennines, found their way onto Ordnance Survey maps where they are still to be found today. Stephenson believes that Bertram may have taken the cue for his forged chronicle from Camden's *Britannica* (Bishop Edmund Gibson's 1695 translation) in which he states that: 'The north part of the country (Staffordshire) rises gently into small hills; which begin here, and like the Apennine in Italy, run through the middle of England in one continued ridge, rising higher and higher, as far as Scotland...'

Before describing Wensleydale, with its six 2,000 foot fells, I will take a brief look at the Yorkshire Dales as a region. Lying to the east of the Lake District, north of the Peak District and south of Hadrian's Wall, the Yorkshire Dales National Park covers 680 square miles of the Pennines taking in the districts of Craven and Richmondshire plus a slice of eastern Cumbria. It is an area of high grassy hills, or fells as they are more commonly called, rising to over 2,000 feet. They are intersected by a number of valleys or dales through which the main rivers of the area run and where most of the scattered population of the area lives. It is pastoral country par excellence. Dales hills, in most cases, are ridges consisting of great rolling moors rather than distinct mountain peaks as found in the Lake District. Tom Stephenson captures this landscape perfectly when he says: '...here are great stretches of shaggy moorland; long ridges dipping sharply to the valleys and gently swelling heights repeating themselves with minor variations into the blue distance; vast solitudes with no sounds other than of running water, or of the wind swishing in the heather or rustling in the grass.'

The hills increase in height gradually from east to west with the highest and most distinctive, in terms of their size and shape, to be found in the north west corner of the national park. Here you find the famous Three Peaks - Whernside, the highest fell in the Yorkshire Dales at 2,415 feet, Ingleborough with its flat top at 2,372 feet and Penyghent at 2,277 feet, so like a crouching lion. A little to the north of this group lies Great Shunner Fell, one of our six portraits, whilst further south and east lie other great fells such as Buckden Pike, Fountains Fell and Great Whernside.

The great valleys of the Yorkshire Dales - Wensleydale, Swaledale, Dentdale, Ribblesdale, Wharfedale and Nidderdale - have many attractive features. Their rivers rise on the great moorland ridges which separate the valleys from one another. The copious rainfall which falls on these hills produces mountain torrents which, in a number of places, tumble over rocky escarpments creating magnificent waterfalls like the famous Hardraw Force and Aysgarth Falls in Wensleydale. Both these waterfalls are notable attractions being visited by many thousands of visitors every year. The hills of the Yorkshire Dales are primarily limestone with a millstone grit capping. The Yorkshire Dales has a more open aspect, with its rolling moors, than the more closed in landscape of the Lake District with its soaring peaks. It is a country of spectacular vistas laid out on a vast, grand scale.

Most dales rise to about the 1,000 foot contour at their heads. They are thinly populated but do have villages and hamlets dotted throughout their length. The four main features of a dale - river, meadowland, pasture and fell - are interdependent in the annual cycle of the farm. Some dales have a market town, bustling with activity, such as Hawes in Wensleydale and Grassington in Wharfedale. Apart from the main roads through the dales there are innumerable paths, connecting neighbouring villages or leading up on to the fell tops. Much wider green roads trail across the fells - many are old drove roads of yesteryear. There could be no more appropriate indigenous symbol of the Yorkshire Dales National Park than the sheep which are to be found everywhere across the landscape. Ruins, such as Castle Bolton in Wensleydale and Bolton Abbey in Wharfedale, give a real sense of history to the area. Dry stone walls reaching up the fellsides signify the hand of man in organising the landscape.

To do justice to the Yorkshire Dales countryside it should be seen in all its moods throughout all the seasons of the year. The exceptional clarity of the light, particularly in winter, picks out the features of this sweeping landscape. In summer when a large storm cloud, over Great Shunner Fell, moves away allowing the sun to flood it with dazzling light the contrast is dramatic. The fell tops are natural viewpoints for watching cloud shadows chase each other across the rolling moors. Around Malham the sun on the crags of the Great Scar Limestone creates a luminescence of rare beauty. This is expansive country with a genuine feeling of space and freedom. From the summits of the fells one can appreciate the stunning views to far horizons and the softer, more intimate association of village, river and meadowland of the dales themselves. For some people, artists have captured the beauty of this landscape successfully on canvas, but for others it can only be really appreciated and understood if it is seen in all its stark beauty.

In looking at Wensleydale in a little more detail it would appear that the origin of its name is a mixture of Old English and Old Norse. The first two parts ‘Waendel’ and ‘leah’ are Old English; the last part ‘dalr’ is Old Norse. Waendel is a personal name, leah means a woodland clearing and dalr a valley. Thus Wensleydale translates into Waendel’s woodland clearing in the valley. The dale itself is wide and spacious rather than winding. As its fells are set back, leaving a broad valley floor, it does not have an enclosed feeling like some of the other more narrow dales such as Swaledale and Garsdale. The hills on the southern side of the dale do not form a continuous barrier as a number of side dales such as Coverdale, Bishopdale and Sleddale, all give access to Wharfedale. Further west Widdale connects Wensleydale with Ribblesdale. Whilst the northern side of the dale gives the appearance of a slightly more forbidding mountain barrier, even here there are a number of high level routes, such as the Buttertubs pass, which gives access to Swaledale. There are good links east-west through Wensleydale as the A684 runs along the valley floor linking the A1 to the M6.

Wensleydale is a pleasing valley with its appealing stone-built villages and its lush green meadows. Part of its attractiveness lies in the shape of its fells with their scars and terraces. Wensleydale’s fells all have their own identifiable features such as their height, profile, escarpments and particular location in the dale. For instance, to the traveller in upper Wensleydale, Addleborough, above Askrigg, looks like a rocky citadel and is visible from a number of different points in the dale. Penhill is another prominent fell its bulk being clearly visible from the A1 trunk road. When driving up Wensleydale it is relatively easy to orientate one's position by reference to the shape of the nearest fell. In reflecting on their shapes it should not be forgotten that, whilst these hills are millions of years old, man's footsteps on them are merely thousands. Wensleydale's hills, like hills elsewhere, existed long before man introduced his activities of sheep farming and mining to their slopes. From time immemorial Wensleydale's hills were nameless until man came to settle and to name features in the landscape, including the fells.

Wensleydale's fells also perform their role as boundaries to neighbouring dales. This is summed up in the proverb: 'There is a hill against a dale, all Wensleydale over.' With the exception of Addleborough, which achieves prominence by being detached from its neighbours, most of Wensleydale's summits, in particular the six over 2,000 feet, are usually the highest point on a long ridge. Drumaldrace, for example, is the highest point on Wether Fell, just as Great Knoutberry Hill is the name given to the highest point on the long ridge of Widdale Fell. Dodd Fell is the highest point on an impressive arc of high ground stretching from Drumaldrace round to Ten End. On the north side of the dale Sails is the most southerly of a number of summits on a long ridge which is part of Abottside Common. Great Shunner Fell and Lovely Seat are the highest points on a long ridge of high moorland which divides Wensleydale from Swaledale.

Finally what all Wensleydale's 2,000 foot fells have in common is the fact that their summits lie some distance back from the broad valley. For the visitor to upper Wensleydale the highest fells are merely content to project their flanks into the heart of the upper dale whilst adopting a shyer, more retiring position for their summits. For the walker who plans to climb them it all adds to a sense of mystery and anticipation.

# 2
# WETHER FELL

I begin the portrait of upper Wensleydale's 2,000 foot fells with Wether Fell whose bulk dominates the market town of Hawes. After a description of the fell's topography I examine the stone quarrying industry in Wensleydale based on the Burtersett stone quarries. Attention then focuses on hill farming across the area following which the chapter concludes with a journey along the Cam High Road which crosses the fell.

## *Overlooking Semerwater*

IF Wether Fell took its name from the term for a castrated ram it is highly appropriate today with the fell being home to thousands of sheep. Interestingly there are other animal names on the fell such as Marsett Cow Pasture and Bear Head. The latter is just to the east of the summit and is more than likely to have evolved from the name Bardale, a valley which cuts into the southerly flank of Wether Fell, than any allusion to the shape of the fell resembling a bear's head.[1] At the upper end of Bardale there is a Bardale Head marked on the map, just below a small plantation of the same name, not far from the Hawes to Kettlewell road. However you should consider the fact that the ancient settlers saw similarities between natural features and animal forms. After all not much more than a century ago Bogg thought Wether Fell looked like a lion when viewed from the Buttertubs Pass.[2]

Drumaldrace is the name given to the highest point on Wether Fell. It is an archaic sounding name, stretching back into the mists of time, which makes it difficult to be precise regarding its origin. In the case of the first part of the name, 'drum', it could, as Robert Gambles has suggested, be the Celtic word for a wooded ridge common to a number of Scottish place names. The second element of the name, 'aldrace', may derive from a personal name as in drumalban which means Alban's ridge.[3] Hence Drumaldrace would mean 'Aldrace's ridge'.

~ ~ ~ ~ ~ ~ ~ ~ ~ ~ ~ ~ ~

Drumaldrace, the actual summit of Wether Fell, lies just over a mile from the junction of the Cam High Road (otherwise known as the Roman Road) with the Hawes to Kettlewell road (Beggarman's Road). By

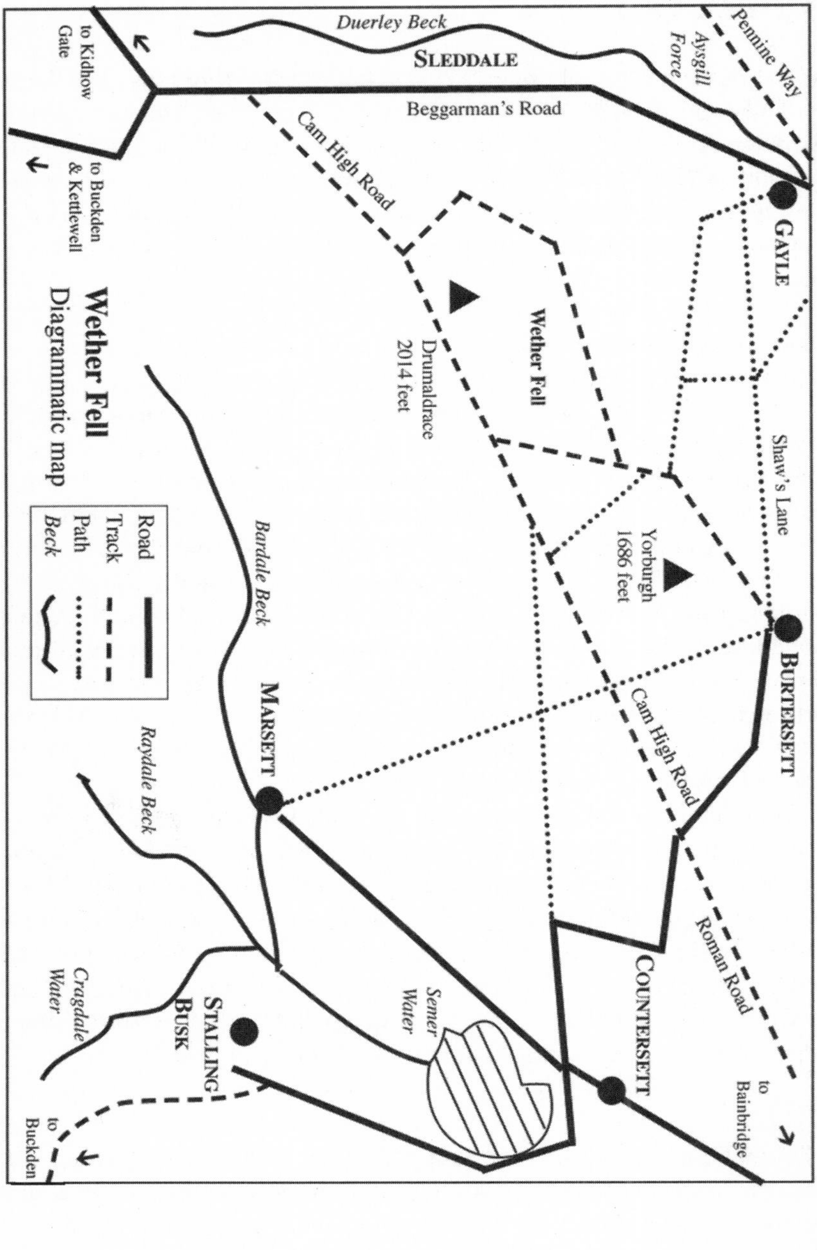
Wether Fell
Diagrammatic map
Road
Track
Path
Beck
Duerley Beck
SLEDDALE
Beggarman's Road
Pennine Way
Aysgill Force
Cam High Road
to Kidhow Gate
to Buckden & Kettlewell
GAYLE
Wether Fell
Drumaldrace 2014 feet
Shaw's Lane
Yorburgh 1686 feet
BURTERSETT
Cam High Road
Bardale Beck
MARSETT
Raydale Beck
Roman Road
COUNTERSETT
to Bainbridge
Semer Water
STALLING BUSK
Cragdale Water
to Buckden

climbing a mere 250 feet from this junction Drumaldrace can be reached by following the wall, on the northern side of the track, to its end and then by climbing up a grassy slope to the small cairn marking the summit. Bardale Beck is Wether Fell's southern boundary flowing some distance below the level of the Cam High Road. Before it enters Semerwater, Wensleydale's only lake, Bardale Beck, becomes Marsett Beck and is joined by Raydale Beck and Cragdale Water after which it becomes Crooks Beck. The valleys of Bardale, Raydale and Cragdale bite deeply into the great moorland mass of Fleet Moss and Cragdale Moor which lie to the south of Wether Fell. To the west of the fell Duerley Beck, which in its lower reaches becomes Gayle Beck, flows down Sleddale which separates Wether Fell from its neighbour Dodd Fell. To the northeast of Drumaldrace lies Wether Fell's outlying summit, the buttress of Yorburgh (1,686 feet), sitting proudly above the village of Burtersett. The northern flank of Wether Fell consists of a series of stepped terraces sloping down to Hawes. From Askrigg Wether Fell has the appearance, according to Marie Hartley and Joan Ingilby, of the limbs and loins of a beast stretched full length filling the horizon.[4] They also say that it often looks blue-black in October under lowering skies.

Peat hags are much in evidence across the wild, extensive plateau of millstone grit which makes up the summit of Wether Fell. Here are large tussocks of mat grass and bilberry interspersed with deep pools of water. Near to the actual summit cairn is a small area of grassland which provides a pleasant contrast to the boggy nature of the rest of the summit terrain. Here amongst the peat hags live the red grouse and the peewit. Above Hawes the deeply indented watercourses frequently carry considerable volumes of water, often over waterfalls, into the river Ure below. For the observer in Hawes the many streams, which burst out of this hillside after heavy rain, can look like the silvery trails of giant snails!

From the summit of Drumaldrace you can look out over a panorama of fells including Ingleborough to the southwest viewed over Dodd Fell's shoulder. To the north Great Shunner Fell and Lovely Seat fill the horizon. To the northeast lie the sweeping moors rolling away towards Swaledale. To the north west Sails can be seen as can Wild Boar Fell with its long flat top. Westwards the Howgills fill the middle distance whilst on the horizon the line of the Lake District fells can be clearly seen. To the east lie Addlebrough and Pen Hill whilst to the southeast our view is filled with the high moorland of the Stake Allotments cradling Semerwater and separating Wensleydale from Wharfedale.

Standing on the summit of Wether Fell it is worth reflecting on the fact that, below your feet, close to the village of Burtersett, a number of men made a living in the nineteenth century digging stone out of the hillside to provide flags for building and roofing. In the section below the quarries' production processes are examined along with their transport methods, working conditions and the rise and fall of the industry.

### *Burtersett Stone Quarries*

QUARRYING for stone to meet local needs has had a long tradition in upper Wensleydale. Sandstone, otherwise known as gritstone, was first quarried for building stone as far back as the sixteenth century; in a few places it was also quarried for millstones. For many villages the most accessible supply of stone was the nearest outcrop of rock. The remains of many, small, hand-worked quarries now grassed over, have taken on the appearance of natural topographical features and are to be found all across the Dales. Just to the east of Burtersett there were two main quarries. The oldest one, not surprisingly, was called the Old Quarry. The other one, the closest to the village, was called Seavy Quarry and probably took its name from an old enclosure in the vicinity called Seavy Fold, (seave is a dialect work for rush so seavy means 'overgrown with rushes'). Of two other workings close to Burtersett, but of less importance, one at Three Hole Brigstone on Raygill Beck offered only poor quality stone and was not in production long. The other at Braygill was worked until 1905 when work ceased due to the poor quality of the stone being quarried.

Wether Fell flags come from the sandstone beds, above Burtersett, which lie at approximately 1,150 feet above sea level. The fifteen foot sandstone bed sat on a shale deposit overlain by a thin coal seam. Unfortunately only the lower six feet of the sandstone bed was of workable quality. The stone, which makes up the flags, is a soft, coarse-grained rock, dark greyish in colour. It is found in layers and can be eased out and cut reasonably easily. In the Yorkshire Dales, whilst thick flags have been traditionally used for paving and flooring, thinner ones have been used for roofing, particularly on farm houses. It has also been the practice to use sandstone flags for footpaths such as those linking Hawes with Hardraw, Gayle and Sedbusk. Such stone was also in demand for lintels, mullions and quoins on Georgian houses. Sandstone flags were also used in wall building and in the construction of cottages, barns and water tanks for farms.

Unlike most quarries those at Burtersett did not have open faces. Instead tunnels were driven into the stone beds from the hillsides to form large underground levels approaching 500 yards long. Many secondary workings led off in a number of directions. As the stone was extracted from the level the 'pillar and post' method of mine support was used which involved stone pillars being left in strategic places to avert roof collapse. Large amounts of waste stone known as 'back fill' were also used for roof support. In many cases timber props, known as puncheons, were used as supplementary support as were lengths of old iron rails. Unfortunately many lateral workings were prone to collapse from time to time, particularly in wide sections, where supports had not been provided. Such collapses, over the years, have made inaccessible large areas of the old workings.

At the Old Quarry a level was driven south into the hillside for 400 yards with the best stone being cut at the far end. Quarry levels were given names such as Red Gate, Savey, Fancy End and Peacock. Seavy Quarry had a tramway serving dressing floors, sheds, loading bays and cranes. The site even had a blacksmith's shop where tools were sharpened and horses shod. The quarrymen were organised in teams of six which then split into two groups of three face workers. The huge (up to six inch thick) slabs of stone were dragged from inside the level by horse drawn, four wheeled bogies, operating on a 27.5 inch narrow gauge railway. The quarried stone was then rough dressed in a shed at the mouth of the tunnel which led into the quarry level.

The two Burtersett quarries sent a large proportion of their dressed stone to the rapidly growing towns of East Lancashire such as Burnley and Colne. Some stone went to London where it is believed it was used for manhole covers over the entrances to the city's sewers. Quarry owners, Richard and Tom Metcalfe, each had two, especially made, four wheeled wagons drawn by two horses. The wagons, alternating between three to four loads per day, carried five to six tons of dressed stone down the hill from Burtersett to Hawes station. The four wagons delivered approximately 80 tons of stone every day to Hawes Station during periods of high demand. Each wagon was fitted with special breaks to prevent it careering downhill out of control.

Stone quarrying was a very hard, demanding industry for the men who worked in it. It was an underground existence with the only light coming from candles which were bought by the hundredweight at a time from Candle Willie of Hawes. The quarrymen worked a six day week with only two days recognised as holidays, Good Friday and a day at Christmas. There is a story of the quarryman who, in his eighteen years working at the quarries, had only one week's holiday during the whole of that time - his honeymoon. Many quarrymen struggled to bring up large families on less than one pound per week. The top wage for a skilled worker, either underground or on the surface, was 18s for a six day week starting at 7.30am and finishing at 4pm with a half-hour dinner break. Many only received 16s per week. It is said that one worker, who walked from Hardraw to Burtersett and back every day, never earned more than 16s per week in the whole of his working life at the quarries.

As a major industry, stone quarrying only developed in the 1870s, with the two quarries at Burtersett flourishing post-1878 after the railway reached Hawes. In fact the coming of the railway triggered a boom in stone quarrying in Wensleydale as its potential for exporting the stone was realised. In 1882 the two quarries produced 6,180 tons of stone rising to 13,000 in 1886. Other quarries in the area produced a further 3,000 tons in the same year. Having reached its peak in the 1880s the industry continued to thrive into the 1890s before demand fell at the end of the century. In the early years of the twentieth century both quarries experienced financial difficulties but managed to survive the fall in demand. Further difficulties followed for both owners in the First World War with one of them going bankrupt in 1916. The industry struggled on through the post-war years but by the early 1930s it had ceased production due to oscillating markets in a period of economic depression.

In 1879 the Midland Company carried 2,664 tons of stone from Hawes Station. When production from the Burtersett Quarries peaked in 1889 stone quarrying had become a major local industry able to sell beyond its local markets. In the same year with six quarries in production in upper Wensleydale the Midland line carried over 13,000 tons of stone. In 1890 15,000 tons of stone left Hawes Station, most of it carried by the Midland Company, with the North East Company carrying the remainder. The railway undoubtedly gave momentum to the stone industry and helped it flourish. As employment prospects for local people improved they did not have to leave the area in search of work.

In 1882 upwards of 80 men worked in upper Wensleydale's quarries rising to 200 in 1890. By that time Burtersett quarries alone employed around 100 men. To meet the needs of the increased work force the two owners built cottages in Burtersett for some quarrymen. Other workers who came from Hawes, Hardraw, Gayle and Sedbusk often walked to work carrying their food for the day. The stone dressers, for example, took their tea in bottles for their midday break. The quarrymen from Sedbusk crossed the Ure by the railway bridge which has long since been demolished. Other workers came from neighbouring Swaledale to work at the quarries.

With the decline of the stone industry a number of unemployed men from the Burtersett quarries found work as farm labourers and in some cases even became farmers. Others found work on the railways or in road construction. A number moved to Lancashire or the West Riding of Yorkshire to find work in the textile mills and coal mines. Some took their chance and emigrated to the USA.

As few business documents survived the closure, or at least have not been found, the detailed history of the quarries at Burtersett is not known or at best is uncertain. A few remains of buildings and entrances to the levels are all that are left of Burtersett quarries today. Gone are the dressing sheds, loading bays and the blacksmith's shop. The quarry faces are now grassed over and are covered with trees and other vegetation. However from what remains you can get a reasonable impression of the original extent of the quarries and the methods used in extracting the stone. The two large spoil heaps on the hillside, just to the east of Burtersett village, identify the sites of the main workings which are approached by access tracks from the road to Countersett. The spoil heaps are not numerous as much of the spoil dug out was used as 'backfill' to support the roofs of the levels.

~ ~ ~ ~ ~ ~ ~ ~ ~ ~ ~ ~ ~

In addition to the quarrying of stone, Wether Fell was quarried for chert and mined for coal and lead. On Flint Hill, not far from the summit of Wether Fell, there is a disused quarry once important for the chert that was quarried there. Chert is an unusual rock consisting of large lumps of flinty stone embedded in limestone. Often the grey chert contrasts sharply with the brownish limestone. It consists of a very fine crystalline variety of quartz somewhat like flint. Whereas limestone scratches, chert does not. It is a very hard rock and is mainly used in the ceramics industry but also for grinding. Not surprisingly early man used it for hand axes and scrapers (although flint was generally regarded as superior).

Coal was mined on Wether Fell at Storth Colliery alongside Beggarman's Road where, at approximately 1,400 feet above sea level, its remains can still be seen.

The hills around Hawes are pock marked by the working of 't'owd man' which is the collective name for generations of lead miners. The evidence on the ground for lead mining however is probably more definitive in Swaledale than in Wensleydale. There was some lead mining on the lower, north eastern slopes of Wether Fell above Burtersett but, more significantly, it was mined on the south eastern slopes of Lovely Seat as you will discover later.

Whilst quarrymen dug the stone from deep inside Wether Fell, farmers worked its surface. In the section below, after a brief history of farming in the Dales, the work of the hill farmer is considered throughout the four seasons of the year.

### *Hill farming through the seasons*

HILL farming and its methods are common right across the hill country of the Yorkshire Dales including upper Wensleydale. Before I take a season by season look at the landscape and the work of the area's hill farmers, it is helpful and instructive to take a brief journey back in time to see how farming commenced and then developed in the Yorkshire Dales. Bronze Age tribes first settled in the Yorkshire Dales some 3,000- 4,000 years ago, clearing the trees that then blanketed the hills, cultivating the land and creating what passed for the first definitive farms in the area. Following further clearance of woodland from the fells the Brigantes, the successors of the earlier Bronze Age tribes, were able to improve crop production particularly cereals. At about the same time they also acquired the technique of smelting iron.

By the time the Romans appeared in the Dales the Iron Age Brigantes were well established in their farms and villages. The vast amount of stone, to be found lying upon the hillsides, was useful, not only for building huts for habitation but also for defensive ramparts. It has been contended that the Romans never completely achieved total domination over the Brigantes. It is also claimed that the Romans contributed little to farming skills and practices in the four centuries of their occupation of these islands. As a result the Brigantes, being farming folk, supplied the Roman army with horses, hides, meat, corn, tallow, wool and timber, possibly as tithes. It is likely that the Roman fort at Bainbridge fell into this supply chain. It is conceivable that the Brigantian hill farmers prospered under the Romans owing to improving economic conditions.

Following the Roman departure from Britain in the early fifth century new invaders, the Angles and Saxons, came to these shores settling down to farm in the eastern counties of England before migrating westwards to areas such as the Yorkshire Dales. Here they cleared the land of trees, boulders and stones in order to grow corn. Like their predecessors they found much of the land in the valley bottoms virtually uncultivable as it was undrained and marshy. Most of the early cultivation carried out by the Angles and Saxons was done on terraces formed by ploughing narrow strips of land, about a furlong in length, on the hillsides. Known as lynchets these strips were ploughed by pairs of oxen.

As time went by the additional dwellings built around individual farms became the forerunners of village development. The village was usually centred around a green area which was at first fenced to keep the livestock safe. Some historians have taken the view that the Anglo-Saxons made more of a contribution to English farming than any other ethnic invaders of these shores. In addition they also contributed many words, to what would later become the English language. Place names ending with -ley, -ton and -ing are also derived from Anglo-Saxon.

In the ninth century the Danes arrived from Scandinavia. After capturing large tracts of territory they settled in eastern England including many Dales valleys. Like all their predecessors the Danes, as settlers, continued to carry out the tasks of forest clearance, cultivation of the land and care of their livestock. Life was not easy as they had to contend with robbers, as well as threats to their livestock from wolves and foxes and damage to their crops by deer and wild pigs.

The second group of invaders to come to these shores from Scandinavia were the Norsemen in the tenth century. They came to England having already established themselves in Iceland, Ireland and Scotland. In Cumbria and Yorkshire they found most valley bottom land was too wet to be farmed or had already been settled. To some extent this forced them to settle on the higher fells around the dale heads, such as upper Wensleydale, in a landscape not too dissimilar to their own Norwegian homeland. Here the Norsemen were able to run their sheep on the hills above the forest cover. Theirs was a transhumance farming regime involving summer pasturing for their cattle on the high moors and winter feeding in the valleys on hay grown in the lower meadows. Norse settlements in the dale heads were little more than scattered farms located on the slopes and terraces of the fells. A typical Norse settlement usually comprised a father and his sons living in one or two buildings. Such settlements were surrounded by meadow land for grazing, adequate arable land for grain and folds not too far away for their sheep. To prevent, where possible, their sheep flocks on the high fells getting mixed up, Norse settlements were never established too close to one another.

As time went by the Norsemen turned from merely shepherding to rearing cows and pigs and caring for meadow and pasture land. Norse settlements usually varied in size from a simple farm to a hamlet. Of those in the former Forest of Wensleydale, Burtersett and Appersett eventually became villages. Down the years Norse words gradually filtered into the English language such as *bekkr* (beck), *gil* (ravine), *thwaite* (clearing), *saetr* (an upland pasture), *sett* (the place where stock were kept in summer pastures) and many more. This prompted Peter Gunn to say that: 'it was these pastoralist Norsemen who have perhaps left the greatest racial impression on life in the Yorkshire Dales in the customs and especially the language.'[5]

Following the Norman conquest in 1066, life in England was harsh and brutal. Firstly, because of resistance to his conquest, William carried out a 'harrying of the north' by which he laid waste to huge tracts of land including the Yorkshire Dales. Both people and animals were indiscriminately slaughtered, farms set on fire and ploughs destroyed. Following the harrying, Dales farmers found it difficult to make a living from the poor soil, the destruction of their infrastructure, new forest laws leading to restrictions on grazing and crop damage by wild animals particularly the deer. The Scots took advantage of the disruption to conduct raids into the Dales. In addition to these tribulations, Dales farmers also had to pay dues in either goods or services to the new feudal lords. As the church increased its land holdings and grazing rights, dues also had to be paid to the bishop. From the Normans right through to the Tudors, despite all the difficulties, village development continued apace, coupled with the first moves towards the enclosure of the land.

By the seventeenth century, as the forest laws were slowly relaxed, there was a significant population increase with more people acquiring rights to land. Although farms were generally small, they all had a dwelling place and grazing rights in the lower pastures or up on the fells. Between 1780 and 1840 the large open fields, the open spaces around villages and the open fells came under a national policy of enclosure. Large enclosures were established on the fellsides by building dry stone walls which created a patterned landscape. The right to enclose land was based on the number of cattle and sheep that were already part of the holding.

By the nineteenth century two industries dominated the Dales countryside - farming and lead mining - with many men actively involved in both. The first half of the twentieth century gave Dales farmers a steady livelihood with the exception of the 1930s slump. New breeds of cattle and sheep led to higher levels of production on farms. The First and Second World Wars were significant factors in increased production through the policy of national self-sufficiency. Of equal significance was the mechanisation of farms which relieved much arduous labour.

In the latter part of the twentieth century Dales farmers had to come to terms with the economics and politics of the global economy. Merely to keep their heads above water they had to increase their efficiency and productivity. Since the agricultural peak at the end of the eighteenth century, thousands of workers have left the land. The Dales farmer has also had to contend with the perennial problem of isolation in his job and all the health and psychological problems this can lead to. The 1950s and 1960s saw milk production increased by using bulls of proven quality to produce good milking cows through artificial insemination. In addition large mature bulls from continental breeds were introduced into the beef industry. In the 1980s and 1990s the Dales farmer struggled through the BSE crisis with its attendant collapse in exports and new government regulations and restrictions. During the 1990s the sheep trade collapsed for various economic and political reasons. Finally in 2001 foot and mouth disease (FMD) hit farming with a vengeance leaving farmers to cope with the fallout of severe restrictions, funeral pyres, restocking and compensation. In addition there was an overwhelming sadness across the Dales - a real 'silence of the lambs'.

On a normal everyday basis the main aim of a Dales hill farmer is to rear young cattle and sheep to sell. He sells his older cows after they have given birth to a number of calves. He also collects a wool crop every year from his sheep even though, more often than not, the value of it is hardly worth the effort put in at shearing time. Dales farms have increased in size over the years for two main reasons. Firstly farmers were able to acquire miners' small holdings as a result of the lead industry's demise. Secondly farmers consolidated their holdings by acquiring their neighbour's land when it came on the market. Unlike his nineteenth century predecessor, today's hill farmer does not have extra income from weaving or mining.

The high fells of the Dales, including those of Wensleydale, provide for pastoral farming with arable farming being confined to the wider eastern ends of the valleys with their lower altitude and warmer climate. The hill farmer is stoical in his battle against Dales' weather with its high rainfall, blizzards, frost and minimal sunshine. Some aspects of a hill farmer's way of life change little. For example, if you visit any upper Wensleydale farm you will see the age old scene of a farmyard full of chickens, ducks, geese and sheepdogs. On the other hand, like many hill farmers, the upper Wensleydale farmer has had to diversify into sidelines like running bed and breakfast, jam production or a host of other small industries.

The blunt truth is that hill farming economics are such that looking after cattle and sheep, in an often inhospitable environment, cannot possibly compete with such activities in gentler, more benign lowland areas. Farming in upper Wensleydale, like other parts of the high Dales, remains viable only through government and EU subsidies and grants which go some way towards off setting the natural disadvantages. At the time of writing even these subsidies are likely to be radically altered between now and 2012 through changes to the Common Agricultural Policy. Society, through the tax system, pays hill farmers and encourages them to stay in farming. Their demise would see hill farming disappear making the Dales landscape, as we know it, unrecognisable within a few years. For example, the loss of sheep would see the fells and dales revert to forest and scrub vegetation. Hill farming is a vital part of the environment for both the Dales population and for tourism.

~ ~ ~ ~ ~ ~ ~ ~ ~ ~ ~ ~ ~ ~

I will now look at the upper Wensleydale farmer through the four seasons of the year and the variety of tasks that he has to perform. Upper Wensleydale is a pastoral area of permanent grass and rough grazing devoted to rearing sheep and cattle. The farmer aims to produce young stock, both sheep and cattle, to send to lower farms for fattening. Our journey will take us from the meadowland at the foot of the fells, through the pastureland of the lower slopes and up on to the high fell tops. We start our journey in the autumn when a new cycle of life begins on the farm with the ewes being put to the tup. For a hill farmer a vital part of his assets and the source of his livelihood is the sheep flock. Flocks can number up to 1,000 breeding ewes which give a good annual crop of lambs. On upper Wensleydale's high fells two main hill breeds predominate - the Swaledale and the Dalesbred. Both were originally bred from the Scottish Blackface, itself an evolved moorland sheep.

The Swaledale was first bred in the northern half of the Dales but is now to be found more widely. Although not accepted as a major breed until the first part of the twentieth century, it is now generally accepted to be the pre-eminent breed in the Dales. It is also one of Britain's toughest breeds of sheep along with the Herdwick (Lake District) and the Rough Fell (Howgills). There are now thought to be 1,500,000 Swaledales in the British Isles. The breed's popularity amongst hill farmers is due to its mobility across rough terrain, its body strength and its tendency not to roam far from its heaf. It is also able to live on poor quality grazing land in the harsh environment of the high fells. Of medium size it has a thick, long, coarse fleece which, as well as keeping out the rain, ensures the animal is warm in winter conditions of frost and snow. Farmers welcome the Swaledale's good mothering instincts in coping with the birth of twin lambs and then rearing them successfully. The Swaledale has a black or dark grey face with lighter patches, a whitish-grey nose and mottled black legs. Both rams and ewes have strong, curving horns.

First bred around 1930, the Dalesbred, whilst being similar to the Swaledale is distinguished from it by the very characteristic clear white patches on either side of its nose. Like the Swaledale both tups and ewes have strong horns. The Dalesbred is now regarded as a breed in its own right and is found more widely in the southern half of the Dales.

In September, as the summer ends, the sheep are rounded up. Ewes which have lambed for four years are sold to lowland farms where they produce lambs for a further one or two years. In November the ewes are gathered from across the fells for the annual tupping. Such major gathers are complex, exhausting operations calling upon all the resources of the farm. Whereas, a generation or so ago, a number of full time shepherds would have been involved, today it is usually the work of father and son using quad bikes, dogs and the assistance of neighbours when time allows. It is worth pointing out that the four-wheeled quad bike has revolutionised life on the hill farm (along with the round bale which has improved fodder quality). Not only is the quad bike an essential tool in sheep gathering, it is also used for carrying, in its attached trailers, fodder, building materials or even a sick ewe. A gather may last all day especially if the weather is poor. Sheep folds, pens and gates are used to manage the sheep numbers.

At tupping time there is always a demand for quality tups and a good Swaledale tup can fetch many thousands of pounds at auction.

Swaledale ewes are first put to the tup as two year old shearlings with approximately 60 ewes serviced by one tup. The tups and the ewes are usually gathered in the pastures on the lower slopes of the high fells. This enables the farmer to more easily make his visits to the tup to add fresh ruddle and to be close at hand when the lambs are born. It is usually the case that, the higher the altitude of the farm, the later the ewes are put to the tup, in the hope that better weather will have arrived by the time the lambs are born.

Both Swaledale and Dalesbred ewes, after some three to four years on the fells, are in prime condition for crossing. It is usual practice to put the ewes of mountain and moorland breeds with lowland rams to produce ewes with a higher birth rate, a better milk yield and better fleshed lambs. A very popular crossing has been the Swaledale or Dalesbred ewe with the lowland Blue-Faced Leicester to produce the Mule or Grey Face. Today it is the most popular crossbreed in the Dales. Teeswaters and Wensleydales are also crossed with the Swaledale or Dalesbred to produce Masham lambs. During the autumn, after lambs have been separated from their mothers, the ewes are returned to the upland pastures. Young ewes, known as gimmers, are mainly kept to replenish the stock but there are sales to lowland farmers who prefer to breed from strong hill ewes. Male lambs, known as wethers, are sold to lowland farms for fattening.

During November, as grass growth in the meadows and pastures slows, the cattle are taken inside for the duration of the winter. The sheep on the other hand remain on the fell. In previous generations cattle were housed in stone barns (or fieldhouses as they were often called) which were often located in the fields some distance from the farmhouse. Food was stored in the hayloft above the stalls where the animals were kept. Today it is a vastly different scene, for the cattle spend the winter months inside large specially built sheds which, in most cases, are near to the farmhouse. The cattle are fed in these sheds and exercised in the adjoining yard. Large modern sheds also have space for storing hay and housing the farm's machinery.

~ ~ ~ ~ ~ ~ ~ ~ ~ ~ ~ ~ ~ ~

Despite the fact that the cows are inside during the winter months (where they are fed on hay, silage, barley and concentrates) milking still has to go on 365 days of the year. Another job that you are likely to see being performed on the hill farm towards the end of the year is muck-spreading. From December onwards, when the ground is frozen, the accumulated muck from the castle shed and barns is regularly spread on the lower pastures to encourage early spring grass growth. During the winter months farmers can also often be seen doing repair jobs on collapsed and damaged walls.

During the winter months the ewes need additional feed especially as lambing time approaches. In addition to extra hay, which is strewn about the fellsides for them, they are given supplements, such as sheep nuts, to increase the chances of a trouble-free lambing and a ready supply of milk. One difficult decision the hill farmer has to make, is deciding when to fetch the sheep down off the fells when bad weather threatens such as the blanketing of the moorland grass by heavy snow. The problem is that a few light snowflakes in the valley may be a raging snowstorm on the tops. As Pennine farms are often 1000 feet above sea level, the land is exposed to severe weather conditions. Farmers often have to dig sheep out of deep drifts with the help of dogs. Fortunately sheep can survive being buried in snow for up to two weeks, sometimes even longer, partly due to the warmth of their thick fleeces. Ewes trapped under a snowdrift may resort to eating their wool but the great danger comes form suffocation. For most hill farmers however rain, rather than snow, is their worst fear. Ewes have an intense dislike of wet ground and, if forced to lie for any length of time on it they get cold, uncomfortable and unhappy; lambs born to such ewes are likely to be weak or even still-born.

~ ~ ~ ~ ~ ~ ~ ~ ~ ~ ~ ~ ~

For many people spring in upper Wensleydale means lambs gambolling in the meadows, the cries of peewits and curlews wheeling and swooping across the slopes of the fells and the cheerful yellow of the daffodil, primrose and celandine. In the high fell country spring often arrives late making it invariably a season of short duration. Gone are the dark days of winter - ahead lies the traditional Pennine summer - often damp, cool, and cloudy. Spring itself can be unpredictable with pleasant warm sunny days alternating with periods of rain. Snow is not uncommon in April; however, during March and April 2003, upper Wensleydale experienced more than six weeks of sunny, dry weather with the sunniest March for over 40 years. Usually by May the trees and bushes are in leaf but, in some years, snow may still be seen in certain north facing hollows by the observant fell watcher.

Lambing time is a busy season. As you walk through the rich meadows surrounding the farms you will encounter ewes waiting to give birth and those that already have. We all love to see the newborn lambs taking their first tentative steps in life. For the ewes it is their longest separation from the moors on which they spend most of the year. Generally speaking lambing in upper Wensleydale begins in earnest in March and lasts through April into early May.

After about twelve weeks of their five month pregnancy most flocks are scanned by a skilled technician to ascertain how many lambs a ewe is carrying. It is common practice to dose the ewes to prevent the disease of liver fluke spreading throughout the flock. During lambing time the farmer has to draw on the skills he has acquired over many lambing seasons. Such skills are crucial to the welfare of both the pregnant ewes and the newborn lambs. In particular those ewes likely to have multiple births need to be carefully monitored. It is vital that the ewe comes through the pregnancy fit and well so she can provide milk for her lambs. There is always the need for the farmer to assist with difficult births such as when the lamb's legs get stuck back. Also high on the farmer's list of priorities are the two year old shearlings who are lambing for the first time. Here the problem may be rejection of the lamb by its mother and then bottle feeding might be required. The farmer will normally make a number of daily visits to his flock plus an occasional night visit. Such is the farmer's lot at lambing time.

The farmer also has to guard against lambs falling ill with peritonitis, hyperthermia, pneumonia and even hunger. Cold and damp weather is the worst combination for new born lambs as they can sometimes die when their wet coat causes a loss of body heat. Lambs found in this condition are often taken into the farm house kitchen to be revived. For the comfort of their pregnant ewes during lambing, many farmers tend to set aside a large barn or shed as a 'maternity ward'. Here the farmer can keep a close watch on the ewes and of course on the new born lambs. For up to four weeks new born lambs are protected by their mother's milk following which they are dosed against worms. To allow the cattle to be released from their winter quarters, to graze the lower pastures and to allow the hay crop to grow, the ewes and their lambs need to be returned to the fell fairly rapidly. Lambs by this time are generally robust and healthy enough to cope with the weather and the rough terrain. By this stage all the lambs are marked and tagged.

Apart from lambing, there are a number of other spring jobs for the hill farmer to take care of. One such job is to continue to provide fodder for his cattle which are kept inside the cattle shed until roughly the middle of May by which time the grass has had a chance to grow. Calvings by caesarean section will normally require the vet to be called in. Spreading the accumulated winter muck from the cattle shed also keeps the farmer busy. Finally the pastures need to be cleared of moles to prevent the soil that they displace contaminating the grassland on which the cattle will graze.

~ ~ ~ ~ ~ ~ ~ ~ ~ ~ ~ ~ ~ ~

By June the meadows of upper Wensleydale are covered with buttercups, marsh marigolds and other wild flowers. Swallows, meadow pipits, skylarks and wheatears are in the sky. Visitors abound in search of scenery - the high fells with their grazing sheep, dry stone walls, rushing becks, tumbling waterfalls, picturesque cottages, flower strewn meadows and ruminating cows. For the hill farmer the pressures of lambing are over along with calving, muck spreading and winter feeding. As the lambs grow some of the males are castrated and become wethers. Sheep are prone to a number of illnesses and diseases such as moss illness, ticks, liver fluke, bracken poisoning and tetanus. Most of these are now treated by vaccination, drenching and good management, usually when they are a few months old. By law sheep are now routinely dipped in a tub, for at least one minute, to rid their fleeces of such parasites as lice, ticks and flies. Sheep scab is caused by a tiny mite which attaches itself to the skin. Although dormant in summer, it is highly active when the weather turns cold, causing a high level of irritation to the sheep. The result is that, because of the intense scratching by the sheep, their fleeces become ragged and almost peel off. The damaged skin can lead to weight loss and in some cases death.

For clipping in June and into July the sheep on the fell are gathered together. Each ewe produces about four pounds of wool. Shearing of the ewes is done by the farmer with the help of his neighbours and increasingly a team of outside contractors. Electric shears are normally used but hand shearing has not entirely disappeared. The farmer's family are heavily involved in channelling the sheep to the shearers and wrapping the fleeces. Wet conditions pose real problems for the shearers as damp fleeces are not only more difficult to clip but also are prone to rot. It is worth pointing out that dirty fleeces lose their market value. An added problem is that clipping often coincides with hay time when manpower resources are stretched. After shearing a sheep is identified by a paint mark and an ear tag to facilitate strays being returned to their rightful owner.

It is important to realise that the sheep on the fells have an instinctive sense of place and rarely stray from their home patch. On unenclosed moorland this saves on shepherding and, whilst not completely eliminating, reduces the spread of disease. Such sheep are known as 'heafed' or 'hefted' sheep. These grazing rights, on the common land of the upper fell slopes such as those of upper Wensleydale, are distributed amongst local farmers. This process of allocation of grazing rights is known as 'stinting'. Each stint relates to the total number of sheep which can be grazed on the common pastures without causing problems through overgrazing. Each farmer's stints mean that he has the right to a set allocation of 'gaits' which he has paid for. It is generally acknowledged that one gait represents the right to graze one sheep and four gaits the right to graze one cow. To prevent the land deteriorating over the years farmers need to adhere to their stinting arrangements by not putting more stock on the grazing areas than their gaits permit. In times gone by shepherds were employed to monitor the stock, for all the farmers sharing a pasture, to ensure that the gaits were correctly used. Nowadays shepherds are rarely employed, farmers tending to shepherd their own stock.

By July haymaking is one of the commonest sights to be seen in the meadows and pastures on the lower slopes of Wensleydale's high fells. The weather is the key to the operation with fine, settled weather essential to the drying of the strewn hay as rain can easily affect its quality. It is imperative that next year's fodder for the stock be harvested at all costs. For earlier generations hay time was a long, tedious process often lasting all summer. Nowadays cutting, whisking and baling are all mechanised. However, in the race to beat the weather, the farmer's family and neighbours all pull together to get the job done.

Some farms in upper Wensleydale come under the Environmentally Sensitive Area (ESA) Scheme and the Countryside Stewardship Scheme (CSS). These schemes are aimed at encouraging less intensive farming by, amongst other things, reducing stock numbers, delaying cutting of the first hay crop until early July and limiting the use of artificial fertilisers. Such practices help to protect both the flora and ground nesting birds of the upper dale. Payments are made to farmers partaking in such schemes.

A common sight, on the lower slopes of the high Wensleydale fells, is the large, heavy, black and white Friesian dairy cow which has replaced the Shorthorn. Its introduction to the fell country has been so successful that virtually all local dairy herds now comprise this breed. Each cow has the potential to produce three gallons of milk or more per day. Today the size of milking herds in upper Wensleydale is upwards of forty cows which live on the most lush pastures of the farm during the summer. Tankers from Hawes creamery (Wensleydale Dairy Products Limited) can be seen visiting the farms, where milking is a commitment, every single day of the year.

Some upper Wensleydale hill farmers keep young beef suckler cattle during the spring and summer. Such young cattle can be put out to graze on the high limestone pastures while still leaving sufficient grass for the sheep. Hill farmers breed this resilient young stock for sale to eastern lowland farms to be fattened. A beef calf born in the spring is suckled through the summer months, weaned and sold in the autumn. As most cows calve in the spring the bull's service is only required for a short summer duration. As a consequence farmers tend to hire rather than buy.

In the late 1930s, prior to the dominance of the Friesian cow, sixty per cent of all milk came from the shorthorn breed which was developed in 1800. By 1900 a beef shorthorn had been bred for meat and likewise a Northern dairy shorthorn for milk. The latter has reportedly been grazing the upland pastures of upper Wensleydale for many years.

Farmers with their tractors and quad bikes are one of the main users of the next subject, the Cam High Road, the main track across the flanks of Wether Fell. The focus falls first on the road network based on the Roman fort at Bainbridge. This is followed by a description of the route taken by the Cam High Road across the fell. We note the skills of the Roman engineers in road construction and identify the types of travellers who have used the road over the centuries. Attention is drawn to the severe weather likely to be encountered on its higher stretches and to the condition of the road surface today. The section concludes with a look at other paths, roads and tracks on the fell which join the Cam High Road.

### *The Cam High Road*

THE Wensleydale village of Bainbridge is situated just to the north of the prominent rocky fell of Addlebrough. The village lies on the confluence of England's shortest river, the Bain, with the river Ure, Wensleydale's main river. On low Brough Hill, just opposite the village green, stood the Roman fort of Virosidum. The fort, whose name means High Seat, was constructed by Governor Julius Agricola (77-85 AD) along with others at Ilkley and Elslack and was designed to keep the local Celtic tribes under control. Its timber buildings were fortified by earthen banks and ditches. Such forts, along with an integrated network of roads to supply the legions stationed in them, were used to keep the Dales under firm military control. Most Roman forts lay on the fringes of the Dales area with only Bainbridge itself and the fort at Reeth well within. Periodic rebuilding and modification of these forts was required to control Brigantian uprisings. In 155AD, after one such uprising amongst the latter, Virosidum was rebuilt with a stone wall beyond its clay ramparts. It is thought that, as a result of being over run and then destroyed by native tribes, the fort may well have been abandoned in 275AD before being rebuilt at the beginning of the fourth century. Today some depressions, where the buildings once were, can be seen on the top of the hill. However all the stone work has been removed, probably for building purposes in and around the village and for dry stone walling.

The fort of Virosidum stood at the strategic junction of two roads. One went to Olicanum (modern Ilkley) taking as its route the winding course over the high moorland of the Stake Allotments between Wensleydale and Wharfedale. Today this route makes for a very pleasant walk between the village of Stalling Busk, above Semerwater, and the hamlet of Cray above Buckden. The other route, known as the Roman Road and the Cam High Road (the Ordnance Survey use both names), went via Ingleton to Ribchester in Lancashire. Its route on leaving Bainbridge follows the Countersett road for a short while before leaving it for a broad, green walled track. This track climbs over Bainbridge High Pasture, the slopes of Crag and Common Allotments, before reaching its maximum height of 1,900 feet just below Drumaldrace the highest point on the boggy plateau of Wether Fell. After passing the summit, the Cam High Road swings southwest to join and then follow the line of Beggarman's Road. After nearly half a mile it heads off to the right, along the slopes of Dodd Fell, following the metalled access road to Kidhow Gate and the isolated settlement of Cam Houses. A short distance beyond the latter, the road forks, with the Cam High Road descending to Gearstones to join the metalled road from Hawes to Ingleton (B6255) whilst the other branch goes to Horton-in-Ribblesdale. At Chapel-le-Dale, just beyond Ribblehead, the Cam High Road leaves the B6255 to follow the minor metalled lane below Twistleton Scars before becoming lost in the farmland around Ingleton.

The skills of the Roman engineers gave the road a good surface and made it wide enough to fulfil its main purpose of transporting troops and their supplies across the Pennines. Although experts are sure the Romans actually built the road it is quite possible that, for surveying purposes, they followed the line of what was an existing ancient British track.

The Cam High Road has been in constant use ever since Roman times and has seen many changes throughout the centuries. From being an ancient Dales route going back into the mists of time, it is today a pleasant road for farmers, horse riders and walkers. One of the main uses to which the Cam High Road has been put since Roman times is cattle droving. It was the main drove road from Askrigg via Bainbridge, Wether Fell, Cam Fell and Ribblehead, to Ingleton and beyond. It also served as a route for the packmen selling their wares across the Dales .

In 1751 a major development in the history of the Cam High Road occurred. In that year Alexander Fothergill of Carr End, on the northern side of Semerwater, surveyed a route for the proposed Richmond to Lancaster turnpike using the alignment of the existing Cam High Road from Bainbridge to Gearstones. This high level route was essential as the valleys tended to be boggy. Although a more direct road from Richmond via Askrigg and Bainbridge to Ribblehead had, up to that time, never been made, within less than half a century it had succumbed to the dangerous winter conditions encountered on Fleet Moss. In 1795 a new road was opened avoiding the high ground above Hawes by going through Widdale the route now followed by the B6255. This new route softened the gradients considerably as well as reducing the maximum height reached by some 500 feet, a significant reduction when considering winter travel.

Conditions in winter on Fleet Moss where the Cam High Road joins Beggarman's Road are not to be lightly dismissed. Farmers using this high level moorland route know very well the extreme conditions to be encountered in the mist, driving rain and blizzards on these isolated heights. Stories are told of how they provided for themselves against the elements by hiding food rations in dry stone walls for emergencies. The huge snow drifts, which block the road, make it easy to see why the Cam High Road was abandoned as the principal route between Richmond and Lancaster in favour of the present valley road. Even in an average winter snow drifts linger up here long after the snow has melted in the valley and from most of the slopes of the surrounding fells.

Even without the severe weather conditions, travel on eighteenth century roads during the decades of 'turnpike trust mania', was anything but pleasant with holes and ruts commonplace. Travellers who did venture along them were not impressed. For example, in 1793, the Honourable John Byng having travelled along the Cam High Road over Wether Fell complained that it was one of the longest, steepest and stoniest roads in Great Britain. However, despite the poor condition of its surface and severe weather likely to be encountered, the Cam High Road was still shown on an 1816 map as an alternative route to the one through Widdale.

Today the Cam High Road, from its junction with the Countersett Road to Green Side high on Wether Fell, is walled on both sides except for two stretches on its northern side. The first of these stretches occurs just below the summit of Drumaldrace, the other just before reaching Beggarman's Road. The Cam High Road is generally some twenty feet wide with a strong central foundation (or agger) about twelve to fifteen feet in width. From the Countersett junction to just below Drumaldrace the Cam High Road follows a completely straight alignment for some three miles. The only kink in this alignment occurs at New Bridge where a stone culvert takes Horton Gill under the road. The Cam High Road stands out both on the ground and on the map by its bold straight line. Today it consists of some stony sections, parts where the surface of hard-packed earth often turns to mud, stretches of exposed limestone pavement and sections bordered by grass verges. The surface condition of the road is sadly often one of deep water-filled ruts caused by tractors, four wheel drive vehicles and motor cycles.

As it cuts its unswerving way over Wether Fell the Cam High Road is one of the most stirring sights in the dale, particularly when viewed from the northern side of the valley on the road between Askrigg and Sedbusk. Equally to walk up it is an exhilarating experience. After climbing up Bainbridge High Pasture and past the scars of Crag there is a sudden glimpse of the valley of Raydale on the left. Later, with greater height having been achieved, the lake of Semerwater comes into view. This is followed, all the way to the summit of the road, by a succession of majestic views of the surrounding fells and moors. As you climb and turn to look back you see laid out before you the beautiful panorama of upper Wensleydale from Bainbridge to Askrigg and beyond. Where the Cam

High Road meets Beggarman's Road the view down Sleddale is one to savour.

The Anglo Saxons, superstitious and suspicious of things Roman, reputedly gave the Cam High Road the name Devil's Highway and would, it was said, only use it by day. Locally the road is known as the Devil's Causeway linking it with a local legend in which a giant and the Devil settled a dispute by hurling boulders at each other from either side of nearby Raydale. The Devil's Stone now lies on the western slopes of Addleborough, whilst that of the giant, the Carlow Stone, sits on the beach at the northeastern end of Semerwater.

~ ~ ~ ~ ~ ~ ~ ~ ~ ~ ~ ~ ~

There are a number of paths linking the Cam High Road to the surrounding villages. One such is the track out of Burtersett over High Pasture and past the buttress of Yorburgh. After passing an old shack and a large gap in a wall, a sunken path veers up hill to the right, climbing gently before dividing into two. The left hand path arrows straight to the Cam High Road. The right hand one by contrast, takes a more circuitous route by swinging along the north face of Wether Fell, just below Drumaldrace the fell's highest point, before finally curving left to join the Cam High Road. Back at the shack and the gap in the wall a faint path bears left of the main sunken track to descend a slight depression before rising gently to join the Cam High Road from where paths to Countersett, Semerwater and Marsett can be followed. Another path out of Burtersett crosses High Rigg before joining the Cam High Road just below Green Scar. Last, but not least, two paths leave the village of Gayle to then merge and join the main track up from Burtersett.

The Cam High Road meets Beggarman's Road, Yorkshire's highest motorised road, high on the bleak uplands of Fleet Moss. This road climbs 1,000 feet out of Gayle in only three miles to reach 1,934 feet above sea level. It follows the western flank of Wether Fell through green pastures with Sleddale far below on the right. Peering down into the latter, Duerley Beck, its source high on Dodd Fell, can be seen snaking its way along the valley bottom.

Beggarman's Road has always presented a challenge to both pedestrians and motorists. Travelling it is an adventure. The last half mile or so, up to where it meets the Cam High Road, is the steepest - the car feels almost vertical. Descending this section when coming over from

Kettlewell is an equally dramatic experience. As one broaches the summit the road suddenly drops away sharply creating the sensation, as the valley comes up to meet you, of being in an aircraft coming in to land. In winter the conditions on these heights are often atrocious. Many a vehicle has failed to make the summit in icy, snowy conditions and, in summer, the conditions are quite often more akin to spring.

Despite its bleak, wild, desolate location the views from the top of Beggarman's Road are nothing if not spectacular. One is also cheered by the sight of violets and primroses blooming on the grass verges. Looking back from the summit of the road you can see the high fells of upper Wensleydale whilst in front you can see along the length of Langstrothdale with Buckden Pike dominating its eastern end. Away to the southwest Ingleborough, majestic as ever, fills the sky dwarfing the tiny remote settlement of Cam Houses.

By virtue of Beggarman's Road there is the opportunity to make an easy ascent of Wether Fell. From the Cam High Road's junction with Beggarman's Road the summit, Drumaldrace, can be reached by walking just over a mile along the former. After the wall on the left is no more it is just a few hundred yards to climb to the cairn marking the summit. About half a mile along the Cam High Road from its junction with Beggarman's Road there is a sign on a small gate in the left hand wall. This informs the public that there is no access to the fellside as it is reserved for the members of the Yorkshire Dales Hang Gliding Club. From the track you may see some members getting ready for take-off while others are already aloft gliding gently on the thermals.

# 3
# Dodd Fell

Following a description of Dodd Fell's topography and the changeable nature of Dales' weather I follow the Cam High Road, West Cam Road and Cam Road across the fell paying particular attention to the packmen who travelled along them. In the final part of the chapter there is a description of the flora to be found across the high ground of upper Wensleydale.

### *Sleddale Sentinel*

ACCORDING to Robert Gambles the name Dodd comes from the mediaeval word 'dodde' meaning a round summit[1]. If you then add the old Norse name 'fjall' meaning hill you get the hill with a round summit. The round summit meaning of the name can often be applied to the shoulder of a much larger hill. That application of the name, however, does not apply in this particular instance as it is Dodd Fell itself which constitutes the high fell with Ten End its lower summit. A mountain with a round summit seems singularly appropriate when describing Dodd Fell as its dome shape is a distinctive feature particularly when viewed from locations such as Sedbusk on the northern side of Wensleydale.

~ ~ ~ ~ ~ ~ ~ ~ ~ ~ ~ ~ ~

Although limestone is a common feature of the upper Wensleydale landscape the summits of the high fells, including Dodd Fell, are capped by a small area of gritstone. A trig point is to be found on Dodd Fell's gritstone summit at 2,192 feet. It is reached after a short walk over tussocky terrain from the Cam High Road or the West Cam Road. Here amongst the peat hags grow cotton grass, bilberry, mat grass and the cloudberry with its green leaves and white flowers.

On the First Series 1:50,000 Ordnance Survey Wensleydale and Wharfedale map Dodd Fell's summit was, like a number of others, given a view point symbol. When the revised second series was published this symbol had been omitted. Phil Clayton believes that its disappearance is connected with the fact that most of the view points were on actual fell summits such as Dodd Fell, Ingleborough, Whernside, Penyghent and Great Knoutberry Hill[2]. He makes the point that, although the views from these fells in clear visibility are spectacular, the changeability of the weather means that they cannot be guaranteed. Alternatively, Clayton believes that the remoteness of some of the summit view points was considered to have been too much of an 'invitation to the unwary or unprepared.' The only view point in this area now shown on the map is on Beggarman's Road just past the turn off to Kidhow Gate and Cam Houses.

For some people the flattish nature of the top of Dodd Fell militates against it being a good view point. They consider its views to be inferior to those to be had from Ten End, Dodd Fell's lower summit at 1,910 feet, a mile or so along the ridge to the north. No doubt people who visit both summits will form their own judgement as to which is the most favourable view point. Indeed many people will find the view from Dodd Fell's summit excellent by any standard. There is a complete panorama taking in the Three Peaks, Hawes, Gayle and the fells on the northern side of Wensleydale including Sails, Great Shunner Fell and Lovely Seat. Just across Sleddale lies the bulk of Wether Fell with Addleborough prominent beyond. From Ten End's summit, it is claimed, you can see ten named North Yorkshire fells. This might go some way towards forming an explanation as to its name.

More often than not, like many Dales fell tops, Dodd Fell's summit is wreathed in cloud. In most years such cloud cover brings copious rainfall to its flanks which rapidly finds its way into the fell's numerous becks. A number of streams on Dodd Fell's southern slopes find their way into Oughtershaw Beck which later becomes the River Wharfe. Most of the water draining off Dodd Fell's other slopes finds its way into the River Ure in Wensleydale by way of Snaizeholme Beck, Little Ing Gill and Duerley Beck. The latter, which becomes Gayle Beck lower down its course, runs over Aisgill Force, an attractive waterfall surrounded by trees and reached by a footpath from Gayle village. The water falls some 30 feet over a smooth sloping slab of rock. When Gayle Beck is in spate the falls are a magnificent sight as the torrent plunges over the lip into the gorge below. Even a slight flow of water falling over the slanting rock creates a most magical effect akin to looking through a lace curtain.

On its way to the Ure from Dodd Fell, Duerley Beck flows through the village of Gayle which shelters under both Dodd Fell and Ten End. Here, in the centre of the village, the beck passes over a cascade before continuing its journey to Hawes where it plunges over a small but dramatic

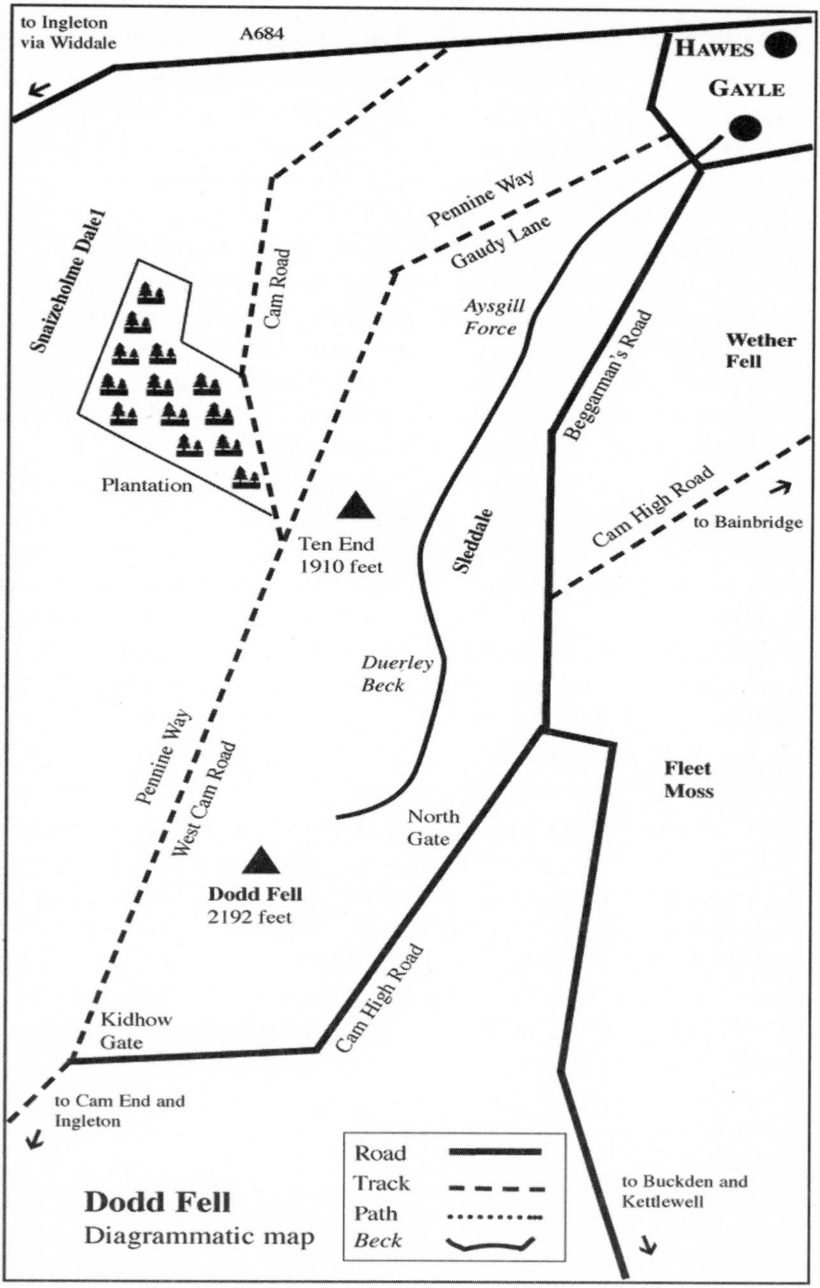
to Ingleton
via Widdale
A684
HAWES
GAYLE
Pennine Way
Gaudy Lane
Cam Road
Snaizeholme Dale1
Aysgill
Force
Beggarman's Road
Wether
Fell
Plantation
Cam High Road
to Bainbridge
Ten End
1910 feet
Sleddale
Duerley
Beck
Pennine Way
West Cam Road
North
Gate
Fleet
Moss
Dodd Fell
2192 feet
Cam High Road
Kidhow
Gate
to Cam End and
Ingleton
Road
Track
Path
Beck
to Buckden and
Kettlewell
Dodd Fell
Diagrammatic map

waterfall. It eventually joins the Ure near Haylands Bridge a little to the north of Hawes. As the strata of the hills of upper Wensleydale consists of alternating layers of limestone, shale and sandstone, erosion and weathering occur at different rates. Such a differential rate of erosion is responsible for the stepped features of the great number of 'forces' or waterfalls in the area such as the ones at Gayle and Hawes.

Dodd Fell stands like a sentinel guarding the head of the deep valley of Sleddale through which flows its main stream Duerley Beck. The spectacular nature of Sleddale, which lies on Dodd Fell's eastern flank, is best appreciated from high on Beggarman's Road near to the junction with the Cam High Road. The valley's farms are well strung out along its lower track which is a no-through road. Other farms are to be found spreading out from Gayle along Beggarman's Road as it clings to the slopes of Wether Fell high above Sleddale.

Snaizeholme, to the west of Dodd Fell, is essentially a side dale of the much larger Widdale. It lies in the embrace of Dodd Fell, Ten End and Snaizeholme Fell (1,793 feet). The dale not only has a number of inhabited dwellings spread out over a mile or so, mostly along a no-through road, but also boasts the Mirk Pot Nature Reserve with its small lake, woodland and wild life. Both the heads of Sleddale and Snaizeholme are bowl-shaped thanks to the massive spurs of Dodd Fell which spread out to the east and the west.

~ ~ ~ ~ ~ ~ ~ ~ ~ ~ ~ ~ ~

All of the six 2,000 foot fells of upper Wensleydale have a substantial layer of peat, formed over many centuries, across their summits. Dodd Fell's main peat grounds lie on its lower summit, Ten End, near to where the Pennine Way parts company with the Cam Road. Many Dalesfolk claimed rights of turbary which allowed them to cut peat from the common land on the fell for their own domestic fuel. In many cases such rights to cut peat can be dated back as far as the twelfth century when turbary rights were granted to Yorkshire monasteries.

For centuries, especially after the forests were cleared, the chief fuel used in the Dales was turf or peat. Most farmhouses kept a store of peat often supplemented by coal from the small, local pits. The hard, dried, peat blocks compared favourably with coal often burning well with small pieces of coal such as that mined at Tan Hill. In Cotterdale, where West Pits supplied coal, some people burned coal fires safe in the knowledge that, if they went out, the coal could be re-lit by borrowing a burning peat from a neighbour. Lead smelters burnt huge quantities of peat cut from the high fells close to the lead veins. Peat was also used in lime kilns and by blacksmiths in their forges.

Peat pits could be deep holes or shallow hollows depending on how far down the diggers had to go to reach the peat layer. Today peat cutting has virtually ceased in the Yorkshire Dales National Park but many holes and hollows on the moors are a testimony to old peat diggings. Many diggings have in fact flooded creating the bonus of small but attractive tarns. For most Dales folk digging for peat was an annual, wearisome chore. Every hamlet and village had its own peat pit. When peat was the chief source of fuel as much as three years' supply was cut in good seasons to provide for poor, wet years. Up to the Second World War peat was still cut at the heads of some dales where the distance from a railway denied access to cheap coal. The same applied where there was an absence of small coal pits and where farms were many miles from public roads.

The first job was always to adequately drain the peat pit to prepare it for cutting in the spring. After the removal of grass and heather from the bed, the peat was cut out in blocks roughly eight to ten inches wide by two inches thick and a foot in length. Cutting started as lambing time was almost finished. It was another job to be done, just like bringing in the hay. After the peat blocks had been cut out of the peat pit they were spread out in close rows on firm, drained ground to dry out. After weeks of hardening, they were set in foots, using up to four peats propped up against each other to allow the wind to blow through them. Just as for hay, wind was considered the best drying agent. In the late summer when the shrunken peats were dry they were finally stacked in a pike which is a circle of peats tapering to a single one at the top. Once stacked they did not spoil and could be shifted by cart in the year they were cut or even the following year. One cart load was generally considered to be one stack. In really wet springs the peat never properly dried out which hindered the whole operation. Whilst older sons helped with the cutting of the peat, younger children helped in the drying process and with placing the peat blocks in the peat house.

A variety of tools were used in the peat gathering process such as a flaying spade for clearing the land. A slicer with a small wing was used to cut one side of the peat wide and one narrow at the same time. Some of the lightly built carts used for moving the peat had wheels whilst others had metal runners like hay sledges and were pulled by a horse.

There were many leases of coal mines on Dodd Fell, Ten End and in Sleddale during the nineteenth century. One such was Bank Gill Colliery north-east of Dodd Fell's summit. The spoil heaps of the various levels are a prominent feature running on the contour of the coal seam around both sides of Sleddale.

The Cam High Road coming up from Horton-in-Ribblesdale to Kidhow Gate traverses the western side of Dodd Fell and Ten End as the West Cam Road. Both this track and its branch, the Cam Road, descend into Hawes. The West Cam Road, travelled for centuries by packmen and their ponies, is today travelled by long distance walkers doing the Pennine Way. This road and its colourful travellers are the subject of the next section of this book.

### *From ribbons to rucksacks*

TO make your way from Wether Fell to Dodd Fell you follow the Cam High Road as it becomes part of Beggarman's Road. After about half a mile or so you part company with the latter to swing right to follow the Cam High Road along Dodd Fell's southern flank. This stretch of the road is metalled as far as the access road to Cam Houses after which it becomes a track descending to Cam End and Gearstones. This metalled section reaches 1,911 feet above sea level at North Gate on Greenside and 1,927 feet on Oughtershaw Side. This high level stretch, along the slopes of Dodd Fell, is a wild, spectacular route. It is also worth noting that from the Cam High Road, as Kidhow Gate is approached, a short walk off to the right over rough pasture leads to the summit of Dodd Fell.

Speaking of Dodd Fell's summit, Phil Clayton suggests it may have been used by the Romans for surveying purposes. The question arises because the virtually dead straight middle section of the Cam High Road, between the Roman fort at Bainbridge and the top of Wether Fell, is perfectly aligned with the summit of Dodd Fell. The case is further supported by a similar alignment to the south west of Dodd Fell where the Cam High Road runs, in a virtually straight line, for two and a half miles between the fell's summit and Cam End. What is amazing about the construction of the Cam High Road by Roman surveyors and engineers was their ability to overcome topographical difficulties and the altitude to produce such a straight course. The road is a tribute to Roman surveying techniques.

The section of the Cam High Road between Beggarman's Road and Gearstones was incorporated into the Richmond to Lancaster turnpike during the eighteenth century thus continuing the road which marches over Wether Fell. Authorised in June 1751, it was the main road south until a lower route was constructed in 1795 through Widdale. At Cam End, at around 1,500 feet, the Cam High Road is joined by another ancient track, the Pennine Way, coming from Horton-in-Ribblesdale. From Cam End northwards, for just over a mile, the Pennine Way and the Dales Way march in step before the latter swings east at Cam Houses leaving the Pennine Way to continue north to Kidhow Gate. The Cam High Road, high on the slopes of Dodd Fell, has, throughout the centuries, been used as a Roman road, eighteenth century turnpike, packhorse route, drove road, farm track and most recently as a long distance footpath.

A word now about Kidhow Gate which has been mentioned hitherto. It is a major junction of ancient tracks and roads which many would regard as one of the most fascinating locations in the Dales. It lies just a mile south west of Dodd Fell's summit at 1,877 feet. Here travellers on the Pennine Way heading north pass from Ribblesdale to Wensleydale. Here also, the Cam High Road continues east towards Beggarman's Road and Wether Fell whilst another track, the West Cam Road, heads north. Two important river systems have their beginnings in the vicinity of Kidhow Gate. A great wedge of land, between Cam Fell and Dodd Fell, separates the source of the Ribble at Gavel Gap from that of the Wharfe in Langstrothdale. The metalled section of the Cam High Road from where it leaves Beggarman's Road gives vehicular access to Kidhow Gate where, on a summer's day, motorists, long distance walkers and strollers just out for the day can enjoy a picnic while admiring the scenery.

The views include one of Penyghent seen over the conifer plantations of High Green Field Knott to the south east. To the south west Whernside and Ingleborough loom large. In the far north west are the rounded Howgill Fells with, if the visibility is good, the Lakeland Fells behind them. Looking north you can see Wild Boar Fell above the valley of Mallerstang. A little north east of the latter lies Great Shunner Fell. To the south east lies Langstrothdale with Buckden Pike 2,303 feet and Great Whernside 2,310 feet at its eastern end. The 'great' part of the latter's name distinguishes it from its neighbour Little Whernside, not from Whernside of the Three Peaks.

A short walk from Kidhow Gate along the Cam High Road, passing Cam Houses on the left and descending towards Cam End, provides a stunning view of the Three Peaks. This is the highlight of a wonderful ridge walk along the slopes of Dodd and Cam Fells. As A. J. Brown has commented from beyond Kidhow Gate down to Gearstones it is the green road of dreams[3].

The walker now picks up again on the enclosed track known as the West Cam Road which heads north from Kidhow Gate. Once a pack-horse and drove road, it now carries the Pennine Way along the western slopes of Dodd Fell. Proceeding along this track you will leave the catchment areas of the Ribble and the Wharfe and enter that of Wensleydale's river Ure. It is a very pleasant high level route which, soon after leaving Kidhow Gate, takes you high above the deep valley of Snaizeholme with its beck one of the main feeders of the Ure. Soon after leaving Kidhow Gate is Dodd Fell's summit off to the right. Probably the easiest access to it is to go about a quarter of a mile from Kidhow Gate, to just past the first gate in the cross wall, before climbing the grassy slope on the right to the trig point.

Between Dodd Fell and Ten End the West Cam Road loses its easterly wall as it crosses the open fell. Just below Ten End's summit it splits into two with the left hand branch known as the Cam Road going directly to Hawes. The right hand track meanwhile continues as the West Cam Road taking the Pennine Way over the slopes of Ten End, Rottenstone Hill, past Gaudy House, along Gaudy Lane to Gayle village and on to Hawes. On the descent from Ten End, whose summit is just a short distance to the north east of the junction with the Cam Road, there is a magnificent panoramic view of upper Wensleydale with Sails, Great Shunner Fell and Lovely Seat all prominent. The Cam Road, on leaving the West Cam Road (Pennine Way), descends past a conifer plantation before going across the rough pastures of Backsides with Widdale and the steep slopes of Widdale Fell to the west. This track, which can be used as a bad weather alternative to the official Pennine Way route over Ten End, eventually enters a wide, walled lane before it joins the B6255 through Widdale just above Hawes.

In centuries past packmen wended their way across the fells of the Yorkshire Dales including those of upper Wensleydale. As has already been mentioned the Cam High Road, West Cam Road and Cam Road running across Dodd Fell and Ten End were important packhorse routes. The packhorse trade was very important from early monastic times until the days of the turnpike. It was the development of markets that led to the rapid growth of the packhorse trade. Clustered around Norman castles were large numbers of soldiers, retainers and craftsmen who needed feeding. Add to that the desires of the nobility for fine wines, spices and other goods unavailable locally and there is a need for a suitable transport system. To meet all these needs it was necessary to have a market to which merchants could bring a variety of goods and to which villagers could bring their small surplus for sale. It was clear that, where large settlements of people were not entirely self sufficient, markets were vital. As their populations increased villages turned more and more to the larger markets for their needs. Thus it was the growth of settlements and the increase in population which brought into existence the packhorse trader who called at villages on his journeyings between market towns in the centuries following the Norman Conquest. The monasteries too were instrumental in developing many packhorse roads as they needed to bring together all the goods and products from their dispersed estates.

Because the sure-footed ponies could negotiate a landscape too difficult for wheeled transport, the packhorse roads followed relatively direct routes between towns and villages. Many packhorse tracks led from one important mediaeval market to another linking villages and hamlets that they passed through. Shorter tracks linked up the more remote hamlets and farms. Most packhorse routes, but not all, as in the case of parts of the Dodd Fell route, crossed the hills below the 1,750 foot contour line as high fell crossings were always liable to encounter soft peat and deep gullies. In addition deep drifts and long-lasting snow cover made higher routes impassable in winter. Even at lower elevations bad weather could cause difficulties with horses unable to maintain their footing in icy conditions and heavy rain turned the roads into quagmires. Ironically in summer, when the roads were at their driest, some packmen were absent from the packhorse routes owing to their involvement with the demands of the hay harvest.

There was a network of Dales tracks and pathways carrying a steady traffic of packhorses between major markets, villages, hamlets and farms. At many of these places the packmen were known and welcomed for their goods, news and gossip from the world outside. Packmen, in addition to crossing Dodd Fell, also followed the Cam High Road over Wether Fell, the Galloway gate over Great Knoutberry, Lady Anne Clifford's Way across Lunds Fell and the Buttertubs Pass between Great Shunner Fell and Lovely Seat.

Rivers and becks were spanned by packhorse bridges some of which were too narrow for the passage of wagons and carts. Such bridges, usually had a single arch, rather than stone piers which would have had to bear the full force of water often in spate. In most cases the parapets of bridges were kept deliberately low so as to ensure that there were no obstacles to the panniers on the flanks of the packhorses.

Packhorse journeys, between important markets, could take many days so inns were established along the routes. Many of these not surprisingly, were called The Packhorse or The Packman. Such inns offered overnight stops where stabling and feed were available for the horses and refreshments for the packmen. Here the horses and ponies could be unburdened of their loads whilst they and the packmen rested. It was not uncommon at these inns for the packmen and their boys to grab some sleep where they could such as amongst their packs. Each packman carried his own basic supply of food consisting of onions, oatmeal and cheese. A packhorse inn lay on the High Way, the old packhorse road from Kirkby Stephen to Hawes. Known as the Horse Paddock it served as an inn until trade diminished with the opening of the turnpike in 1825.

Many of these packhorse inns were situated in remote areas where the local constables' authority did not run and toll collection was, at times, poor. As a result there was probably something akin to a rough frontier atmosphere in these isolated spots. For instance the story goes that three Scottish peddlers, well known in the area, were murdered by the mother and daughter of the inn where they were staying in Middlesmoor in Nidderdale. The inn stood on a hill and as a result of this incident acquired the unattractive name of Dead Man Hill, which it still carries today. In modern times the vast majority of these remote packhorse inns have closed and in many cases been demolished.

At the height of the packhorse trade, packhorse traffic was to be seen everywhere in the Dales fell country. Such traffic ranged from one packman and his pony to whole strings of horses forming packhorse trains. A typical packman, with the help of one or two assistants, would act as the driver of a train of anything up to forty packhorses. The leading pony always had a bell or multiple bells whose ringing signalled the approach of the lead horse and was a help in keeping the other horses in the train together as they followed the sound. The bell also had the important function of providing a warning to other travellers, in particular other packhorse trains, so that a passing place could quickly be found. This was of crucial importance as packhorse tracks were often narrow in places making it quite difficult, if not impossible in some cases, for two loaded packhorses to pass. With the lead horse fitted with bells, at the head of anything up to forty horses one behind the other, a packhorse train must have been a splendid sight as it made its way across the hills.

The packmen and their trains moved goods of all descriptions including hides, fuel, fish and wool, the latter of crucial importance. Even at the end of the eighteenth century the packhorse trade, although in decline, continued to carry the necessities of life such as coal, salt and textiles at one shilling (5p) per ton per mile. There were seasonal adjustments to charges to allow for the adverse travelling conditions in winter and the shortness of the days. Packhorses were also involved in the transport of minerals. In the mid-nineteenth century they could be seen working the lead mining areas of the Dales. They carried lead ore to the smelt mills, coal from the mines and pigs of lead to where they were required. During the nineteenth century hand loom weaving continued in and around Hawes with pieces being transported to Settle by packhorse train from where they would return with yarn. Packhorse transport survived for a long time in this part of the Dales owing to the fact that, before the Hawes railway branch opened in 1878, the town was sixteen miles from the nearest station at Sedbergh.

The name 'badger' was given to a peddler or small trader with a licence to sell corn in small amounts in the surrounding villages. It is almost certain that he also carried a wide variety of other goods in addition to the corn. The badger was such a familiar figure that some green roads were even named Badger Gate or Badger Stile. His appearances were very important for those people whose needs did not always merit a regular, long journey to a market. The badger was in fact the friendly country packman who carried his own pack or alternatively used a pony or a horse to carry it for him. His visit to a farm was an exciting event for the farmer and his family, his labourers and his neighbours, for carried in his pack were sewing materials, basic medicines, spices, not to mention, lace, ribbons and perfumes. Of equal importance to country folk was the fact that the badger, like all visitors, brought news and gossip from the outside world.

The early success and development of the wool trade in places like Kendal and Halifax was dependent to a large extent upon the 'brogger'. With his two horses the one thing he had in common with the badger was the fact that he visited scattered farms and hamlets all across the Dales countryside. However, unlike the badger, he was not in the business of selling wares but rather that of buying small quantities of wool which he then supplied to clothiers in the woollen towns.

As Raistrick has written, the impression is sometimes given that the world of the packman was one of violent incidents taking place along the hundreds of miles of packhorse roads across the Dales[4]. We know that thousands of folk, including packmen, spent a great deal of time journeying along such roads over one of the wildest, most remote landscapes in England. Not only did they carry goods of considerable value but also large sums of money. However, over a period of two centuries or more, it would appear that only three stories of violence have come to public knowledge. It is generally believed that people, whilst being rough and ready in their manners, were basically honest. If theft and violence had been such a significant part of their lives as it is sometimes alleged, then both the packhorse and droving trades could not have been carried on to the extent that they were, nor for that matter could they have survived for so long.

Packhorses, ponies and even pack mules formed the main transport in the Yorkshire Dales for probably some 600 years with many thousands of them operating across the Dales countryside when the trade was at its peak. In the Dales, packhorses were usually called Galloways after their place of origin in the lowlands of south west Scotland where, at some stage in the past, they were a distinctive breed. It is thought that some Scottish Galloways were even bred in Swaledale and Arkengarthdale. Galloways had brown bodies, black legs and stood about fourteen hands high. Although small, they were robust and resilient enough to cope with rough ground. Some packhorse roads were called 'jagger' roads after the packman, or jaggerman, in charge of a team of packhorses. The name is a derivation of 'jaeger' the name given to the strong German hunting pony.

Two panniers or baskets were used to carry a packhorse's load. The size of such panniers depended on the type of goods being transported. For instance, at 2s 6d (12.5p) per dozen, small panniers were adequate for carrying coal. When it came to the transport of salt, corn, charcoal and peat, larger panniers were needed at 7s 6d (37.5p) per dozen. The wooden panniers were connected to a harness which was fitted to the packhorse. The panniers perched on a ledge which jutted out on each side of the horse. The weight of a packhorse load could be anything up to two hundredweight although some horses have been known to carry 22 stones of lead ore.

Dales packhorses could negotiate the steep slopes and rough tracks of the fells with greater facility than horse-drawn wheeled wagons and carts. In fact wheeled transport in the Dales was rarely seen until the coming of the turnpike. Metalled roads and the railways brought about the demise of the packhorse trade as the carriage of goods gradually transferred to these new, quicker, more efficient methods of transport. Many packhorse roads and tracks are today green lanes and bridleways. Where once the packman travelled the Cam High Road carrying ribbons for the ladies, today you are more likely to encounter the Pennine Way walker carrying a rucksack.

Sitting on the grass on a sunny day at Kidhow Gate, it is easy to let one's thoughts drift back, to a time two centuries or more ago, and picture a packhorse train coming up from Gearstones. It may even be the case that the imagined sound of the horses' hooves and the tinkling of a bell will seem real enough to jolt you from your reverie.

~ ~ ~ ~ ~ ~ ~ ~ ~ ~ ~ ~ ~

The Pennine Way coming up from Horton in Ribblesdale follows the West Cam Road along the western flank of Dodd Fell. The concept of one continuous footpath from the Peak District to the Scottish border was first mooted in 1935. At that time there was little or no chance of supportive parliamentary legislation nor the prospect of any concessions from the water authorities or the owners of the grouse moors. In fact, as Tom Stephenson has reported, the water engineers were of the opinion that 'ramblers on a gathering ground might lead to a typhoid epidemic'[5]. It was in this atmosphere that, in June 1935, Stephenson wrote a newspaper article putting forward the case for a continuous Pennine path. This was at a time when proposed sections of the Pennine Way, such as Kinder and Bleaklow, had no rights of way across them. One of the interesting contributory factors that prompted Stephenson to give credence to such a route was a letter from two American girls requesting advice on a proposed walking trip in England. It was their reference to the Appalachian Trail, a 3,200 kilometre long distance path through the eastern United States from Maine to Georgia, which kindled Stephenson's interest in a long distance path in England[6].

Stephenson's proposal led to a strong popular demand across Britain for the creation of such a path. This led, in 1938, to a number of representatives from certain open air organisations meeting at Hope in

Derbyshire out of which the Pennine Way Association was formed. Local committees then took over to survey the variety of Roman roads, miners' tracks, packhorse routes, drove roads and footpaths which would comprise the projected route. By 1939 there existed somewhere in the region of 180 miles of presumed rights of way with approximately another 70 miles still to be negotiated.

In 1949 the National Parks and Access to the Countryside Act set up a National Parks Commission. One of the tasks it was given was that of drafting proposals to the government for the creation of long distance footpaths. It started with the Pennine Way adopting, with only minor changes, the route that the ramblers had initially surveyed in 1939. It is worth quoting from the commission's second annual report to see how it foresaw not just the route of the Pennine Way but its whole concept. It said that: "the Pennine Way will be a strenuous high-level route through predominantly wild country and is intended for walkers of some experience. It will involve a fair element of physical exertion and a willingness to endure rough going. While the greater part of the way is across existing well-trodden tracks, the route in places crosses expanses of wild moorland devoid of prominent landmarks and consisting largely of peat, heather, bog and tussocks of rough grass. These sections of the route can be traversed only by strong walkers and in bad weather they can be safely negotiated only by people who can steer a course by map and compass."

On the 6th of July 1951 the Labour Government approved the route put forward by the commission following which all the local authorities involved finalised the new rights of way. Excitement and anticipation were palpable on the 24th April 1965, when the then chairman of the National Parks Commission, Lord Strang, the Minister of Land and Natural Resources, Mr F. T. Willey and the secretary of the Ramblers' Association, Tom Stephenson, addressed an assembled crowd of more than 2,000 people on Malham Moor to celebrate the completion of the Pennine Way in England. The Scottish section of the way was finally completed in 1977. Today the Pennine Way follows a route from Derbyshire through Yorkshire and Cumbria, across Durham to the Roman wall, before crossing the Cheviots to reach the Scottish border. It was the first long distance right of way to be completed in Britain - 270 miles long and offering 32,000 feet of ascent.

Anyone travelling along the Pennine Way today will, if he of she is wise, keep a weather eye open as, apart from its potential severity, the weather can change dramatically within minutes often producing weather akin to four seasons in one day. With that in mind, it is to the weather of the high fells of the Yorkshire Dales that I now turn.

### *Four seasons in one day*

THIS section considers the weather of the high fells of the Yorkshire dales. The material set out here applies to all the six upper Wensleydale 2,000 foot fells with examples of specific weather features and conditions being taken from the whole area. Often cloudy and humid with a high proportion of days with measurable rain, aptly sums up the weather of the high Pennines of which the Dales are a part. The writer Van Greaves would seem to concur with this view judging by his comment that, to him, it rains more in the Pennines than many other places[7]. Compared with many lowland and eastern locations this is true but Pennine rainfall is matched and often exceeded by such mountainous areas as Snowdonia, the Lake District and the Scottish Highlands. The cause of such wet weather can be laid at the door of the seemingly endless stream of Atlantic depressions which move across Britain. As they reach the Pennines their associated air is cooled, by being forced to rise, causing water vapour to be released as rain on the upward western slopes and the summits themselves. Precipitation totals much less on the downward slopes. The most persistent and heaviest precipitation tends to fall when the heavily, moisture laden southwesterly winds, with their long Atlantic sea fetch, blow across the country.

As rainfall is closely related to altitude the higher the land the greater the total rainfall. Thus rainfall totals increase with the steady elevation of the land surface from the west coast of England to the high western slopes of the Pennines. Such an altitude rise can have a very dramatic effect. For example the Cross Fell range, part of the Pennines to the north of the Dales, receives some 60 inches of rain per annum with Cross Fell itself, the highest summit in the Pennines, receiving an annual total of some 78 inches. The high fells of upper Wensleydale lie in the north west corner of the Yorkshire Dales National Park where they receive about 60 of inches of rain per year on average. This is comparable to the amounts received in many parts of the Lake District. Garsdale Station, at 1,135 feet above sea level, on the border of Wensleydale and Garsdale is one of the wettest parts of the Dales receiving an average of 64 inches per annum. Another area of high rainfall in upper Wensleydale is the high ridge which separates the latter from Wharfedale. This ridge, which includes Dodd Fell, receives over 80 inches per annum. Whilst the town of Hawes receives about 60 inches of rain per annum, middle Nidderdale, a little further east, receives only two thirds of this at 40 inches. The year 2002 was particularly wet in upper Wensleydale with Hawes receiving 70.28 inches. 2004 was even wetter with Hawes recording 76 inches.

It is interesting to compare the annual rainfall figures in inches (see table below) for three upper Wensleydale villages:

| | **Burtersett** | **Bainbridge** | **Askrigg** |
|---|---|---|---|
| 1997 | 52.72 | 44.62 | 39.55 |
| 1998 | 60.76 | 54.20 | 49.15 |
| 1999 | 62.41 | 56.90 | 51.48 |

The figures show the decreasing rainfall as one moves from Burtersett, situated on Wether Fell's north facing slopes, towards Askrigg some four miles to the east on the northern side of Wensleydale. On these figures Burtersett, (although slightly higher than the other two villages) received 13.17, 11.61 and 10.93 inches more rainfall than Askrigg. Here you have two factors at work. Firstly you have a situation called a rain shadow whereby the prevailing south westerly winds drop most of their precipitation on the Wether Fell and Dodd Fell massif before they cross the valley towards Askrigg. Secondly the figures illustrate the difference between the higher rainfall in the west of upper Wensleydale with that in the east, even over a distance of a mere few miles.

Just to the south west of Hawes the valley of Snaizeholme has the highest weather recording station in the upper Wensleydale rainfall catchment area. Here the annual rainfall is much higher on average than that at Stalling Busk only a few miles away to the east. One of the wettest, if not the wettest, location in the Dales is Ribblehead. Situated just below Ingleborough and Whernside, it has an average annual rainfall of 70 inches. However, in 1954, it surpassed itself recording 109.5 inches. In upper Wensleydale, February, April, May and June tend to have less than average amounts of rain with August to January wetter than average. The heaviest rain often falls in thunderstorms during July and August the two warmest months of the year.

In winter much of this precipitation can fall as snow. Blizzards and the disruption they cause, although much less frequent, are just as harsh on the Pennines as on the Scottish mountains. This is due to the strong, westerly winds which regularly blow across the range. Added to these are the seasonal severe gusts, such as that recorded on Great Dun Fell in

1968, when the wind speed touched 134 miles per hour. Snow, cleared from a high moorland road at an elevation of upwards of a 1,000 feet, may be quickly blown back to form deep drifts. Snow cover can last a long time in the Pennines, the Cross Fell range for example having between 100 and 140 days per annum. Snow also comes early to the Pennines, sometimes as early as October, although falls are usually light and short lived at this time of the year - as I write Great Shunner Fell has a light October covering. Amazingly summer falls of snow on the high Pennines are not unknown, Cross Fell receiving a covering on 16 June 1860. On 7 August 1889 Great Shunner Fell and its neighbours were covered in snow during a violent thunder storm. Snow was reported on the high fells of the Dales on 3 June 1953 and on 8 June 1985 Buckden Pike in Wharfedale had a two inch fall.

~ ~ ~ ~ ~ ~ ~ ~ ~ ~ ~ ~ ~ ~

It is difficult to imagine the intensity of the Arctic cold that prevails in the more elevated parts of upper Wensleydale unless one has had first hand experience of it. I remember one particular winter's day in 1986, on the slopes of Great Shunner Fell above Cotterdale, battling through deep snow against an east wind that threatened to cut me in half with its Siberian edge. Needless to say the harsh elements won and I had to retreat to the less severe conditions of the valley. Dales fells offer little protection from the weather on their long, exposed moorland crossings where shelter is at a premium. The exposed tops of the high Dales country experience some of the severest conditions known in Britain. Here sub-Arctic conditions of ice, snow and wind chill can cause death from exposure. In 1947, one of the harshest winters the Dales has ever known, many remote villages were cut off. In 1951 Cam Houses farm, just to the south of Dodd Fell, was cut off by snow for twelve days and similarly from Christmas until late February 1979 when the Army cut a way through. In 1963 Hardraw Force turned into a column of ice. 1987 was another cold year with blizzards as was 1991 when the Dales experienced a widespread snowfall of over fifteen inches. The severe snowstorm of 1895 led to the deaths of people on the fells, not to mention the heavy loss of livestock.

It is not unknown for dead sheep to be discovered, by shepherds and farmers, when the last snowdrifts behind the dry stone walls and gullies have melted. Some idea of the severity of Dales weather can be gauged from the incidents related by Harry Speight[8]. He tells of a man dying from severe cold on Cam End, his body being recovered the next morning. The same writer also relates the story of the man who crossed the fells from Dent Head en route for Hawes in mid winter. The cold was so severe that his limbs became so numb that they were to some degree paralysed. On reaching his destination he could not speak for nearly a quarter of an hour as his jaws were frozen. The man recalled that the sensation he had for a time was one of barely knowing he was alive. Anyone, he claimed, might have knocked his head off his shoulders as it felt like a mere lump of ice. In winters past, the cold on the snowy fell tops has been so penetrating that shepherds, after attending to their flocks, have been forced to come down to their homes to thaw their hats from their heads in front of the fire!

Dales winters, as well as frequently being bitterly cold, are often long. On the highest and most exposed of the Dales fells snow may lie for a third or more of the year. Farmers bring their sheep down to lower pastures when blizzards threaten the fell tops. Driving sheep down off the fell to the safety of lower ground in a snowstorm is not a task farmers relish as invariably they get wet through and chilled to the marrow. It is an especially miserable experience for the farmer if the sheep, through their stubbornness, become difficult to manage. Ewes carry their lambs through winter combating snow, ice and temperatures often below zero. Sheep have a better knowledge of the landscape than the farmer and can usually be relied upon to find shelter in a torrential rainstorm or a blizzard. However, it goes without saying, that in a severe winter Dales farmers will be called upon to recover their sheep buried in deep snow drifts. Amazingly sheep can live buried under drifts in hollows where, through the heat from their bodies, the snow has thawed. In fact many sheep, whilst buried under the snow, stay alive for quite remarkable lengths of time by living on the grass and other vegetation around them. It is essential however that farmers locate their buried sheep before the main thaw sets in as melting snow in its sloppy, wet state can cause them to suffocate. It is worth stating that on the plus side, despite the unfortunate loss of stock and thankfully rare human fatalities which can occur in severe winter conditions, the sun shining on upper Wensleydale's hills after a heavy snowfall, is a truly magical, memorable sight.

~ ~ ~ ~ ~ ~ ~ ~ ~ ~ ~ ~ ~ ~

The Yorkshire Dales climate is essentially one of cool, moist winters and short, mild summers. Like all Pennine weather, that in the Dales is

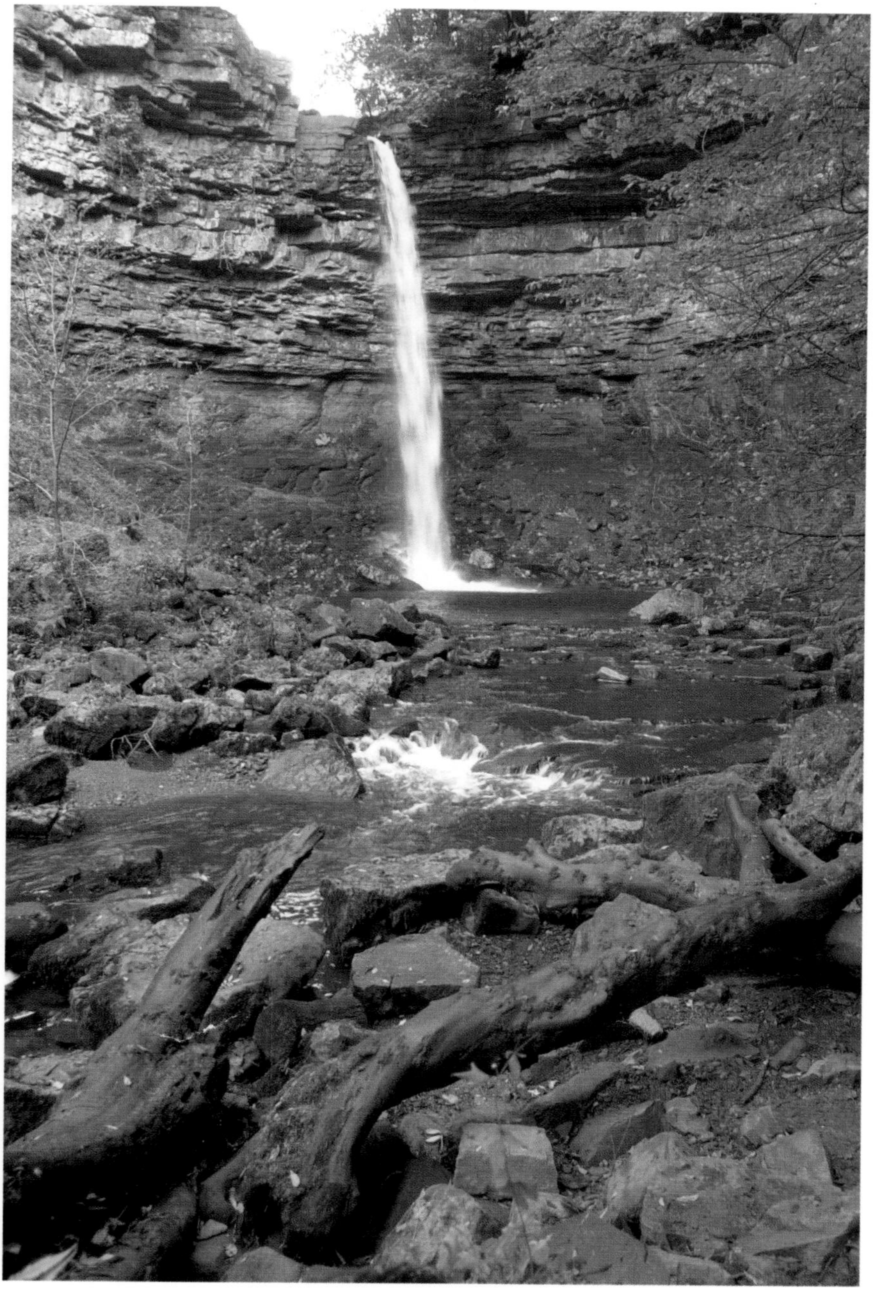

*Hardraw Force with its 100 foot single drop set in a magnificent gorge.*

*Above, Cliff Beck below the Buttertubs divides Great Shunner Fell on the left from Lovely Seat on the right.*

*Below, a steam falling into the Buttertubs.*

*Above, the famous profile of Ingleborough viewed from the Cam High Road on Dodd Fell.*

*Below, looking down the Coal Road in the direction of Dent Station.*

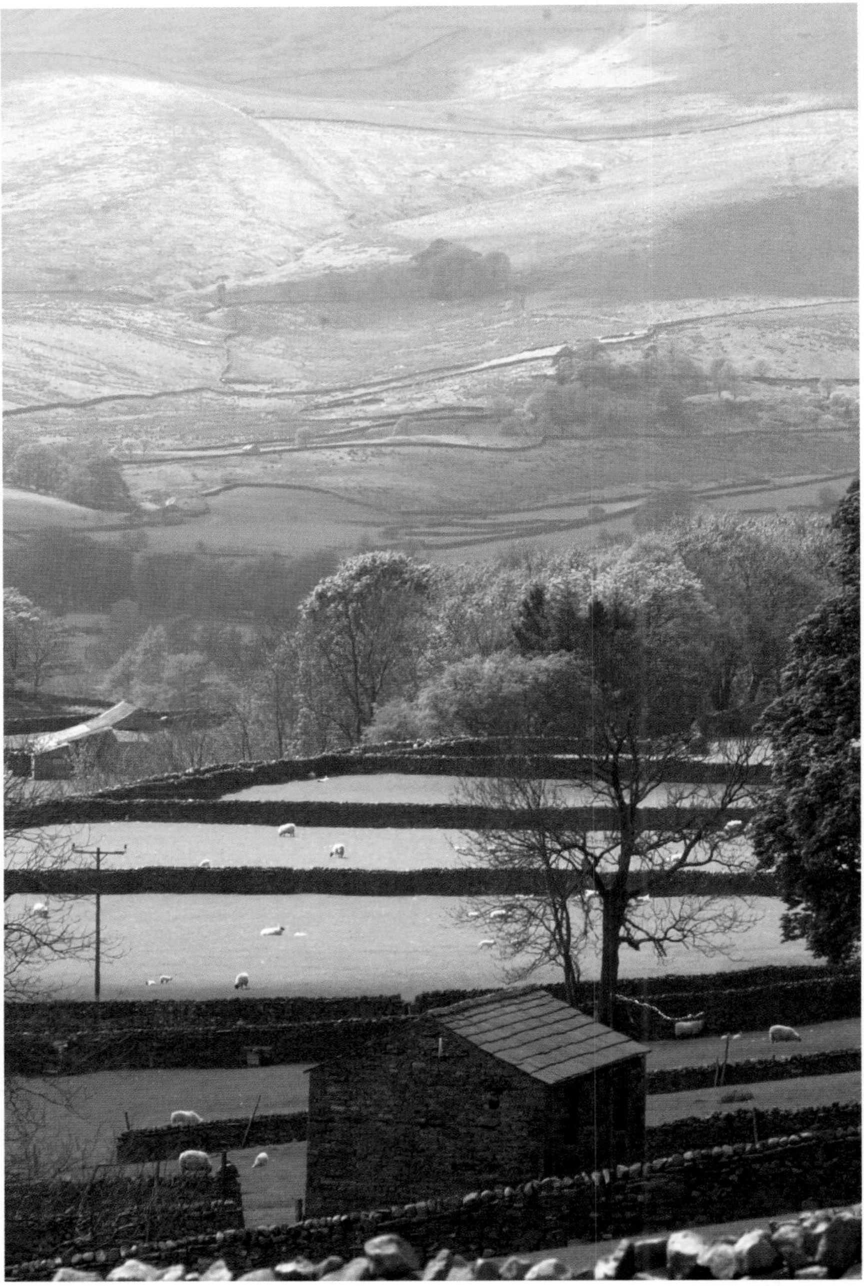

*A typical upper Wensleydate scene with its barns, dry stone walls, meadows and pastures.*

essentially unsettled with rapid changes often occurring in the space of 24 hours. Hence the title of this section *Four seasons in one day!* For example a spring day might start frosty, have warm summer sunshine between April showers during the afternoon before ending up with a rather misty, cool, autumnal evening. Such changeability provides a kaleidoscope of weather features. One such is the variety of changes in the light which makes a particular vista never look quite the same on any two consecutive days. A summer's day may be bathed in glorious sunshine, the next cloudy with a persistent drizzle falling, making it more reminiscent of November. A day of heavy snow can be rewarded 24 hours later by the sun shining out of a deep blue sky on a scene of sparkling white.

Equally there are enormous variations from place to place sometimes only a few miles apart. For example, in May 1959, a cloudburst at the head of Wensleydale and Garsdale affected the Widdale and Snaizeholme areas. Numerous streams sprang out of the slopes of Widdale Fell (1,923 feet) a sight not seen before in living memory. These found their way into the River Ure causing serious flooding of pasture and meadowland. Amazingly, in Hawes, just three miles away, the sun shone nearly all day.

As one crosses the high western summits of the Dales to descend to the eastern valleys the moderating influence of the Atlantic is left behind making the climate a little cooler in winter and a little warmer in summer. Given the pattern of the weather regime in the Dales, rain and snow fall heavily over the western slopes. Thus the region is considerably wetter in the west and over high ground than the lower ground to the east. Compared with that of the Plain of York the Dales climate is wetter and colder but, compared with that of the Lake District, it is colder but a little drier. Some places in the eastern Dales receive only 25 inches of rain per annum which is very similar to rainfall totals in Kent. Interestingly, where the Dales and the Vale of York meet, the climate has a certain similarity to that of the low hills of the Cotswolds or the Chilterns.

Spring in the Dales arrives later than west of the Pennines but it is drier than winter and is a good time for walking the fells. Pennine summers are generally cool and wet with extensive cloud cover. For example, in July 1960, rain was reported to have fallen on every day of the month. It is worth noting that certain summers in the 1990s, and early in the twenty-first century, have broken the Dales pattern by being sunnier and drier. Whether these are normal exceptions to the general pattern of Dales weather, or the first signs of fundamental climate change in association with global warming, only time will tell. Early summer, is the best time for birds and flowers. With summers being short, autumns are often early in the Dales but it can stay mild until November.

Temperature plays an important part in Pennine weather as it can determine the start and the length of the growing season for grass and other crops. The growing season is taken as the period during which the daily average temperature rises above 42 degrees Fahrenheit (six degrees Celsius) allowing the grass grazed by farm stock to naturally replenish itself. The short growing season, the heavy rain and the frequency of cloudy days make for a very short grazing season on the high Pennines with grass growth often late. In most high, exposed locations the growing season only lasts for approximately one third of the year whereas in the valleys it is probably more like two hundred days. The shorter the growing season the less time there is to grow the fodder to feed the farmer's stock during the winter.

An important weather demarcation boundary in the Dales is the 1,000 foot contour line. Above it conditions are usually too harsh to allow arable crops to be cultivated. Instead the emphasis is on maintaining a sheep flock with some cattle and the growing of hay for winter feed. Modern silage-making methods have removed the need for warm sunshine to dry the cut hay. One of the prime jobs is to get the ewes into the best possible condition to give birth and then suckle their lambs. This means maximum advantage being taken of the short grazing season on the high fells with grazing starting early and finishing late. Equally the growing and gathering of hay is often beset with bad weather making the whole operation drag on into the early autumn.

The changeability of Dales weather, not just throughout the year but from one place to another, ensures a wide range of habitats for plants and wild life. On the high fells plant species, left over from the Ice Ages, still linger. Erosion is virtually a permanent feature of the fells through the agents of wind, rain and frost. The variability of the weather has led the folk of the Dales to adapt their activities to take account of its changing patterns. Not only has the climate shaped the Dales landscape but also the lives of its people. For example the harsh conditions of the heads of the valleys have caused those living there to adapt to the short growing season. The weather is an integral part of Dales life and provides unlimited scope for conversation. In fact Dales folk have invented their own dialect words for aspects of the weather. For example 'snizy' means raw, a cutting edge to cold weather; 'clashy' means stormy with rain lashed by an angry wind; 'glishy' refers to a gleaming sun leading to rain; 'dowly' means dull and 'maguey' means misty. There is even a rhyme about the weather of upper Wensleydale entitled 'Hawes Weather Lore'[9]. Its first six lines are as follows and provide a poetic end to this section on the weather:

*When Dodd Fell wears a cap of cloud;*
*the roar of Gayle Beck will be loud;*
*when mists come down on Widdale Fell;*
*a drenching day grey heads foretell;*
*when Stags Fell frowns on Abbotside;*
*the rain will pour both far and wide.*

When considering the landscape of upper Wensleydale, it is difficult to underestimate the effect of the weather on its flora. In the next section the flowers and plants which the climate allows to grow and survive on Wensleydale's high fells is examined.

### *Flora*

THE plant life of the six 2,000 foot fells of upper Wensleydale is fairly uniform across them all so this section will consider the flora of the whole area. Following the end of the Ice Age, some 10,000 years ago, a number of climatic changes introduced a variety of flora to the Yorkshire dales. First an increasingly warm climate took hold which enabled pine and hazel forests to develop. In the somewhat drier conditions which followed lime, ash and silver birch flourished. Then, around 500BC, a wetter, colder climate returned, broadly the climate we have today.

Wensleydale's varied vegetation has been determined by its climate, soil and rocks. The vegetation ranges from the grass on the heavily grazed limestone pastures to the heather on the millstone grit moors. After its original soil was dispersed by glacial action during the Ice Age its new young soils were only formed when the ice finally melted. Basic soils consisting of limestone, sandstone, shales and glacial till slowly established themselves. On the higher slopes and the tops of the high fells the area of limestone is comparatively small. It is often covered by till which is a glacial deposit consisting of rock fragments of various sizes of which the most common is boulder clay.

Flowers common to an Arctic climate grow on the rocky escarpments of the hills. With the exception of the interceding warmer climatic periods, the landscape of the high fells of upper Wensleydale must have been similar to that found in the frozen tundra areas of the world today. On the tops of the fells the conditions come close to being sub-Arctic. Here can still be found the descendants of plants which took hold as the ice sheets melted. One such is the Alpine bistort, another the blue spiny gentian. Other plants which like the high fells are the sea plantain, sea pink, and water crowfoot. Juniper, found in the coniferous forest which covered much of the region at the end of the Ice Age, still exists in isolated pockets today. As a relative improvement in the climate occurred, mixed woodland was established up to 2,000 feet. Although such extensive woodland has long gone, some of its native plants - wood anemone, wood sorrel and bluebell - can still be found in sheltered ravines on the high fells.

As you stride across upper Wensleydale's 2,000 foot fells you are likely to come across heather, bilberry, cloudberry, sphagnum, cotton grass, bent and sheep's fescue. The cloudberry, a type of bramble, has bright green leaves and distinctive white flowers. In summer cotton grass forms tussocks which makes for difficult, tiring walking. Mat grass is also found, albeit on drier ground. The relatively flat summits of the high fells are poorly drained and it is here that you are most likely to come across peat which, because of its black colour, often creates a rather sombre environment. It is in this environment that the lack of calcium in the soil is a problem. Without the calcium, needed to break down the organic material which collects in the gritstone soils, drainage is seriously hampered. Consequently such soils become very heavy due to a lack of oxygen and humus. Sheep are closely related to goats and enjoy eating shrubs and trees as well as grass. On the high fells they forage on any young shoots, and few trees are found on or near the summits. Those that do cling on are those growing in crevices the sheep can't reach such as rowan, hawthorn and ash. Below the summits, on the higher slopes, hazel, holly and birch thrive. Rather attractive copses or small woods hug the limestone scars and thrive in ravines alongside becks.

Following the retreat of the ice and the various changes in climate, peat bogs developed as did woodlands of alder, willow, oak and elm. The most characteristic plants of boggy terrain are sphagnum and cotton grass with its little white plumes which bob in the wind. Where mosses or bogs are the dominant feature there is often a standard vegetation consisting of bog myrtle, bog asphodel, butterwort, cloudberry, crowberry and the rare bog rosemary. In the spring sheep feed on the cotton grass which in the early summer months tends to brighten the bogs and mosses. In some localities where the higher ground is better drained, ling (heather) or bilberry may thrive. On the edge of the mosses extensive purple moor grass may be seen rippling in the wind. The often boggy nature of the summits and moors offer a stark contrast to the close-cropped grassland of the limestone slopes and terraces.

Moorland streams have carved myriad channels in the peat, in some cases many feet deep. The criss-crossing of streams, assisted by the erosive power of the wind, often creates isolated hummocks topped with heather or bilberry. A not uncommon feature of the high moors and fells of upper Wensleydale are the man-made ditches, such as those on Lovely Seat, which march across the landscape in serried rows. This practice is called 'gripping' which means cutting trenches to supplement the existing drainage channels. There is an increasing worry about the damage these ditches are causing to some upland habitats especially in very boggy, peaty areas, which tend to hold heavy rainfall and release it slowly into the streams. Improved drainage brings the danger that heavy rain is quickly channelled down the fell sides causing flood damage to villages and a likelihood that stock will be swept away and drowned. The problem has been highlighted by wet seasons in the last few years. Recently the River Ure has consistently broken its banks in the vicinity of Hawes. Lead mining activities in earlier centuries, such as diverting streams (hushing), sometimes led to the rapid draining of bogs. It was also not uncommon for a similar thing to happen as a result of the drainage work of gamekeepers in charge of grouse moors in the nineteenth century.

On the steeper slopes, where good drainage can be relied upon, there is a rich flora. Plants such as the cross-leaved heather, bilberry, crowberry, together with some sedges, rushes and grasses all flourish on better drained land. It is worth noting that when peat does dry out the cotton grass gradually dries out too.

On the inaccessible limestone cliffs, which even the sheep cannot reach, live many ferns and plants such as herb Robert, bedstraw and brittle bladder. In upper Wensleydale green pastures are to be found along the limestone of the valley sides. These are home to such limestone plants as the birds-eye primrose with its lilac-pink flowers, the globe flower, the bloody cranesbill, the yellow mountain pansy, the yellow common rock rose and the wild orchid. On the thin, well-drained but alkaline soil of the scree slopes lives the mossy saxifrage usually found on shady, north-facing hillsides. On the rich soil, lower down, can be found flowers such as the purple orchid, cowslip, and marjoram. In the copses and small woods primroses, bluebells, wild garlic, violets and St John's wort may be seen.

Around the 800 foot contour the limestone's thin alkaline soil supports good sheep pastures. Endless grazing takes its toll on many plants but tough ones like the daisy, creeping buttercup and speedwell cope reasonably well. The well-drained, slightly acidic soils, found on the lower slopes of the high fells, are rich in the minerals which have leached down from the upper slopes. Such soils are home to bedstraw, milkwort, harebell and tormentil. The dampness and shade to be found in the grykes of the limestone pavements are similar conditions to those found in woods and alongside streams. Here, protected from the sheep, thrive herb Robert, cranesbill, wood anemone, wood sorrel, lily-of-the-valley, spleenwort, brittle bladder and hart's tongue.

Good grazing is to be found along the moor edges where a variety of grasses, the most prevalent being white mat grass, grow. Blue-moor grass can be found where the soil has a little moisture in it. Other grasses are sheep's fescue, silver hair-grass, common bent, trefoil and vetch, all of which provide good pasturage. More than the gritstone the limestone terraces offer good, nourishing grassland of sheep's fescue and meadow grass both of which are able to cope with constant sheep grazing.

As heather thrives at an altitude of between 700 and 1,700 feet above sea level there are vast tracts of it across the high moors of Wensleydale and Swaledale. Such moors are the home of the red grouse which is indigenous to north west Britain. The acid soil of these moorlands supports thousands of acres of heather and bracken of which a high percentage is common grazing. In fact many of the finest grouse moors are a result of the joint techniques of grazing sheep and burning off the old heather in order to produce the best feed for both the sheep and the young grouse. Heather seems to flourish on gentle slopes and on better drained peat beds. There are two forms of heather - the bell and the cross-leaved. Burning produces the patchwork appearance of the heather moor with its sooty-black colour in winter, green re-growth in early summer and the intense purple-mauve as the plants flower in August and September. Other plants which share the moor with the heather are the yellow tormentil, creeping bedstraw, bilberry, cranberry, rushes, sedges and bracken.

Heather has a tendency to grow high and bushy if it is left untended.

Heather in this condition provides little food for the sheep or the grouse. One of the prime maintenance tasks in looking after a grouse moor is to carry out a controlled burning or 'swaling' of the heather between October and the middle of April. This involves burning off all the plant above the ground to encourage the growth of the succulent young heather shoots which the grouse depend on. Burning the heather brings about a quick regeneration of a grouse moor as, once the light is let in, the seeds in the ground can germinate. By early spring when the grass is only in the early stages of growth the sheep share the moor with the grouse, the former gaining their protein by eating young heather shoots. In addition to burning, care is required in carrying out good drainage and ensuring that the right amount of lime is applied. Burning should not occur too often nor should a moor be over-grazed as this may lead to it reverting to mat grass which tends to be tussocky. Grouse also like the older, mature heather as it provides them with some degree of protection and shelter.

The Yorkshire Dales heather moors are maintained for grouse shooting. This maintenance is carried out by gamekeepers on behalf of landowners whose aim is to provide grouse for their shoots. Some owners of large estates have their own moors whilst other moors may be managed for a syndicate of both owners and tenants. Access to the moors during the nesting and shooting seasons is usually restricted which sometimes leads to difficult relations between owners and walkers. To guarantee new, strong heather growth, very thorough management of the moor is essential. This means that the gamekeeper and the farmer have a mutual interest in looking after the grouse moor.

# 4
# GREAT KNOUTBERRY HILL

Great Knoutberry Hill's topography and location are dealt with first in this chapter. Then, after a detailed look at the Dent 'marble' industry there is a section on the old drove road, the Galloway Gate, which highlights its features and the drovers who used it. Finally the chapter focuses on the famous Settle-Carlisle railway line with its viaducts, tunnels and stations.

## *Tarns and Gulls*

ACCORDING to Robert Gambles the Old Norse word 'knottr-ber' means knotberry or cloudberry and the word 'berie' is Old English for berry[1]. It seems that, to all intents and purposes, what could have been called Cloudberry Hill became Knoutberry Hill as the northern dialect word for the cloudberry is the knotberry. The cloudberry is a plant which flourishes on the high fells and produces a fruit not unlike a strawberry.

Sometimes Great Knoutberry Hill is called Widdale Fell after the long, high escarpment which runs north east from it. The word Widdale was, according to Gambles, written 'withdale' in 1217. It is derived from the Old Norse 'vithr' and 'dalr' which means the wooded valley. Today Widdale is still heavily forested with conifer plantations. The name Widdale also appears a number of times on the fell - for example Widdale Foot, Widdale Side, Widdale Bridge, Widdale Carr Plantation and Widdale Fell End.

Great Knoutberry Hill reaches an elevation of 2,205 feet above sea level and is the highest point of an extensive tract of hill country between Widdale in the east, Dentdale to the south and west and Garsdale and Wensleydale to the north. From the road through Widdale, the A684, Widdale Fell presents itself as a long ridge of which Great Knoutberry Hill is its highest point (although from the road the summit is not visible). Lying on the Pennine watershed, Great Knoutberry looms over the village of Appersett 'like a great beast keeping guard'[2]. The county boundary between North Yorkshire and Cumbria runs across the summit of the fell in a general north-south direction.

Great Knoutberry's millstone grit summit, like many other high fell

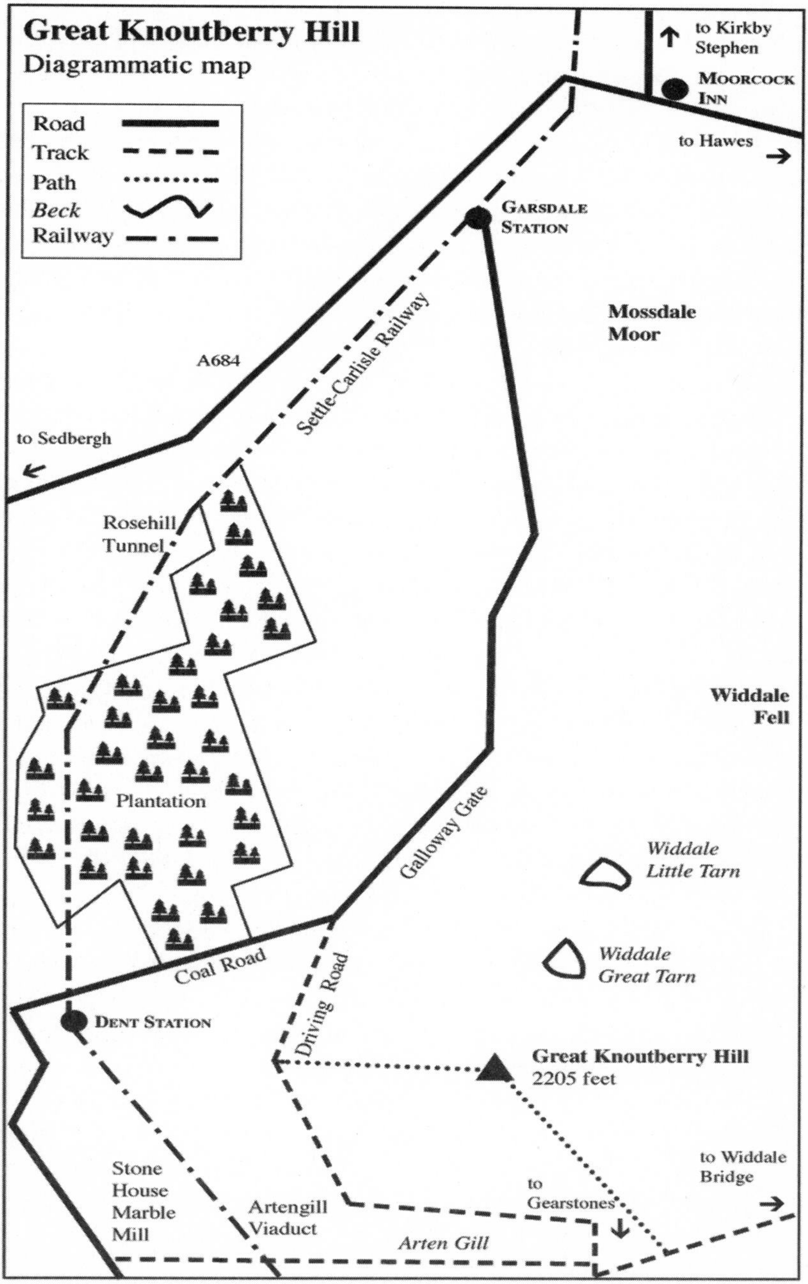
Great Knoutberry Hill
Diagrammatic map
Road
Track
Path
Beck
Railway
to Kirkby Stephen
MOORCOCK INN
to Hawes
GARSDALE STATION
Mossdale Moor
Settle-Carlisle Railway
A684
to Sedbergh
Rosehill Tunnel
Widdale Fell
Plantation
Galloway Gate
Widdale Little Tarn
Widdale Great Tarn
Coal Road
Driving Road
DENT STATION
Great Knoutberry Hill
2205 feet
Stone House Marble Mill
Artengill Viaduct
Arten Gill
to Gearstones
to Widdale Bridge

tops, consists of peaty hollows and large tussocks which makes walking tough going. What distinguishes it from four of the other five 2,000 foot fells of upper Wensleydale is that, together with Great Shunner Fell, it has two tarns - Widdale Great Tarn and Widdale Little Tarn. They lie about a fifth of a mile apart to the north east of the summit. The only other 2,000 foot fell in upper Wensleydale which has a tarn of any significance is Lunds Fell. Pontefract and Hartley reflect on the fact that, because there are two tarns, they lack the feeling of desolation of most single moorland tarns. However they do point to the melancholy lapping of the water against the sides of the tarns. Black headed gulls are known to nest here in the spring.

The main stream flowing through Widdale is Widdale Beck. Although it is fed by numerous small becks, which pour off the vast bulk of Widdale Fell and Great Knoutberry, its main feeder is Snaizeholme Beck which merges with it not far from Widdale Side. Widdale Beck, after beginning life as a number of mountain streams, flows through beautiful meadows and woodland before dropping gradually, via a series of steps in its riverbed, to join the Ure near Appersett. Here it may be said is where the Ure, having absorbed Widdale Beck, loses its youthful abandon to begin its life as a mature river. Oyster catchers and sandpipers haunt Widdale Beck with redshanks favouring some of its adjacent boggy areas.

The story is told that, somewhere up Widdale Beck in the early part of the nineteenth century, there lived a very old man known as John o' t' Bog who tended sheep on Widdale Moor[3]. He was the tenant of an ancient cottage which, when it was re-roofed in about 1865, revealed a hoard of silver coins of the Stuart period.

Over on the northern side of Great Knoutberry Hill the wild, yet attractive Mossdale Gill has cut a deep ravine into the northern edge of the huge expanse of Mossdale Moor. The gill has two splendid waterfalls, the lowest falling over a low cliff, the higher one leaping over a bare ledge of rock into a pool. The lower falls, with its tumbling waters, is spectacular after heavy rain. When the foliage surrounding the lower falls is not too dense it can be glimpsed from high on the Hawes-Sedbergh road. It is believed that Turner was so impressed with the beauty of the gill that he painted there. In 1888 the swollen gill swept away many dry stone walls as several large boulders weighing many tons were brought down from the gill head. A kitchen garden, belonging to the farm at Mossdale Head, had several dozen berry trees completely washed away.

Widdale Fell's vast expanse has a rather sad, melancholy link to the last war. It was here that a Lancaster bomber, after a successful mission over France, crashed as it was returning to Leeming. Badly off course the crew decided to drop below the low cloud base to ascertain their position and in so doing the plane struck the fell and turned over in peaty terrain. Of the five crew only two, the navigator and the rear gunner, survived. Making for the sounds of passing trains the rear gunner found the Galloway Gate track which he followed down to Dent station. There the stationmaster notified the police who in turn informed the RAF.

On the most northerly edge of Great Knoutberry's Mossdale Moor lies the Moorcock Inn at the junction of the Hawes-Sedbergh road with the road to Kirkby Stephen through Mallerstang. In days gone by it served a clientele made up principally of railwaymen and farmers. Named after the red grouse it was part of the large Mossdale estate. The inn once owned 60 acres of land which meant that the landlord could double as a farmer if he so wished. Electricity was provided by a large diesel engine whilst water flowed to the building from a large tank kept filled by a pump powered by a windmill. It was the meeting point for the Lunesdale fox hunt whilst the tiny school at Lunds, a mile away, hosted the hunt ball.

In 1910 ten people were killed in a dreadful crash between Garsdale station and Aisgill on the Settle-Carlisle railway line not far from the Moorcock Inn. The accident happened when the *Scotchman* express from St.Pancras to Glasgow ran into the back of two pilot engines returning to Carlisle. The bodies of the victims were taken to the Moorcock where they were laid in the cellar. The inn acted as a temporary mortuary until identification had been completed and relatives had claimed the bodies. A poem titled 'The Wreck of the Scotch Express' was written a year later and has two verses which refer to the Moorcock:

*Sad, were the hearts of their comrades,*
*And many a tear was shed,*
*As they slowly bore to the Moorcock*
*All that remained of the dead.*

*And there in that moorland chamber,*
*Far from home and from all they loved best,*
*They waited 'for someone' to claim them,*
*Before passing to their final rest.* *JTH, 1911*

After recovering from a fire in 1975 the Moorcock continued as a public house and today is a friendly, atmospheric country inn.

~ ~ ~ ~ ~ ~ ~ ~ ~ ~ ~ ~ ~ ~

One of the easiest ways of gaining access to the summit of Great Knoutberry Hill is to follow the track up Arten Gill from Stonehouse Farm in Dentdale passing under the viaduct en route. Where the track makes a sharp turn to the left higher up the fell, you carry straight on. When the track becomes completely unenclosed you follow a wall on the left, up the fell side, for about three quarters of a mile to reach the summit. Equally easy access to the summit can be had by leaving the metalled Galloway Gate road (linking Garsdale with Dentdale) and striking out along the green road that winds along the western flank of the fell. After a short walk along this green road, about which there will be more details later, you leave it at a sign on the left indicating a path and right of access. From here you follow the path alongside the fence on your left to reach the summit relatively quickly and without too much pain. Another pleasant walk, this time around Great Knoutberry Hill, involves leaving the Galloway Gate at its junction with the green road. You then follow the latter over the shoulder of the fell down its eastern slopes into Widdale to meet the Ingleton-Hawes road at Widdale Bridge.

The view from the summit of Great Knoutberry Hill must be one of the most extensive in the Yorkshire Dales, encompassing an area bounded by Roseberry Topping in the far north east to Morecambe Bay in the south west. The finest view to be had is from the summit trig point where two fences and a wall meet. Hills fan out all around you to all points of the compass. To Ella Pontefract and Marie Hartley, Great Knoutberry offers the best, panoramic summit view of all the fells above Hawes. For them it is '...a perfect circle, and you can work round it again and again, and each time find some fresh hill or corner of a valley.'

To the west, the view takes in Dentdale sheltered by Great Coum and Rise Hill. Working round to the north west you see the rounded Howgill Fells and if really clear the Lake District mountains beyond. To the north lies the huge bulk of Baugh Fell and its neighbours Swarth Fell and flat-topped Wild Boar Fell. Then come the Mallerstang fells including Lunds Fell with Sails its highest point. To the north east lie Great Shunner Fell and Lovely Seat. On the far northern horizon, but only when the visibility is good, you can pick out Mickle Fell which used to be Yorkshire's highest hill until it was transferred to County Durham in 1974. To the south in an east-west arc you will see Penyghent's lion couchant profile, flat-topped Ingleborough and the great bulk of Whernside. On the sky-line to the south, beyond these three famous peaks, Lancashire's Pendle Hill can be clearly seen. To the south east lie the Wharfedale fells including Great Whernside. There are other fells in the frame not included here which, with the help of the appropriate maps, should be easily identified.

From Great Knoutberry's summit it is also easy to trace the line of the various dales in a clockwise direction starting in the west - Dentdale, Garsdale, Wensleydale, Widdale and Ribblesdale. To appreciate Great Knoutberry's wonderful vistas, clear visibility is a must. Disappointments in this respect I know to my cost, having set out on a number of occasions, on what looked like perfect days for taking in the views, only to find visibility on the summit to be average or distinctly poor. The best weather conditions, in which to make the easy climb to the summit from the Galloway Gate, to take in the view, are those which occur when a cold front has just passed through pulling in colder, clearer air from the north west.

~ ~ ~ ~ ~ ~ ~ ~ ~ ~ ~ ~ ~ ~

Along the Galloway Gate, or the Coal Road as it is often called locally, a number of grass covered mounds can be seen in the vicinity of Hugh's Moss, Cowgill Head and Windy Hill. These spoil heaps indicate the old workings where coal was once mined by Garsdale Colliery. The large number of them gives a clear indication of the extent of this former mining operation. Tracks, now long since grassed over, linked the pits to each other and to the Galloway Gate. Lying either side of the latter, high up on the western flank of Great Knoutberry, these coal pits make up one of the most extensive areas of old coal mines in the high fell country at the heads of Wensleydale, Garsdale and Dentdale.

Garsdale Colliery was worked for two centuries or more before it closed. For example a lease was granted in 1742 to search for coal in 'Mosedale' (Mossdale). Then, in 1783, another lease was given for fifteen years for mining coal on Mossdale Moor. This was followed in 1797 by a much wider lease covering not only coal but lead and copper where found; it was renewed in 1801.

There was little need for much in the way of pithead buildings at Garsdale Colliery as the workings were reached by small shafts where the winding was done by the simple hand turned 'jack roller' which consisted of two wooden uprights with a roller between them around which a rope was wound. The shallow pits led to seven or eight inch seams of hard brittle coal which the miners worked by candlelight on hands and knees for about 14s (70p) a week. The hewed coal was brought out in tubs.

In the early days of Garsdale Colliery, coal was transported along the Galloway Gate to hamlets in the valley by packhorse and then later, in the nineteenth century, by horse and cart. Horses had to be trained to control a full load of coal to prevent the cart running downhill out of control. Coal was burnt domestically in the Dent, Garsdale and Sedbergh areas during the eighteenth and nineteenth centuries. At one point a ten hundredweight load was sold for 5s (25p). Some coal was used for lime burning with field kilns being built both close to and often below the pits to make for the easy transport of coal. Scores of such kilns are still to be seen across the Dales - one such being built into the wall running along the eastern side of the Galloway Gate not far from the remains of the pits. Coal mining came to an end on Great Knoutberry about 1860-65 for two reasons. Firstly the workings became waterlogged and secondly the Settle-Carlisle railway brought in cheaper and better quality coal from other areas.

In addition to being mined for its coal, Great Knoutberry was also quarried for its dark grey limestone known as Dent 'marble' which became the reason for the development of an industry based on a mill in upper Dentdale. After defining the nature of the marble in the next section the focus shifts to the industry's production processes, its products, their transportation and the industry's demise. Finally the story of Dent 'marble' is concluded by reflecting on a young solicitor who, on a visit to Dentdale, became fascinated with the supply of water power to the marble mill. He went on to study hydraulic engineering before forming a huge engineering empire on Tyneside.

### *Dent Marble*

BLACK 'marble', or Dent 'marble' as it was more commonly known, is not a true marble but a Yoredale limestone with a high carbon content. Predominantly dark grey to black it is hard enough to be polished and the fossils in it delineated by a definitive white outline. It was discovered in 1760 and was widely used, for over a hundred years, for ornaments but also for fireplace surrounds and staircases. The stone was found on steep hillsides and in gills where the seams were exposed. The quarries, from which Dent marble was dug, were to be found across Dentdale in particular at Arten Gill and Dent Head and on Great Coum and Rise Hill. As the limestone needed very careful handling explosives were banned in the quarries. This was due to the fact that a severe jolt, or the use of a very heavy hammer, might make the rock unsuitable for polishing and susceptible to weathering if the block was to be used externally.

Between 1760 and 1810 the development and organisation of the marble industry progressed steadily so that, by the end of the eighteenth century, the marble trade was well established. When it expanded rapidly in the first half of the nineteenth century it centred on two mills, High Mill and Low Mill, at the bottom of Arten Gill. By 1830 many men were employed in the industry's quarries and mills. The arrival of the railway in the last quarter of the nineteenth century gave a further stimulus to the industry.

The Stone House Marble Mill, owned by two partners Nixon and Denton, stood at the bottom of Arten Gill. (Later the mill was owned by Blackmore and Company, the Blackmores living at Broadfield House lower down the dale.) Paul Nixon (1765-1850), lived in Stone House, the largest of the houses at Arten Gill. He was a Cumbrian man and a well known sculptor of his time. The marble works was formed out of the conversion of two former woollen mills once used for spinning and carding. Built originally in the eighteenth century the change to marble production seems to have occurred by 1812. The works flourished in the nineteenth century at a time when marble chimney pieces, staircases and monuments were fashionable. In mid-Victorian times Stone House Marble Mill was a major employer. As old people remarked, the mill was 'a gay busy shop i' them days.' By 1812 High Mill's remarkable 60 foot diameter water wheel had switched, from driving spinning jennies in the eighteenth century, to operating marble cutting saws in the nineteenth. Low Mill too had a water wheel near to Stone House Bridge.

The mill at Stone House developed links with London firms of monumental masons and through Paul Nixon with the marble works in Carlisle. At one point Stone House Marble Mill employed around forty men of whom thirteen were skilled marble masons. Sadly the local marble industry went into a slow decline with only eight or nine men employed. What hit Stone House Marble Mill particularly hard was the removal of the import tariff on Italian marble. All production ceased around 1900 with demolition of the two mills following in 1928.

It is interesting to examine the production processes at Stone House Marble Mill in earlier times. It was there that the marble was cut and polished. At High Mill the marble was cut by saws covered in sand and water before being polished at Low Mill. It is believed that Low Mill later acquired its own cutting equipment. When both mills were in full production the waters of Widdale Great Tarn were used as a water supply. In times of drought an old man was employed by the company to climb the fell to turn the water on in the morning and then to climb the fell again in the evening to turn it off for the night. It would seem that the water was fed to the two mills via a system of underground culverts.

Dent marble was highly valued in the nineteenth century for interior decorative purposes. To meet this demand Stone House Marble Mill turned out fireplaces, tombstones, fonts, staircases, marble-topped tables and many small objects such as bowls, inkstands and painters' pallets. It even supplied Ingleborough Hall at Clapham with ornamental columns of polished rock which displayed the fossils beautifully. Fireplaces and floors, not only across the Dales but as far afield as Newcastle, Liverpool and London, were made from Dent marble. As many as five chimney pieces made from the stone were installed in the Cowgill Vicarage in Dentdale. In Bradford the Cartwright Memorial Hall's staircases were all built of Dent marble as were many fireplaces in station waiting rooms on the Settle-Carlisle railway. It was also used for the staircase in Owen's College in Manchester and those in London's Inns of Court. Dent marble was used in the construction of Arten Gill viaduct. On a smaller scale items like two beautiful chess tables were skillfully made out of Dent marble.

During the mill's productive life its products were sent by road, canal, rail and sea to London, Newcastle, Carlisle and Preston. In the early days packhorse trains were used to transport the products with one, for example, going to Gargrave where the Leeds-Liverpool Canal could be used to reach distant parts of the country. Following the arrival of the Settle-Carlisle railway the delicate blocks of marble were trundled up to Dent Station for transportation.

The chief rival to Dent marble products were the imported, cheap, coloured Italian marbles. These imports virtually killed off the Dent industry towards the end of the nineteenth century by making Dent marble quarrying unprofitable. At this period in time Stone House Marble Mill itself took in Italian marble which it realised the public preferred to the local stone. From this imported Italian marble the company continued to make a wide range of products such as inkstands and tombstones. Sadly this only postponed the inevitable and, as I have noted, Stone House Marble Mill finally closed. The boost the coming of the railway brought to the industry was nullified by the importation of the cheaper Italian marble at about the same time. Shortage of labour was another added difficulty. The final factor was that, whilst once a very popular stone, Dent marble went out of fashion.

Finally, before I leave the subject of Dent marble, it is important to refer to the unusual, but important, link between the industry and William George Armstrong. In 1835 William George Armstrong, then 25 years old, came to upper Dentdale on his honeymoon. While he was fishing in Artengill Beck he became intrigued by the way that the workers at Stone House Marble Mill used the local water supply to generate power. He visited the mill and noted its waterwheel. He also visited local quarries and studied the machinery in use at them. In Arten Gill he saw Dent marble being extracted from its bed and given a high polish to enable the fossils to stand out. More importantly it was the way that the water was being harnessed to generate water power that got him thinking. He calculated that only about one twentieth of Artengill Beck's power was being used.

On returning to Newcastle he gave up all thought of becoming a solicitor and pursuing a career in the law. Instead he made a special study of water power with reference to hydraulic machinery. Later he took up the study of steam power and finally electric power to become one of the foremost engineers of his day. His initiatives in these fields led him to set up his own business which later turned into the huge Armstrong engineering empire on Tyneside.

It is quite likely that Dent marble products, which left Stone House Marble Mill by packhorse train, travelled along the Galloway Gate. This drove road was part of the network of such roads along which cattle were moved from Scotland to England. In the next section this road's features, its breathtaking views, its severe weather and its main branch, a green road, known as the Driving Road, are explored.

## *The Galloway Gate*

REFERRED to locally and on some old maps as the Coal Road the Galloway Gate is some four miles long. Commencing at Lea Yeat in upper Dentdale it goes up the hillside to Dent Station from where it continues across the western flank of Great Knoutberry Hill. It then passes through an area of disused coal pits before reaching its highest point of 1,760 feet above sea level in the vicinity of Cowgill Head and Shaking Moss. From there it begins its descent past Garsdale Common and Garsdale Station before joining the A684 which runs through Wensleydale and Garsdale linking the A1 with the M6.

Close to Blea Grin Gill and not far from where the large plantation comes right up to the western side of the Galloway Gate a branch of the latter, known as the Driving Road, turns off to follow a grassy ledge along Great Knoutberry's western flank just below the cairns on Pikes Edge. This green road, after about two miles, combines with the Arten Gill track, coming up from the valley, to continue as the well-defined ancient route from Dentdale across the eastern side of Great Knoutberry. It eventually joins the Ingleton-Hawes road after crossing Widdale Beck at Widdale Bridge once used by packhorses.

The Galloway Gate is a scenic and historic route. It is a former packhorse and drove road and was once part of the ancient cattle route from Scotland to England via Mallerstang. The origin of its name is debatable deriving either from the Galloways, a breed of ponies used as packhorses in the movement of coal and other goods, or from the Scottish Galloway cattle driven along it. A late twelfth century charter refers to a road, in roughly the same part of the country, called the Galwaithegate which ran south from near Tebay to Kirkby Lonsdale. There appears to be some evidence, in the form of old deeds and manuscripts, for the Galloway Gate to have been called the Coal Road some time in its past. This name, also used by locals, more than likely originated with the fact that the Galloway Gate gave access to Garsdale Colliery's coal pits.

Today, the traveller coming from Dent Town, passes Cowgill Chapel before turning left to climb up the notoriously steep 600 feet or so to Dent Station. Given a metalled surface in 1954 it also has, for much of its length, good grass verges which help vehicles grip in bad weather. Today it is essentially a minor road with a relatively good surface used, for the most part, by summer visitors. In winter ice can make it a very hazardous place for a motorist. It is often blocked by snowdrifts which linger on behind the walls long after the snow has melted in Dentdale and Garsdale, the two valleys it connects. In fact winter conditions, on its highest stretches, are sufficiently dangerous for signs to have been erected near to both Dent and Garsdale stations which read: 'Altitude 1,750 feet. Winter conditions can be dangerous.'

It is more than likely that a significant proportion of the 100,000 beasts, driven annually from Scotland to England by a whole host of traditional routes, were moved along the Galloway Gate. Geoffrey Wright has identified the routes followed[4]. Scottish drovers converged on Carlisle from where the route continued to Penrith. From there one route went to Kirkby Lonsdale whilst another went south east to follow the line of the A66 to Appleby. There the route split again with the eastern arm going to Brough, across Stainmore and on to Scotch Corner where it met other drove roads coming in from Corbridge. The western arm from Appleby went to Kirkby Stephen then on to Shoregill, in Mallerstang, from where the drovers followed The High Way along the flanks of Lunds Fell to Garsdale and the Galloway Gate. Another important route, from the north, went to Richmond via Alston, Teesdale, Bowes, Arkengarthdale and Reeth. For Scottish drovers heading for the Dales, Kirkby Stephen, Brough and Bowes were key towns on the routes. Of the cattle on the move at any given moment a large number were being driven to Malham where cattle fairs were held. At the latter's Great Close as many as 5,000 head of Scottish cattle were sometimes gathered to be fattened for markets or sold to butchers.

The Driving Road, possibly got its name because driving was a corruption of droving. This route branches off the surfaced Galloway Gate. As part of one of the former drove routes from Scotland it keeps well below the summit of Great Knoutberry but still manages to reach an altitude of about 1,700 feet only slightly lower than the highest point on the Galloway Gate itself. As a drove road it had the advantage of being both level and relatively dry contrasting strongly with the Arten Gill track. Drovers liked to follow such familiar, well-defined routes whose elevation kept them well clear of farms and enclosed fields in the valleys. After following the Driving Road around Great Knoutberry drovers then headed for Gearstones, not far from Ribblehead, by working there way down the eastern side of Wold Fell, Great Knoutberry's neighbour.

In prehistoric times livestock was moved from one grazing area to another. Roman engineers sometimes followed the line of these ancient livestock movements for their early roads. Throughout the Middle Ages and right up until the Enclosure Movement got under way roads, including drove roads, were un-walled and un-surfaced; today many of them are the green roads so beloved of walkers. Drove roads were usually wide enough for bunched cattle to move along. Old drovers' routes became the earliest roads, preserved by virtue of the continuous usage by herds of cattle and sheep over the centuries. Drove roads were thus an integral part of the road network of the country and cattle often shared these routes with wagons and packhorses. It was no surprise therefore that, with the growth of towns in the sixteenth century and the resulting increase in the demand for larger meat supplies, drove roads, such as the Galloway Gate and the one between Horton-in-Ribblesdale and Hawes, grew in importance.

As described earlier the views from the summit of Great Knoutberry are nothing if not impressive. Whilst not as extensive as those to be had from the summit, the views from the Galloway Gate and the Driving Road are splendid in either direction. In my opinion the most dramatic view is to be had from the Galloway Gate, at the point where, just above Dent Station, it begins its descent. In front of you the bulk of Whernside fills the south western horizon together with the noble profile of Great Coum. Beyond these majestic fells you can see Calf Top and the Barbon Fells. Immediately to the west lies Rise Hill dividing beautiful, green Dentdale from narrow Garsdale, the latter hemmed in on its northern side by Baugh Fell. The eye wanders down Garsdale and can pick out the Howgills and beyond the distant Lake District peaks.

When travelling north over the Galloway Gate the best views are to be had as you descend towards Garsdale Station. As you begin the descent into Garsdale an unfolding panorama opens up that compels you to stop. If the view south impressed with the feeling of great height and the great contrast between the intimate detail of pastoral Dentdale and the powerful looming presence of Whernside and its neighbours, the view north impresses with the vast panorama of fells both near and distant. In an arc from west to east you can see Garsdale flanked by Rise Hill and Baugh Fell. Beyond them, in the far west, are the shapely Howgills and the Lake District mountains. To the north lies Swarth Fell and Wild Boar Fell with its distinctive flat top. Across Mallerstang lies the gently rounded summit of Lunds Fell with its highest point Sails. Further east lies the expansive summit of Great Shunner Fell which with Lovely Seat guards the Buttertubs pass. Finally if you look across Garsdale to the north west you should be able to identify the lonely, hanging valley of Grisedale made famous by the book written many years ago entitled *The Dale That Died.*

Drovers came along the Galloway Gate and in the next section I consider the need for droving and take a detailed look at the development of the industry, the controls placed on it, the drovers' working methods and the reasons leading to the industry's decline.

### *The Drovers*

ALTHOUGH it is not clear when droving first began, it is safe to assume that, from the earliest times, cattle and sheep have been moved around to find better pastures. Such movements of stock continued through the Middle Ages up to the fourteenth century. By then drovers had acquired a reputation not much higher than that of cattle thieves which some people believed many of them were. A big boost to the growth of droving occurred in the sixteenth century. It was then that each town and city discovered it had a major problem in providing its burgeoning population with meat from its own immediate rural hinterland. Added to this were the ever spiralling demands of the navy for fresh meat. To deal with these two major problems an ever increasing number of cattle were moved around the country highlighting the urgent need for drovers and by definition their importance. The result was that, during the reigns of Mary and Elizabeth I, drovers became so numerous that controls had to be introduced. A drover now had to be thirty years of age, married and a householder; more significantly he had to carry an annually renewable licence. A fine of five pounds was imposed on any drover breaking these laws. The tightening up of the trade, with these new controls, also had the beneficial effect of giving reputable drovers enhanced status.

By the late seventeenth century the demand for meat in England, particularly in the south, grew dramatically thereby once more increasing the need for drovers to drive more and more cattle south from Scotland. In 1672 the abolition of tolls had the effect of establishing the droving trade on a sound financial basis. During the reign of Queen Anne a law was passed preventing a drover from declaring himself bankrupt and thereby avoiding all his financial obligations. An earlier seventeenth century law prohibited Sunday droving presumably in the belief that work should not be performed on the Sabbath.

By this time drovers were, not only controlling the movement of large numbers of livestock, but increasingly being entrusted to carry messages and handle financial transactions. Droving reached its peak in the early decades of the nineteenth century before the coming of the railway resulted in the easier, quicker and more convenient shipment of cattle over long distances. There is little doubt that the transport of cattle by rail to new cattle centres brought to an end the era of the drover or 'kilted cowboy' as he was otherwise known. The other major change which, like the railway, affected droving was the Enclosure Movement which swept across the countryside in the nineteenth century, its miles of walls and improvements to the land effectively preventing passage by herds of cattle and sheep.

~ ~ ~ ~ ~ ~ ~ ~ ~ ~ ~ ~ ~

By 1800, at the height of the droving trade, some 100,000 cattle a year were driven from Scotland into England. Almost certainly many would have passed through the Dales possibly along the Galloway Gate. In Scotland young cattle were collected from around the highlands to be assembled at fairs at such places as Falkirk and Dumfries. From there they would be driven south to be sold at fairs and gatherings in the north of England one of which, as we saw earlier, was at Great Close near Malham. From such large Dales fairs and gatherings cattle, bought by Dales farmers for winter fattening on their hill pastures, were sold the following year at local markets. In addition Dales markets were regularly frequented by dealers from the Midlands and the South who bought cattle for fattening and selling in their own areas.

How did drovers operate - what methods and tactics did they employ to control their stock? Some drovers were in the regular employ of a dealer, others were hired for a particular drive. Most cattle drives would consist of 200 head or more. Small groups of drovers, with only a few head of cattle, would often join forces with a larger drive. One drover with the help of his dogs, a boy and a couple of mules to carry his provisions, could manage 50 cattle or 500 sheep. The drover used his dogs to control the livestock in his charge much as the modern farmer uses them in sheep management on the fells. As Geoffrey Wright has noted if a drover, after finishing a drive, had to stay on an extra day or two to conclude his business his dogs would be sent home ahead of him on their own. It is believed that they even followed the same route as on the outward journey receiving food at the same inns.

Although most drove roads were wide enough for herds to move forward bunched together most drovers, for easier control and management of the herd, preferred their cattle to move slowly rarely more than three abreast. If they moved slowly the livestock could also graze as they walked so that they did not lose fitness. Drovers cared for their animals day and night taking them along quiet drove roads across the fells and moors being careful to avoid towns, villages and land under the plough. They crossed streams at their narrowest points which usually meant near their sources and rivers by well established fords. The inclination of the drover was to stick with the familiar, wide, well defined routes which were known to have inns for themselves and overnight pasturage for their stock.

It was in a drover's interest to do his best to ensure that his beasts arrived in the best possible condition at the big markets in the Midlands or London's Smithfield. Driving up to 200 cattle and 2,000 sheep meant progress was inevitably slow with a great deal of hard work required on the part of man and beast. Generally, given the gentle pace of a herd on the move, the maximum distance covered in any one day was usually about twelve miles with overnight rests often occurring after six days. Although beasts did eat along the route a midday stop was made to ensure that the cattle got a little grazing. By early evening a good sheltered spot was found with water and grass for the overnight stop. In the late eighteenth century, for a small charge, some inns and cottages would provide good pasturage in small enclosures of which the often ruined walls can still be seen on the fells. As a drive covered some several hundred miles the hooves of the cattle were shod. A complete shoeing cost one shilling per animal in 1850. The shoeing did not apply to sheep which, instead, had their hooves hardened by a mixture of sand, tar and sawdust.

On most nights drovers slept in the open air wrapped only in their woollen tartan plaids. On some occasions they lodged in inns such as High Dike on the High Way with their stock pastured close by. At some inns they would enjoy a merry night of conviviality with music and drinking. The basic food of the drover was oatmeal, his basic dress a traditional plaid, his language Gaelic. It is said that when cattle strayed the drovers stripped naked to round them up!

It must be remembered that the drover, on behalf of the owner, was the custodian of a large sum of money in terms of what the animals were worth. It was soon realised that beasts were less easy to steal than money carried in cash on the drover's person. So, at the end of the drive, a drover would pay the merchant's costs out of the money raised from the sale of the animals. As times changed and droving rose in status it was not unknown for trusted drovers to carry messages and be allowed to carry money, raised by the sale of the animals, back to their masters. Drovers, dealers and merchants often used promissory notes or bills of exchange which, in effect, provided a system of credit within the droving trade. At some of the major fairs and markets temporary banking facilities were set up to facilitate the exchange of promissory notes and bills.

Both the costs incurred and the income received from a cattle drive fluctuated for two reasons. One was the vagaries of the weather, the other the condition the beasts were in at the end of the drive. On an average drive of two hundred cattle each animal could fetch between 2s 6d (12.5p) and 5s (25p) a head in the early nineteenth century. Drovers were paid between 3s-4s (15-20p) per day at the end of the nineteenth century which was about twice as much as a farm labourer. Out of his wages the drover had to pay for his own lodgings which could be as much as 9d (4p) a night in winter, half this amount in summer. The drover was paid 10s (50p) for his journey home.

~ ~ ~ ~ ~ ~ ~ ~ ~ ~ ~ ~ ~

As has been seen, one of the main reasons for the decline of droving and the use of drove roads was the coming of the railway. When trains started running along the Settle-Carlisle railway the Galloway Gate ceased to function as a drove road. In the next section I travel along the stretch of the line which runs along the flanks of Great Knoutberry, noting its many engineering features and the severe weather conditions to which it is prone. I also consider the functions and the working practices of both Dent and Garsdale stations whilst not forgetting the latter's role as a centre for the social life of the area.

## *The Settle-Carlisle Railway*

THE seventy-two mile stretch of the Settle-Carlisle Railway - a tribute to the brilliant constructional skills of Victorian engineers - cuts a north-south route through the hills and dales of the Pennines. Built between

1869 and 1876 it was a hugely challenging and exacting venture, both to construct and to maintain, in an area which regularly received seventy inches of rain per annum and was often blanketed by heavy snow. The section of line which lies in the area covered by this book is that between the two viaducts of Artengill and Dandrymire, a distance of some five miles, along a ledge cut from the side of Great Knoutberry Hill. After crossing the viaduct over Artengill Beck the line makes a grand left-hand curve towards Dent Station from where it enters Risehill tunnel. On emerging from the tunnel it runs along a ridge to Garsdale Station before crossing Dandrymire Viaduct. Of the six 2,000 foot fells of upper Wensleydale, Great Knoutberry is the only one with a railway on its slopes. For many people this stretch of the Settle-Carlisle railway ranks as one of the most breathtakingly scenic routes in England. As trains cross Artengill Viaduct passengers have, on their left hand, an aerial view of pastoral Dentdale stretching away to the west with its green fields, dry stone walls and hedges. The dale lies enclosed by the massive bulk of Whernside, Great Coum, the Barbon fells, the rounded Howgills and the long ridge of Rise Hill.

When the line was being built many concerned voices were raised at the harm powerful steam locomotives would have on such a peaceful, tranquil environment. Today the general consensus is that the line has blended in with its surroundings. For example, apart from their portals, the tunnels are hidden under the grassy slopes of the fells and the large viaducts, bridging the gills, have an air of elegance about them with their high, rounded archways. Even today a fully lit train, high up on the flanks of Great Knoutberry, still looks a strange phenomenon when at night it appears to be detached from the ground over which it is travelling. On a positive note the line does have the effect of linking the dale with the world outside by bringing tourists in and enabling dalesfolk to travel further afield.

This is not the place to examine in detail the pros and cons of closing the Settle-Carlisle railway as this has been well-documented elsewhere. In the end the Transport Minister, in April 1989 after many years of uncertainty throughout the decade, refused British Rail consent to close the line. Today the line has a regular passenger service and is also used by freight traffic. In addition it is often used for re-routed traffic when there are problems on the West Coast main line. There are also the occasional nostalgic steam specials which have the capacity to bring out railway enthusiasts in their thousands.

The Settle-Carlisle railway line is famous for its fine features of Victorian engineering with 21 viaducts, 14 tunnels and 325 bridges along its length. Of these Great Knoutberry plays host to Artengill Viaduct, Dandrymire Viaduct and Risehill Tunnel. It also has two stations at Dent and Garsdale. I begin my look at these engineering wonders with Artengill Viaduct.

Artengill Viaduct, completed in 1875 after four years work, spans Artengill Beck which flows down the gully separating Great Knoutberry Hill from its southerly neighbour Wold Fell. It is 220 yards long, 117 feet high and has eleven arches. By contrast Dent Head Viaduct, a little to the south, is 199 yards long, 104 feet high and has one arch less. Artengill's arches have a span of 45 feet and the tallest pier, from the ground to rail level, is 129 feet. All the piers at their base measure 38 feet in circumference by 15 feet in diameter with the exception of one which is 42 feet by 28 feet. Lifting the stones into position on the piers proved a difficult operation due to the breakdown of the lifting gear. This was not surprising when you hear that one stone measured fourteen and a half feet by six feet, was twelve inches thick and weighed over eight tons.

As with many of the engineering works on the Settle-Carlisle line the Victorian engineers met with a number of problems. In the case of Artengill Viaduct the problem lay in securing its foundations. In order to find solid rock on which to stand the piers, shafts had to be sunk, some 55 feet through the thick bed of shale, to find the limestone bed. In addition the shafts had to be continually pumped clear of water to enable the men to work in them and then lined with timber to prevent landslips. The beck flowing down Arten Gill was channelled under the viaduct by a culvert. The viaduct was built with 50,000 tons of Dent 'marble' from local quarries, stone normally used for more ornamental purposes.

Risehill Tunnel was driven through the narrow neck of land linking the north western slopes of Great Knoutberry with the eastern end of Rise Hill. The tunnel, which is 1,213 yards long, was constructed from both ends and from two shafts each 170 feet deep. When excavation was completed the tunnel was strengthened by lining its length throughout with masonry blocks. The construction proved no easy task for over one hundred men, working by the light of candles, to blast a way through the rock using drills, hammers and dynamite. Material dug from the tunnel workings was sent up the shafts in large iron buckets to be used in embankment construction or merely dumped in spoil heaps.

The navvies who worked on the construction of the Settle-Carlisle railway lived in temporary settlements or shanty towns such as the one located on Rise Hill not far from the tunnel workings. The settlement, at approximately 1,130 feet above sea level, consisted of a number of wooden huts linked to a similar settlement at Raygill lower down in Garsdale. The link between the two shanty towns, which between them housed some 350 workers, was a 600 yard long tramway used by a winding engine operated by steam. This winding gear was used to bring food, coal and equipment, needed in the construction of the tunnel, up from the valley. At the upper settlement, near to the two tunnel shafts, were a dozen or so huts, a blacksmith's shop, a communal hut for the men, a room for storage, facilities for making mortar and an engine house. The engine was used for blowing fresh, clean air into the tunnel and for hauling the excavated material up the shafts. At the valley settlement there were stables, another blacksmith's shop, a weighing machine and more huts.

One can only marvel at the stoicism and stamina of the men who lived and worked in the hostile environment of the high Pennines. For example it was not unknown for workers and family members to be killed by the tramway through trucks overturning. In the settlements navvies and their families lived in vastly overcrowded accommodation. Serious illnesses seemed to have been prevented, despite the poor drainage and sanitation, by the healthy fresh air of the fells and an abundance of food. Measures taken by the health authorities to prevent serious diseases, such as smallpox, included fewer persons to a hut, regular washing of the huts using lime, the use of disinfectants and the cutting of open ditches for improved drainage.

Drink was always a problem in such settlements as it led to fighting with bare fists with injuries common and fatalities not unknown. Much of the alcohol drunk, in such temporary settlements as Rise Hill, was drunk without the knowledge of the fiscal authorities. Many of the navvies of Rise Hill went down to the hamlet of Lea Yeat where, while the construction work on the line was going on, a brewery was established. Two miles further up the dale there was a licensed cottage named Scow where the navvies drank and fought. For a time it was known as the 'Wonder Inn'. As was the nature of navvies working on the Settle-Carlisle line they tended to disappear during severe winters and at haymaking time.

On the northern slopes of Great Knoutberry, at Garsdale Head, lies the fell's second impressive viaduct - Dandrymire. Here the engineer's original plan was to build an embankment. However, after tipping thousands upon thousands of cubic yards of material fruitlessly into Dandry Mire itself, the engineers resorted to a viaduct. Dandrymire viaduct has twelve arches and from its deep foundations rises some 50 feet above the bog.

At around 1,150 feet above sea level Dent Station perches on a ledge on the western slopes of Great Knoutberry. This makes it, reputedly, the highest main line station in England. The Midland Company's original plan to locate the station at Dent Head was finally rejected as it would have placed Dent Town not four and a half miles from its station but seven! This distance, between the town and its station, has often puzzled people down the generations giving rise to a number of wry, sardonic responses. For example the story goes that when a visitor once enquired why Dent station was such a long way from Dent town the reply was 'It'll be so it's near t'tracks.' The station is reached by climbing some six hundred feet up the Galloway Gate from Lea Yeat.

Apart from its height, Dent station is also known for its fences of upended railway sleepers on the fell side just to the east of the station. Placed there to prevent snow blowing on to the tracks their usefulness has been questioned from time to time. Some people took the view that, when a blizzard blew down from Great Knoutberry, they were not particularly effective as drifts soon built up behind them from which the wind duly blew snow on to the tracks. When snow was not the problem sparks from steam locomotives were, as the fences often caught fire.

Opened in 1877 the station at Dent had, apart from the station buildings, a signal box and small siding. Its main buildings, today in private hands, were made in the Midland Company's Victorian Gothic style with steep roofs. Its main waiting room was given a fireplace mantel shelf made of Dent 'marble'. Across the tracks on the 'up' platform the waiting room, or platform shelter as it was known, was built into the side of the hill and required the support of a rear wall.

Although Dent Station has lost its signal box the stationmaster's house sits proudly at the northern end of the station exposed to the elements. The house was built with double windows and slate-clad walls to keep out the bitter winds which sweep the fell. When the house was built in the 1890s bathrooms were a rare internal facility. As a consequence whoever was stationmaster at Dent had to brave the cold and the winds to reach the external wash house and privy. Also provided at Dent Station was a stone cabin for use by men clearing snow off the line. It was affectionately called the 'Dent Hotel' as in severe winter conditions it provided the snow clearers with a good fire, food and drink. Today such cabins along the trackside receive much less use owing to milder winters. Dent Station, today, is still a very special place for as Norman Duerden points out, where else in Britain can you stand on a railway platform in June and watch a ring ouzel feedings its fledglings?[5]

Most goods reaching the dale, such as coal from the South Yorkshire coal field, corn, lard, fireplaces, mowing machines and bedsteads came in through Dent Station. Many of the cattle shipments in the area were dealt with by Garsdale Station as Dent Station's facilities were inadequate for the handling of large numbers of stock.

The Dent section of the Settle-Carlisle line, including Dent Station itself has, over the years, suffered its fair share of snow. Around Dent and Garsdale it was said that there was that much snow you didn't know where to put it when you'd cleared it. Bill Mitchell cites a number of incidents which give a flavour of what winter conditions were like in the environment of Dent Station.[6] One permanent way man claimed that the snow was so deep that he walked up the roof of the waiting room at Dent only later realising what he had done. In 1947 the Dent section was blocked for eight weeks. Even moderate snow falls posed problems because the unceasing wind blew the snow off the fells filling the railway cuttings and forming dangerous cornices on drifts twenty feet high. Sometimes snow removed from a cutting was taken by train and thrown over the side of Artengill Viaduct. Forty foot drifts have been known between the station and Rise Hill. The Dent section was ploughed out whenever possible but it was not unusual for trains, even the ploughs themselves, to be buried in drifts. Winter conditions around Dent and the higher parts of the Settle-Carlisle line in general were best summed up by the Settle-Carlisle man who, in response to another man's boast that, in his district the snow covered the rails, retorted that in his area it didn't just cover the rails, it covered the bloody engines as well.

~ ~ ~ ~ ~ ~ ~ ~ ~ ~ ~ ~ ~ ~

Due north of Dent lies Garsdale Station. It is here that the Midland Company's scenic branch line from Hawes joined the main Settle-Carlisle line. The Hawes branch, five miles 1,577 yards long, opened in

1878. The line followed the southern side of Wensleydale, running along the northern slopes of Great Knoutberry for much of its length. Leaving Hawes at 800 feet the line climbed steadily to reach over 1,000 feet at Garsdale. In 1900 Garsdale Station changed its name from 'Hawes Junction' to 'Hawes Junction and Garsdale'. Then, in 1933, it was renamed 'Garsdale (for Hawes).' To avoid confusion by switching from one name to another the name Garsdale will be used throughout this section.

The Midland Company's branch line from Garsdale met that of the North East Railway Company at Hawes where a joint company station was built. The line ran through lovely, but technically demanding, countryside where several cuttings, two viaducts and a tunnel were required. One of the viaducts had five arches and crossed Widdale Beck at Appersett whilst the other, crossing Mossdale Beck, had four arches. Near to the latter a short tunnel, 245 yards long, was built the only one, surprisingly, required between Hawes and Garsdale. People living along the Hawes branch line became so attached to their trains that they gave them names. For example the name 'Bonnyface' was given to the engine which hauled the afternoon train between Hawes and Garsdale. Sadly, throughout the life of the Hawes branch line, passenger traffic was never high. In its first full year of operation, 1879, 6,845 tickets were sold.[7] Between 1880-1920 tickets sales ranged between 7,000 and 9,000 per annum with a peak of 9,193 in 1891. From the 1920s it was a story of slow decline until closure came in 1959. With the closure of the Hawes branch line Garsdale lost its junction status. The stopping trains serving Garsdale on the Settle-Carlisle line ceased in 1970.

Returning to the heyday of Garsdale Station when traffic on the Settle-Carlisle line was at its peak and it served as a junction for those wishing to visit Hawes and stations to Northallerton. The Midland Company gave the station no main buildings due to its remote location. It considered it merely a junction (albeit the only real junction on the Settle-Carlisle line) serving no specific local community. Later plans to turn Garsdale into a model of Hellifield, by building an engine shed for 24 locomotives with living accommodation for the work force, were dropped when the costs became too high. That said Garsdale did have a sizeable signal box with 24 levers, a water tank and troughs, a turntable and an engine shed. The latter, after being destroyed by fire in 1917, was finally closed prior to the Second World War. The turntable was for turning the locomotives, used to double head the trains up to the summit of the line (1,169 feet) at Aisgill, so that they could return to either Hellifield or Carlisle.

The story is told that, on one very windy night, those operating the turning of a locomotive lost control of the turntable. The locomotive spun round and round for hours before the revolving turntable was halted by sand and grit being thrown into its mechanism. After this incident upright sleepers were erected around the turntable to prevent it from spinning in future high winds. Apart from having its own reservoir water supply from springs on the fell, which it purified itself, Garsdale Station also had a 43,000 gallon water tank from which the water troughs, lying between the station and Risehill Tunnel, were fed. The troughs, believed to be the highest in the world, were about half a mile long and six inches deep in the middle. Water flowed from the reservoir to an engine house from where it was pumped into the troughs. Engines took in the water without stopping, often at speeds of up to 60mph, by lowering a scoop. Railwaymen considered the troughs unreliable as they were often frozen in winter, dry in summer and blocked with leaves in the autumn.

Whilst the 'down' platform building at Garsdale was built to conform to the typical Midland architectural style the 'up' platform building had a different feature. Here there was a long, stone waiting room with iron and glass awnings. Unfortunately problems with this awning led to it being taken down in 1957 to be replaced with a flat, wooden canopy attached to the building's north end. Its purpose was to give protection from the weather to passengers on both sides of the station's island platform. Whilst both waiting rooms had fireplaces, the ladies waiting room also had a library of some 200 books placed there for the use of railway employees and passengers. Most of the books had been donated by two elderly ladies from Wensleydale as they felt sorry for the railwaymen who lived in such a remote spot. The books were looked after by the stationmaster who acted as the librarian. The main waiting room was also used to hold religious services and had an organ and hymn books. Next to the station a row of terraced houses, built as homes for railway employees, were only connected to the mains water supply in 1951.

Underneath the huge water tank was the Tank House. Originally used for engine repairs it became, in the years between the two World Wars, Garsdale Welfare Institute. It acted as a centre for a wide range of social activities including dances, concerts, dominoes, whist drives and potato pie suppers. It was a long, high-ceilinged room lit by oil-lamps and heated by two large coal-burning stoves. It had a small kitchen and upholstered seats taken from an old railway carriage which, minus its wheels, was used to serve refreshments. The station became the heart of the community - the focus for social activities for both railway employees and surrounding dalesfolk.

Garsdale Station is terribly exposed in bad weather with winds gusting up to 100mph making the opening of carriage doors a difficult operation. Jessica Lofthouse described Garsdale as '...a railway station cast upon the mountains, the plaything of all the elements. We looked out into nothing but cloud. When we tried to open the carriage door the gale would have nothing of it. The combined station staff had to wrench it open against the force of the north wester. Rain lashed us into the shelter of the little waiting-room-cum-lending library...'[8]

Given Garsdale's isolated position people have, in earlier times on very dark and sometimes stormy nights, missed alighting there. Snow, too, has often played havoc with the line close to the station blocking it frequently. Opening the line has often involved many men in snow clearance operations. The line to Hawes was also prone to being blocked by snow when a north-northeaster blew in.

Today Garsdale is a much less busy station than before the Second World War. Its turntable has gone, so too its sidings, water troughs, engine shed and Tank House. Sadly, gone too from the Settle-Carlisle line, apart from a monthly special, are the steam trains that gave us that wonderful smell of engine smoke.

# 5
# LUND'S FELL

After looking at Lunds Fell's topography, particularly with regard to the sources of the Ure and Eden, I follow the route of Lady Anne Clifford's Way and note the various travellers who used it. I also consider woodland policy for the Dales and conclude with a look at lime kilns and dry stone walls.

## *Pennine watershed*

THE name Lunds is derived from the Norse word 'lundr' meaning a wood. The name almost certainly originated in the days of the Norse invasions when the area presented a somewhat different landscape to that of today. Instead of bare hillsides the area was part forested with thorn, rowan, ash and oak trees and part covered by a dense growth of small trees and shrubs not to mention bogs. In addition to the name Lunds being given to the fell, it was also given to the tiny hamlet on its south western flank. The latter was probably a Norse settlement as many villages in Norway and Sweden are called Lunds. In fact the whole area from the Moorcock Inn up to Hell Gill has a number of Scandinavian place names. It is believed that a form of Norse dialect was spoken on and around the fell up to the time of Elizabeth I. In fact Norse words are still used today in the area - a barn for example is called a laithe. Old documents refer to Lunds as The Lundes; local dalesfolk still tend to use the prefix and refer to it as The Lunds.

Sails, the summit of Lunds Fell at 2,185 feet above sea level, is the most southerly 2,000 foot fell on a long ridge of such fells stretching to the north - Hugh Seat 2,260 feet, Archy Styrigg 2,280 feet and High Seat 2,326 feet. To the south of Lunds Fell the terrain falls away towards Wensleydale encompassing the not insignificant heights of Bubble Hill and Tarn Hill, the lonely seagull-haunted Cotter End Tarn at 1,650 feet and Thwaite Bridge Common. The most southerly point of the ridge is Cotter End, its name probably derived from the Tudor scholar and traveller Leland's reference, in his itinerary, to Lunds Fell as Coterine or Cotoren Hill. Below Cotter End lie the cliffs of Cotter Clints along which runs the High Way, better known today as Lady Anne Clifford's Way.

Just as Drumaldrace is the name given to the summit of Wether Fell so Sails is the name given to the summit of Lunds Fell although the topography is not as clear cut as in the case of the former. Although Sails is what we might describe as the most clearly defined summit of Lunds Fell, thanks to its cairn and the decision of the Ordnance Survey to locate one of their trig points on it, it is not the definitive mathematical summit. Just half a mile further north Little Fell Brae rises to a height of 2,188 feet some three feet higher than Sails. To confuse matters further Ure Head, again a little further north than Sails although lower than the latter, sometimes gets credited with being the summit of Lunds Fell because Wensleydale's river Ure rises on its western flank giving it a degree of significance. Why Sails received the Ordnance Survey trig point is probably due to nothing more than the fact that it is considered to have the best views.

From Sails the view is a vast panorama of high rolling fells. Some have claimed that, when walking south along this great ridge, the view from Sails is better than anything seen since leaving High Pike Hill some four miles to the north. To the east Great Shunner Fell's bulk is all encompassing. To the south Penyghent, Ingleborough and Whernside dominate the horizon. Across Mallerstang to the west Wild Boar Fell looms large and impressive. On a clear day the Lake District fells may be seen. Being the most southerly of the Mallerstang ridge summits Sails overlooks Wensleydale and is thus part of its landscape. The most surprising view from the summit is the one to be had looking south east, straight down Cotterdale, to the market town of Hawes with its prominent church tower. So from the summit of Sails, close to where Wensleydale's river Ure rises, you can see Hawes, the first town on its course, where the river becomes wide and strong flowing. From Sails the hamlets of Aisgill and Garsdale Head can also be seen.

The summit of Sails is broad and mossy indicating limestone overlaid by gritstone on which heather grows and on which are to be found peat beds. Merry mountain streams provide a little interest on what is generally regarded as rather featureless sheep grazing terrain. The whole of Lunds Fell lies on what is called Abbotside Common, a large area of sheep pasture, stretching to the slopes of Lovely Seat a few miles to the east.

Most of the rain falling on the Lunds Fell catchment area finds its way to the North Sea. The streams rising on Lunds Fell, apart from those on its north west flank, flow directly into the Ure or via West Gill. The latter then becomes Cotterdale Beck and joins the Ure a few miles to the south east. The streams on the fell's north west flank flow westwards via the Eden river and its tributaries to the Irish Sea. The watershed on Lunds Fell runs north-south on a line through Hell Gill Bridge and Jingling Sike Cave. The two major rivers, Ure and Eden, rise within half a mile or so of each other, the former on Lunds Fell, the Eden on Hugh Seat.

Lunds Fell is crossed by a number of footpaths. In addition to the High Way, the main track along the fell's western flank, another major footpath reaching 1,750 feet above sea level links High Dike, a former drovers' inn, with Cotterdale village. It crosses the moors of Tarn Hill, Lunds Fell's southern ridge, its route marked by a line of shooting butts. By leaving it at the point where two fences meet, one coming from the south west and one from the south east, a relatively easy climb to the summit of Sails can be made by walking due north over Bubble Hill. From High Dike another path goes down the hillside to Lunds church, to which many generations of Cotterdale folk have carried their dead for burial, Cotterdale having no church of its own.

Another ascent of Sails can be made by simply finding a convenient point, for example from High Hall, at which to leave the High Way and climb up the gradual slope of the fell side. This should not present too many difficulties as the sheer gritstone cliffs of Mallerstang Edge to the north, which prevent easy access to the high fells, are not a feature here. For those who require a little more variety in the climb to the summit of Sails the water eroded little valleys of the infant Ure and Washer Gill, from where they cross The High Way, can be followed to their source before striking out across the moor to the summit cairn.

~ ~ ~ ~ ~ ~ ~ ~ ~ ~ ~ ~ ~

The name Ure seems to have been adopted as a name for the river in 1140 before changing to Yeure in 1530. All the names - Eure, Yeure, Yure, Yore, Yer, Yor, Jor and Ure - can be traced back to variations of the old word for water. It may even be the case that Ure is derived from Isura, which generally means physical or spiritual power, giving rise to the suggestion that the name Ure may mean the strong or holy river.

The River Ure rises on Ure Head approximately a quarter of a mile from Sails. Like many river sources it is not the easiest to identify as it

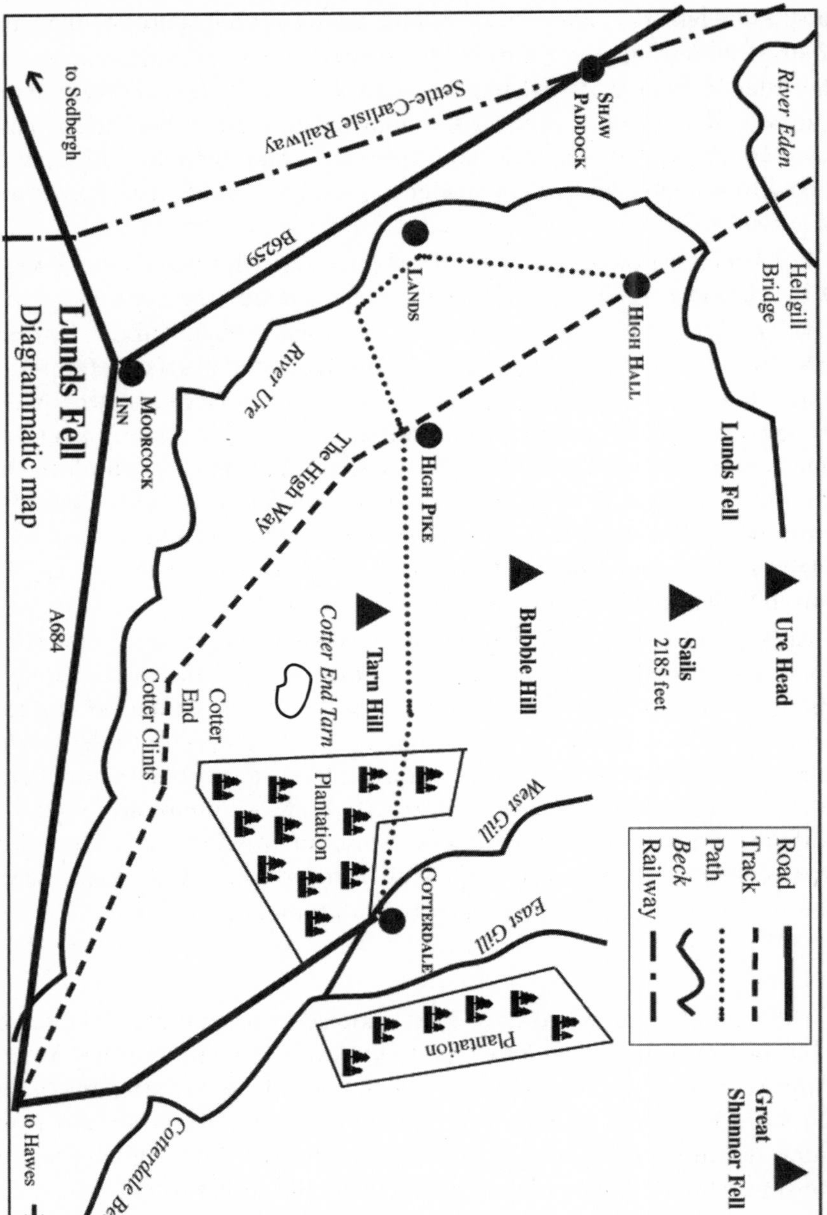
Lunds Fell
Diagrammatic map
to Sedbergh
Settle-Carlisle Railway
SHAW PADDOCK
River Eden
Hellgill Bridge
B6259
LANDS
HIGH HALL
MOORCOCK INN
River Ure
Lunds Fell
HIGH PIKE
The High Way
Ure Head
Sails
2185 feet
Bubble Hill
Tarn Hill
Cotter End Tarn
Cotter
End
Cotter Clints
A684
Plantation
West Gill
COTTERDALE
East Gill
Plantation
Road
Track
Path
Beck
Railway
Great Shunner Fell
to Hawes
Cotterdale Beck

rises as one runnel amongst many in a boggy area of peat hags, hummocks and hollows. This trickle, which passes for the source of the Ure, is, in its initial stages, so narrow that a person can easily stride across it. It begins its infant life struggling through sphagnum moss and bent grass before flowing down a ravine and disappearing underground for a short distance. At this point its dry bed is littered with fallen rocks. Bird cherry and rowan trees grow where they can establish a hold. Ella Pontefract described where the stream goes underground as an eerie spot.[1]

The Ure's source is in a wild, bleak, sparsely populated area of high fells. Camden, the Elizabethan historian and traveller, described the countryside around Lunds Fell as a 'dreary waste and horrid silent wilderness.' He even claimed that the area was a retreat for deer, stags and goats all of which had large horns. In more recent times Ella Pontefract, in her description of a walk up to the source of the Ure, refers to the 'stillness' and 'calm' of an 'unchanging' landscape. To many walkers it is an area not without its appeal particularly those who appreciate the beauty of vast expanses of high rolling moorland across which cloud shadows chase one another on bright sunny days.

Both the infant rivers Ure and Eden flow towards each other before the latter swings north and the Ure turns south. A little south of Hell Gill whilst walking along the High Way a small stream is crossed without realising that it is the infant Ure beginning its journey down the western flank of Lunds Fell. After flowing west-south west to Ure Crook it then turns due south down Mallerstang where, just south of Cobbles Hill, it turns eastwards to flow through Wensleydale. The first of the Ure's significant tributaries is Mossdale Gill which joins the Ure a short distance below Thwaite Bridge. A little further downstream Cotterdale Beck flows into the Ure at Holme Heads Bridge as does Widdale Beck at Appersett. Just north of Hawes, Gayle Beck joins the Ure at Haylands Bridge.

A short distance from its source it is difficult to come to terms with the fact that this narrow, bubbling beck, leaping merrily over rocks, is the source of the broad full-flowing River Ure that curves its way serenely through Wensleydale. After flowing through the latter the Ure joins the Swale near Aldborough to become the Ouse. The latter then flows via York and Selby into the Humber completing, for that initial trickle of water on Lunds Fell, a course under its various names of some 120 miles.

Although the River Eden rises outside the area covered by this book it has been included as its south westerly course, through the gorge at Hell Gill, is an integral feature of the north western slopes of Lunds Fell. The Eden in fact rises on the slopes of Hugh Seat which, at 2,260 feet above sea level, is the next highest point north of Lunds Fell. Despite claims in the past that the Eden rose on Wild Boar Fell it is now generally accepted that, high on the slopes of Hugh Seat, Red Gill flowing into Hell Gill Beck is the main source. This places the Eden's source just under two miles north, as the crow flies, of the source of the Ure on Lunds Fell. Just like the terrain at the source of the Ure the Eden rises in a landscape of wild fells and crags under wide expansive skies.

When walking along the High Way, Hell Gill Bridge takes you across the young Eden. At this point a thought may cross your mind that the name Eden seems at odds with the reality of its turbulent passage through Hell Gill gorge and the wild terrain in which it rises. As it rolls down the fell side the infant Eden increases in size and strength to become a torrent. Later it becomes more in keeping with its name when after, flowing south west for two to three miles from its source, negotiating Hell Gill gorge and Hell Gill Force it turns north to become a beautiful serene river. It flows through Mallerstang's meadows and pastures for several miles to reach Kirkby Stephen and Appleby before emptying into the Solway just below Carlisle. For a time the young Eden as Hell Gill Beck forms the boundary between Cumbria and North Yorkshire. The Eden is one of the few English rivers to flow northwards.

The long, narrow, deep gorge called Hell Gill, running north east-south west on the slopes of Lunds Fell, is not the result of cave collapse but more to do with the opening up of a geological fault line by a stream eating into the limestone rocks. Many thousands of years ago Hell Gill Beck flowed into the Ure before glacial debris, at the end of the last Ice Age, forced it to alter its southerly course for today's more northerly one down Mallerstang.

Hell Gill gorge is over a third of a mile long. At Hell Gill Bridge it is forty feet deep, fifty in other places. Although the stream bed, in the bottom of the gorge, broadens out a little the walls at the top are generally about eight to ten feet wide narrowing sufficiently in one or two places to be leapt across. Over time Hell Gill Beck's turbulent passage through the gorge has created enough erosive power to gouge out hollows in its bed, shallow grooves on its walls and a variety of interesting rock shapes. In summer it is so choked with vegetation growing out from its walls that obtaining a good view of the gorge and Hell Gill Beck is difficult. In cold winters icicles hang in profusion from the walls. The often peat-stained beck, a raging torrent after heavy rain, roars and rushes through the bottom of the gorge tumbling over a number of small waterfalls. After having scoured its way through the limestone it emerges from the gorge to flow across a relatively flat bed of rock before plunging over a small cliff as Hellgill Force into a pool below. In dry spells, mainly in summer, the beck might be caught in a slightly less boisterous mood.

Hell Gill Bridge (known in the past as Devil's Bridge) carries the High Way over Hell Gill Beck to link North Yorkshire with Cumbria. It has a single stone arch dating from 1825, when the bridge was built, to replace an earlier one which records say cost £3.10s (£3.50) to build in 1676. In the middle of the bridge a stone marks the old county boundary between North Yorkshire (North Riding pre-1974) and Cumbria (Westmorland pre-1974). There is a legend that Dick Turpin, to escape arrest by the Westmorland authorities, jumped his horse Black Bess over the gorge at Hell Gill. His intention was to escape into Yorkshire where the Westmorland warrant had no legal force. Other people believe that this feat was actually performed by Swift Nick Nevison, another highway-man, who frequented High Dike. No one seems to know for sure which of the two can claim the feat.

Of Hell Gill itself Camden said it '...falleth down to such a depth that it striketh a certain horror to as many as look down.' Leland also commented that, 'there is a beck cawled Hell Gille because it runneth in such a deadly place.' Camden claimed that the little streams which flowed off Lunds Fell and its neighbours were called by the local dalesfolk 'Hell-becks', that is rivers or streams of hell. However one interpretation of the word 'hell' in this context is that it means clear. Another interpretation claims that the word 'hell' has no fiendish application - it simply means over shadowed or hemmed in.

One feature which is etched across the topography of Lunds Fell is the track known as the High Way which is more popularly known as Lady Anne Clifford's Way. In the next section the route, from Cotter End to the River Eden, is followed noting such places of interest as High Dike and Lunds Church plus the colourful characters who travelled the route particularly Lady Anne Clifford herself.

## *A highway for Lady Anne*

IT may officially be named the High Way by the Ordnance Survey but for many people, both locals and visitors, the wide track which crosses the southern and western slopes of Lunds Fell is always affectionately referred to as Lady Anne Clifford's Way. The High Way was probably used by Bronze Age tribes as a route through the Pennines before the Romans took it over and developed it as a military road linking their fort at Bainbridge in Wensleydale with the one at Appleby in Cumbria. In the Lunds area of Mallerstang the High Way is also known as the Street or Streets perhaps suggesting its use as a Roman marching road. The fact that, in 1926, a hoard of Roman coins (138 *denarii*) were found close to the track suggests an obvious Roman presence in the area. As a major route the High Way was only supplanted in the early nineteenth century when the lower altitude road was built through the valley of Mallerstang.

The High Way ranges from an altitude of over 1,300 feet at Hell Gill, on the North Yorkshire-Cumbria border, to 1,600 feet on Cotter End overlooking Wensleydale. It follows a wild, dramatic but delightfully scenic route along the western edge of Lunds Fell below its summit of Sails. From Cotter End the track crosses the infant rivers Ure and Eden before descending gently into Mallerstang to join the main valley road just over a mile south of the ruins of Pendragon Castle.

For my purpose I shall only be concerned with the section of the High Way that runs between Cotter End and Hell Gill Bridge. I pick it up a little over a mile beyond Appersett near to Collier Holme Farm at the junction of the road up Cotterdale with that of the A684. Here, on the left, a steep bridleway follows the wall uphill for a short distance to reach a large limekiln. It then levels out to run along a limestone terrace, for more than three miles, with open moorland above and enclosed rough pasture below. Before the turnpike was built through Mallerstang and the Eden valley in 1826 the quickest route from Hawes to Kirkby Stephen, for a whole variety of travellers, was via the High Way. Although easier a much longer route would have been through Sedbergh and Ravenstonedale.

For centuries the High Way's altitude and wildness has impressed all those who have travelled it. This would likely be true of Lady Anne Clifford herself who travelled this route on a number of occasions on her way to her castles in what is now Cumbria. I like to think that she would have been impressed by the view of Wild Boar Fell across the valley.

The High Way must have presented a colourful scene in its heyday with farmers, packmen, drovers and gypsies all making use of this high-level route. Amongst the more well known persons to have travelled it was Sir Hugh de Morville, knight and peripatetic judge for Northumberland and Cumberland in Henry II's reign. The 2,000 foot fell Hugh Seat high above his home, Pendragon Castle, was named after him. He is infamous for being one of the four knights involved in the murder of Thomas Beckett, the Archbishop of Canterbury. It should be said that Sir Hugh did not actually carry out the deed himself as his job was to act as look-out and prevent any interference with the murder undertaken by his three fellow knights. Following the murder the four knights fled, via Scotland, to Pendragon Castle. When Henry discovered what the knights had done Sir Hugh was suspended from his judicial duties and lost his estates.

On Richard I's accession to the throne Sir Hugh joined him on the Third Crusade. During the journey home from the Middle East Sir Hugh was taken prisoner, along with the King, by Leopold of Austria. After eventually getting back to England Sir Hugh returned to the Holy Land where he died around 1202 being buried in the then Templar's Church at Jerusalem. I wonder if Sir Hugh de Morville actually galloped along the High Way during the course of his judicial duties. Did his more macabre journey home from the scene of his crime in Canterbury take him along the High Way?

Another notable figure to travel the High Way was Mary, Queen of Scots. In 1568, accompanied by her guards and servants, she made her way along the route to imprisonment in isolated Bolton Castle. One cannot imagine Mary, given the other things on her mind, being impressed by the scenery.

In the fourteenth century timber, to be used in the building of Bolton Castle the home of the Scrope family, was transported along the High Way in wagons. By the late eighteenth and early nineteenth centuries the High Way was an important route for packmen carrying not only a range of goods but news, not to mention chatter, from the wider world. For centuries the Scots came down the High Way, initially as raiders, then as drovers driving cattle to English markets. One can picture them urging their beasts along the route perhaps looking for a comfortable stop for the night. Every year when Brough Hill Fair was held in Westmorland there was a continuous cavalcade of people journeying along the High Way including farmers, horse dealers, packmen, drovers, tinkers and ordinary folk. So many folk in fact passed along the route that a number of local farmers' wives set out their stalls and sold homemade cakes, beer and gingerbread. It was a service much appreciated by many hungry and thirsty travellers.

By the end of the eighteenth century so many people were travelling along the High Way that highwaymen, such as Swift Nick Nevison who we met earlier at Hell Gill, considered it lucrative to frequent it. He is reputed to have made the Drovers Inn at High Dike his favourite haunt and refuge. One of his tricks was to get his horse to walk backwards so that the confusion of hoof prints would make it difficult for his pursuers to work out which direction he had taken. Despite his reputation people said of him that he was 'a very gentlemanly man'.

One of the largest movements of people along the High Way, in the second half of the seventeenth century, would have been the several hundred strong retinue accompanying Lady Anne Clifford on her journeys to her castles in Cumbria - Pendragon, Brough, Appleby and Brougham. Local folk would remember such a procession of people, passing along the track, for a long time after the event occurred.

High up on its ridge and suffused in memories the High Way is today one of the most impressive ridge walks in the Dales. Apart from farmers and walkers, the latter striding out on its springy turf, the track is now silent. Walking the High Way today you walk with ghosts from the past - packmen, drovers, farmers and their wives, tinkers, gypsies, horse dealers and even the great lady herself, Lady Anne Clifford, to whose story we now turn.

~ ~ ~ ~ ~ ~ ~ ~ ~ ~ ~ ~ ~ ~

Lady Anne Clifford was born in 1590 at Skipton Castle. She was the third and only surviving child of George Clifford, third Earl of Cumberland and his wife Margaret. Her mother was the daughter of Francis Russell, second Earl of Bedford. When her father became the Queen's jousting champion the family moved to London where she was brought up by her mother and educated by tutors. This was to prepare her for a position in the Queen's Household which she first undertook at the age of thirteen. She was fifteen when her father died leaving her the very large sum for those days of £15,000. The problem was that he did not recognise her as his legitimate successor despite the fact that she was his only direct heir. His vast estates, 100,000 acres in Westmorland and

Yorkshire, were left to his brother Francis, Anne's uncle. Anne would only inherit if her uncle had no sons. Estates normally passed through the male line but, in the case of the Cliffords, Edward II had made an entail to an earlier Clifford that the descent of the estate was to go to the direct heir even if female. Her mother now took up Anne's cause for the restoration of her land and properties. In 1607 mother and daughter visited the estate's castles, Brougham, Appleby, Brough, Pendragon and Skipton.

Lady Anne Clifford was married and widowed twice. In 1609, at the age of nineteen, she married Richard Sackville who later became third Earl of Dorset making her a countess. They had five children, three sons and two daughters, of whom only the latter survived. In 1630, six years after Richard died, she became the Countess of Pembroke following her marriage to Philip Herbert the future Earl of Pembroke. When her first husband died, after a not completely unhappy marriage, she was left with her two daughters to bring up. Her second marriage was not particularly successful and she lived apart from her husband from 1634 until his death in 1650. Neither husband had given much more than lukewarm support for her inheritance claim which she had pursued all these years initially with the help of her mother until the latter's death in 1616.

Finally in 1643, when she was 53, Henry, the sole remaining Clifford died. This at a stroke removed the last hurdle preventing Lady Anne claiming her inheritance. An immediate return to the north was out of the question due to the Civil War and fears for her safety. When she was able to return, after the execution of Charles I in 1649, she found all her castles were in urgent need of repair and restoration. She made it clear that her intention was to repair her five castles, which she would live in on a fairly regular basis, plus Barden Tower, seven churches, and a number of schools and bridges. With her inheritance came judicial responsibilities and as the Sheriffess of Westmorland she had to generally see that the rule of law prevailed throughout her vast territories. For the rest of her life Lady Anne travelled around all her properties supervising the repair work. All the castles were repaired and restored in the early 1660s usually to the original style.

Lady Anne travelled frequently from one restoration programme to another for over a quarter of a century. The roads she used were often in very poor condition. In 1663 she left Skipton to return to Westmorland by a route which turned out to be one with considerable hazards. She travelled up Wharfedale and crossed into Wensleydale where she spent the second night of her journey at Nappa Hall the home of her cousin Thomas Metcalfe. The next day she went over Cotter End 'where I think a coach never went before,' crossed Hell Gill Bridge and on to Pendragon Castle. This latter part of her route was the High Way which now, unofficially, takes her name. Despite the enormous difficulties to be encountered on this route Lady Anne continued to use it when travelling between her Yorkshire estates and those in Westmorland. Anybody who has walked this route will find it hard to imagine anybody braving the weather and the terrain in a springless coach pulled by six horses particularly a lady over sixty.

The High Way was in continual need of repair as Lady Anne discovered. It seemed that her four-wheeled carriage was the first to go along the track. Even today there are still places where it is impossible for a wheeled vehicle to pass. There are many entries in the book of the Constabulary of Bainbridge for 'repairing the Lunds road.' It appears that the attitude of many travellers, including Lady Anne, was that, poor as it was for a coach, the High Way was better than any alternative. This speaks volumes for the state of alternative roads in the area.

Lady Anne Clifford died in 1676 aged 86 and was buried in Appleby at St. Lawrence's Church. Sadly, with the exception of Skipton and Appleby, her family did not carry out maintenance on the estate properties which gradually fell into ruins. Such was the fate of Pendragon Castle on the banks of the Eden in Mallerstang. Lady Anne was a proud, powerful lady with a strong personality. She was fiercely proud of her family's ancestry but sadly she was the last of the Cliffords. She was also benevolent and even today, over three hundred years on, she is still held in great esteem.

~ ~ ~ ~ ~ ~ ~ ~ ~ ~ ~ ~ ~ ~

The High Way goes past High Dike which, although now partly used as a barn, was once an inn until, it is believed, 1877. Built in the late eighteenth century, with mullioned windows, it once had a fine appearance. Its location was such as to catch the passing drovers' and jaggermens' custom. All wayfarers were welcome to rest and take refreshment. At one point it also served as Lunds School, teaching taking place in a cottage attached to the inn. Children from the hamlet climbed the hill for lessons. As we saw earlier it was also supposedly the favourite haunt of the famous highwayman Swift Nick Nevison. Now minus a roof and engaged in constant battles with the wind, it has been a long time since passing travellers laughed and sang inside. From what is left today one can see that High Dike once had a number of outbuildings some of which would undoubtedly have been stables. To the front of the building, on the south side, it had a paved courtyard with many small walled enclosures close by most likely for stock. Memories, of the various travellers who took refreshment there and listened eagerly to the local gossip, still surround High Dike. You can almost hear the voices of the packmen and hear the clatter of their horses' hooves. As Mike Harding has mused, 'It is hard to imagine that not so very long ago these walls would have rung to the sound of laughter, singing and fiddle music and the clanking of pots of ale.'[2]

After High Dike the track continues above the buildings of Shaws and High Way (the latter is not to be confused with the track called the High Way). Shaws was the home of R. A. Scott McFie for some fourteen years during which he was the editor of the *Gypsy Lore Journal*. Situated on the slopes of the fell, just below the High Way, it had a fine waterfall at its rear. McFie bridged the beck and linked Shaws to the road through Mallerstang with an avenue lined with trees. Later, after McFie's death, Shaws became Garsdale Youth Hostel receiving its food and fuel by tractor. Sadly, its later losses led to its closure. Near to the ruins of High Way the track passes Horse Paddock where a walled area of some four acres encloses a small ruined building. It was probably a halt for drovers and packmen on long journeys where animals could safely graze, packs could be stored in the building and the men could find shelter. Such enclosures were a common feature of Pennine drove and packhorse routes. It has been suggested that Horse Paddock fulfiled the role of a stage house similar to that of Tan Hill and Dale Head Farm on the side of Penyghent.

Just beyond High Way and Horse Paddock is High Hall, another ruined farmhouse, once believed to have been an inn. Just below High Hall lies West End the birth place of John Blades. In 1779 he went to London with 2s 6d (12.5p) in his pocket and got a job as a porter to a glass merchant. Later he married his employer's daughter, inherited the ornamental cut glass business before becoming Sheriff of London in 1813. On the lower slopes of Lunds Fell below the High Way, but still at over a thousand feet above sea level, lies Shaw Paddock. A broad grassy track from

Hell Gill descends the hillside to it. For a very long time now it has been a farmhouse but up to the end of the nineteenth century it was Shaw Paddock Inn having originally been known as the Bull in the 1820s. Lying just off the High Way it was a popular stopping place for those drovers who were heading for Gearstones and Ribblesdale.

Just below High Dike lies the tiny hamlet of Lunds consisting of a few scattered dwellings and a church. One path links it to High Dike whilst another goes from the church up the fell side to join the High Way at High Hall near Washer Gill. Until it ceased to hold services some years ago Lunds Church was once one of the plainest, unadorned churches in England. It lies at 1,100 feet above sea level on the western slopes of Lunds Fell whose summit Sails rises high above it. Across Mallerstang, Swarth Fell and the vast bulk of the imposing Wild Boar Fell seem to stand guard over the church. In its heyday it was the focus for the whole of the upper valley not merely the tiny hamlet consisting of some two or three houses. Tradition has it that, prior to the church being built, services were held on the nearby hill of Course Haw with people being summoned by the ringing of a bell or the banging of an iron pan. Some believe that large stones and traces of an enclosure on the summit of Course Haw may indicate the presence of a preaching cross as well.

When Lunds Church was built is not accurately known but as a curate was licensed to practice there in 1713 and church registers began in 1749 it probably dates from the early eighteenth century. By 1839 the church, which had been built by the parishioners' own hands, was in a very dilapidated state with no door, a holed roof and a broken bell. Following an increase in the population in the Forest of Wensleydale the Askrigg Parish was divided into four separate parishes. These comprised Askrigg, Hawes, Hardraw-Lunds and Stalling Busk. Hawes received its chapel in the late fifteenth century, the latter two at the beginning of the seventeenth. The mother church was at Aysgarth some sixteen miles to the east. In 1858 Lunds Church united with Hardraw Church following which the vicar from the latter conducted a Sunday service at Lunds. The very early incumbent vicars at Lunds Church were also schoolmasters at Lunds School which is on the Moorcock Inn to Kirkby Stephen road. The problem with this arrangement was that when there were frequent changes of vicar the school had no schoolmaster. In 1946, with fewer and fewer children on its roll, the school closed. After the Settle-Carlisle railway came many parishioners at Lunds were railway folk living away from their own parishes. As time went on Lunds' regular parishioners became fewer and fewer but more came on special occasions.

The ruined church lies in a large churchyard often surrounded by cattle and sheep grazing amongst its old gravestones. But for its bell-turret or cote the tiny church could easily be mistaken for a barn. In the building's very rough exterior were set two circular windows and a door but no porch. For many years the story was told that as the church lacked a door a large thorn bush was used to prevent cattle venturing inside. Once, when the bell was broken, the sexton had to call the faithful to prayer by climbing up the tower and shouting. In more modern times Lunds Church, by then having received electricity, held its services under electric lights with radiators providing the warmth. In addition to the pews there was a vestry, a font, a reading desk and a small organ. A visitor, at a winter service in Lunds in 1839, found the seats and floor covered with two to three inches of snow. This had probably come in through the roof or through the opening where a door should have been. Up to 1933, when it could seat 60, it had no access by road merely a track over the moors. However when McFie built the road to his house at Shaws, people could use this to get to the church. As was noted earlier the Cotterdale dead were taken along the old corpse road to Lunds Church. In the graveyard are buried two interesting characters whom we have already met - John Blades and R. A. Scott McFie (the latter died in 1935).

Walking along the High Way is an ideal way to observe the natural and man-made features common to Lunds Fell and the other high fells in upper Wensleydale. One natural feature is the rash of coniferous plantations, which have spread across the slopes of the fells, whilst two man-made features are the kilns built to produce lime for use as a fertiliser on the meadows and pastures and the ubiquitous dry stone walls which criss-cross them. In the next three sections we take a detailed look at each of these features.

### *Woodlands*

THE high fells of upper Wensleydale, like many other areas of the Yorkshire Dales, are not richly endowed with woodland apart from a number of conifer plantations. In fact total woodland cover in the National Park comprises a mere 3.6% of its total area, a figure on the low side compared with the other National Parks. Of this figure semi-natural woodland accounts for around 1.3% made up of semi-natural ancient woodland (1%), replanted ancient woodland (0.2%) and new indigenous woodland (0.1%). Broadleaved woods take up 0.3% and conifers 2%. It is also worth noting that, today, 63% of all woods in the Dales are less than four hectares in size. Even the most expansive of all the dales, Wensleydale, has limited woodland with what it has being confined to scattered shelter belts, that growing on its valley side scars and that fringing the gills in its side dales.

Over the centuries the woodlands of the Yorkshire Dales have been cleared with the timber being put to a variety of uses such as fuel, fencing, building and tools. Where woodland has remained it has been put to many economic uses such as shelter for livestock and shooting for game. It is also believed that trees were often planted to denote the edges of fields. Woodland is considered an important home to indigenous flora and fauna, particularly pheasants, during the winter. The use, care and management of woodland provides employment for local people and income for owners.

Of the semi-natural woodland its most important element is the ancient woodland dating back at least four centuries and in some instances as far back as the last Ice Age. Such ancient woodland can be divided into two types semi-natural and replanted. The former consists of trees that have not been deliberately planted and have distinct shrubs associated with them. The 1,700 hectares of this type of woodland in the national park amount to what is left of the dales very earliest forests. Such ancient woodlands with their stable soils have promoted important plant and animal life. They are dominated by oak and ash with the latter being particularly common in the limestone dales. On steep limestone slopes, particularly those facing south, the yew, although rare, may be found. Other rare woodlands are those of alder, birch and willow found on poorly drained, damp soils. Hawthorn, ash, sycamore and rowan tend to be found on the steep sides of gills. Whilst juniper is not completely absent, gorse cover in the dales seems somewhat sparse.

The second type of ancient woodland, the re-planted, consists of coniferous or mixed broadleaved trees on ancient woodland sites amounting to some 380 hectares. Such re-planted areas contain aspects of the ancient ground flora which helps to create varied woodland cover.

The remaining semi-natural non ancient woodland includes relatively newly established locations which are likely to become wildlife habitats over time. For example mixed conifer and broadleaved plantations provide nesting locations for a range of birds and a refuge for small animals. This type of woodland in the national park is found scattered in gills or on the steep valley sides where they are out of reach of grazing animals. Half of such woods are now found in Swaledale and Wharfedale. As the new native woodlands develop it is hoped that a varied ground flora will also develop similar to that found in ancient semi-natural woodland. Broadleaved plantations amount to approximately 500 hectares within the national park consisting of indigenous and non-native trees. Such plantations are often dominated by beech and sycamore with a noticeable absence of shrubs. Nonetheless such broadleaved woods add to the dales landscape. These mixed broadleaved woods are to be found in the south and southeastern areas of the national park where they provide timber, wind protection and cover for game.

There are a number of coniferous plantations in the Yorkshire Dales National Park which were encouraged by tax incentives and government policies in the 1960s and 1970s. Consisting mainly of Sitka spruce they have become established in those dales branching off the main valley of Wensleydale such as Cotterdale and Widdale. Such coniferous plantations are today the most extensive type of woodland in the dales and the most important economically. Conifers, while planted essentially for commercial timber, also provide an alternative habitat for a few indigenous plants and animals such as the deer and the red squirrel. On the latter point, it is worth noting that the red squirrel is now to be to be found in the north west corner of the park.

One of the most extensive of the Yorkshire Dales National Park's more mature conifer plantations is to be found at Greenfield in upper Langstrothdale. Other younger plantations are to be found in Grisedale, Dentdale, Widdale and Cotterdale. Some of the conifers planted in the 1970s have been thinned in recent years such as those on the eastern slopes of Lunds Fell in Cotterdale.

Over the years grazing by sheep, rabbits and deer has posed a threat to the variety of woodland plant and animal life. A survey undertaken of semi-natural woodland between 1990-93 by the Yorkshire Dales National Park Authority and English Nature showed that 50% of it was grazed by sheep, 60% by rabbits and 15% by deer. Surprisingly only 35% of woodland surveyed had boundaries to keep stock out. It was also found that, where regeneration of woodland did occur, it was confined to such areas as steep slopes where stock could not reach and where fencing had been erected.

Woodland can add variety and beauty to the farmed landscape of the dales. For example each dale can be recognised by its woodlands which provide a link with its past. Trees often add to the attractiveness of a village's location. Where appropriate the planting of new native woodland can improve the landscape by creating variety without destroying the wildness of the bare fells. In the past large tracts of woodland pasture existed in the middle or lower part of the various dales which we refer to today as parkland.

Many semi-natural woodlands are not particularly healthy owing to regeneration being prevented by over grazing. What is needed is a greater variety of woodland landscapes with more habitats created. A step in the right direction is the agreement between the national parks and the Forestry Commission to both protect and increase native woodland. An increase in woodland in the Yorkshire Dales National Park would add to the already attractive nature of the landscape, contribute to plant and animal diversity, increase tourism and recreational opportunities and create more jobs. The aim of the Yorkshire Dales National Park Authority is to encourage the increase and management of the special, but limited, semi-natural woodland. Such woodlands provide a home for plants and animals not found in other types of woodland and are therefore important in terms of conservation. The Yorkshire Dales National Park Authority's Woodlands Strategy 1999-2004 has been set up to offer guidance to every organisation in the park that is working with woodlands. This has already resulted in some 200 hectares of new native woodland being planted and careful management of existing woodland.

## *Limestone and lime kilns*

THE earliest lime kilns, that is those of the thirteenth and fourteenth centuries, were often to be found, not on the fell sides as they later would be, but in castles, towns and monasteries where they were used for the production of lime mortar for use in building. Following the completion of a specific building job it was often the case that the kiln was never used again. In the sixteenth century lime use changed significantly with the important discovery that its use as a manure brought a significant improvement to poor acidic land. By the second quarter of the seventeenth century lime production was well established and its application to the land widespread. Eighteenth century land enclosure on the edge of the moor led to heather and bracken being burnt off, the land drained and then limed to sweeten the sour soil and bring about viable land for pasture. Between the years 1750-1850 kiln building probably peaked as lime was used widely in an effort to improve moorland soils following Parliamentary enclosure. We should never underestimate the value of lime to the farmer in the recovery of moorland for pasture.

There was another factor at this time which added to the pressure for more pasturage and led to the rapid spread of kilns and an increase in lime production. This was the growing number of Scottish cattle herds being driven south to dales markets. This encouraged farmers with good outcrops of limestone on their land to construct kilns to produce the lime for use on the pastures on which the Scottish cattle would graze. Lime kilns spread like a rash all over the limestone uplands of the dales at this time. It should be pointed out however that, whilst most lime produced was used on the fields and pastures, a lesser amount went into the production of lime mortar.

It is clear that considerable amounts of lime were needed for the fields and pastures for use as a manure and to lessen its acidic composition. Limestone had to be processed to produce lime for which kilns were required. Kilns were usually built close to a small limestone outcrop or quarry from which the limestone could be taken relatively easily to them. Some kilns were close enough to their limestone source for the latter to be tipped straight in. Where the kiln was solely for local use it tended to be located on the highest part of the farm for the simple convenience of being able to transport all materials downhill. The ideal location for a kiln was close to a limestone outcrop whilst not being far from a thin coal seam. A farmer who had limestone on his land would build a small field kiln for himself. Alternatively he would share a kiln with one or two other farmers. By and large farmers obtained their lime from the innumerable small field kilns usually built and operated by themselves.

Lime burning was heavily dependent upon a good supply of coal no matter what its quality. Much of it came from the high fells (along with peat) from collieries which opened in the eighteenth century. Many of these flourished in the nineteenth century due to the demand from the lime burners for coal irrespective of the fact that a high proportion of it was low grade. The higher quality coal found its way to the many remote hamlets and farms where it was used for household fires. Some collieries were essentially a local pit supplying just one kiln. For example the coal needed for firing the large kiln high on Cotter End must have been supplied in sufficient quantities when required. When mined the coal from the fells was taken down the hillsides to the kilns. These were built along the valley sides on the lower limestone terraces which lay between the walled fields and the rough pastures and moorland. From the kilns the lime was taken to be spread on the fields below.

Whilst kiln dimensions did vary a little between dales the fundamental structure of kilns, given their purpose and operational process, did not vary much. The basic field kiln is a solid turret-like construction of dry stone walling either curved or square. It is some fifteen to twenty feet in diameter and about the same in height. Kilns were built with large, distinctive entrances with pointed, rounded or flat arches. At the core of a kiln was a cylindrical or circular sandstone lined bowl eight to ten feet in diameter. The upper six to eight feet of the core had parallel sides whilst the lower eight feet tapered to a diameter of three feet. Below the bowl was a grate or hearth which, after the removal of the lime, could be cleared of its ash by raking. The grate was at the end of a short tunnel which led to the entrance of the kiln.

In the burning process limestone needs only about a quarter of its weight of coal. A kiln's function is to burn limestone to produce lime by using one of two methods. One method is to have one single burning of a large quantity of limestone; the other is to have a more continuous process in which limestone is regularly fed to the kiln with the lime being drawn off regularly over a given short or long period of time. Those kilns which in a single burning consumed very large amounts of limestone, usually that cleared from the land, are called pye kilns or pits; those used in a continuous process of burning are called running kilns. When the demand for lime was at its height conditions were such that 'selling' kilns were established where two or three men were kept continuously employed as lime burners. Farmers without a kiln of their own could buy what the lime they wanted from these selling kilns. Some of these kilns were built on a huge scale with the lime being sold at the kiln mouth or carried and distributed by 'limers' with trains of packhorses.

When fired a kiln consisted of alternate layers of quarried limestone and coal. Whilst a field kiln might burn for two or three days a large commercial kiln might burn for a week or more. For a long slow burn layers of limestone and fuel were fed in at the top of the kiln. At night kilns often glowed red through their porous walls lighting up the hill-sides. A few days firing could yield up to 300 horse-loads of lime (each load weighing two and a half hundredweight) for a farmer's own use or for selling at 4d (1.5p) a load. Four loads equalled a cartful - enough to lime one acre of land.

Today the grass-covered pit heaps across the dales uplands remind us of the many collieries which supplied the kilns with coal. Little physical evidence of pit buildings remains primarily due to the fact that they had little in the way of pithead structures. For example if a shaft required winding gear it was provided by means of a jack roller. By contrast, whilst local collieries may have left behind nothing more than a few traces on the ground, lime kilns have left a solid, masonry structure. There are, it is believed, some 600 abandoned lime kilns in the Yorkshire Dales National Park which means that today's visitors, to upper Wensleydale's high fells, will have a reasonable chance of coming across one. Unfortunately many kilns are inaccessible being located in quarries or on the edge of the moors and therefore remote. On the other hand because kilns, like dry stone walls, are ubiquitous across the fells they are often taken for granted with little attention being given to their purpose or historical origin. What we can say, for certain, is that together the collier and the farmer (limer) have provided us with much of the pasturage that makes up so much of the upper Wensleydale landscape today.

### *Walls and wallers*

ALL six of Wensleydale's 2,000 foot fells, like all the fells in the Yorkshire Dales, have dry stone walls running across them. Most of these walls were built between 1750 and 1850 to give effect on the ground to the lines on maps drawn up by surveyors. It would not be exaggerating to say that no other single activity brought about such a change in the physical appearance of the dales landscape whilst at the same time adding to its scenic charm. The walls which spread across the landscape during the enclosure process looked, in the words of Muir and Colbeck, as though 'a gigantic spider had scuttled across the scene, binding meadow, pasture and common together in a petrified web.'[3] The Acts of Enclosure, passed by Parliament during this period, made for a planned, systematic and orderly programme of enclosure. Initially the common fields and meadows were separated into smaller lots which were then enclosed. This was soon followed by enclosure of the higher fellsides and the rolling acres of the moors themselves. Whilst the enclosure of the dales countryside might have peaked between 1750 and 1850 it is worth remembering that the enclosure process began in the late sixteenth century and carried on throughout the seventeenth. During these latter two centuries, whilst most enclosure involved building walls to form crofts or folds around villages, sections of both the common land and the waste land were also being enclosed.

Enclosure in the eighteenth and nineteenth centuries stemmed from the wish of leading landowners in the parish or township to enclose the open fields that remained. To be granted the right to enclose landowners had to petition Parliament to obtain an Act of Enclosure for the parish. Authority was rarely if ever refused even when the major owners of the land were tiny in number compared with the great mass of smallholders and tenants. Once the enclosure process was set in motion all the land held by the peasants, whether meadow land, land under the plough or common land, was irretrievably lost. Once an Enclosure Order was granted commissioners, usually made up of the squire, the parson and a leading freeholder, were appointed. Such local worthies would then go about the business of appointing a surveyor and a valuer whose jobs were to demarcate and then value each holding. They would then draw up a plan for the newly enclosed land. A person who received a newly enclosed holding had an obligation to ensure that the dry stone walls were actually built often within a set time limit. Where the new boundaries of a newly proposed enclosure of a piece of land happened to follow the pre-enclosure boundary, then it was likely the walls would not be geometrically straight. This was the exception to the rule with virtually all the landscape displaying mainly straight-edged fields, the boundary walls having been drawn as lines on a map in a surveyor's office.

One of the processes of enclosure involved a division of the large common fields of the villages and townships into clearly demarcated private walled fields under individual ownership. Where long walls were built to separate clearly the common land from the newly enclosed private land and to clearly delineate the boundaries between neighbouring townships, the building of walls and their upkeep was the responsibility of all the local commissioners involved. Many Acts of Enclosure also had clauses written into them which provided for lime kilns to be constructed near to local limestone outcrops and for parish and township quarries to be kept open. At the height of the enclosure process there must have been hectic activity as an army of wallers spread across the dales. They could be seen in the meadows, the pastures and on the high fells. Local limestone scars and quarries must also have seen much activity given the demand for an endless supply of stone.

Under enclosure reorganisation the first to lose his land rights was the squatter and cottager. Next to go was the small farmer whose receipt of a small, restricted landholding was inadequate compensation for his loss of rights and access to the land held in common which, over many centuries, had provided fuel and bedding. Many farmers were unclear about what obligations the enclosure policy required of them whilst others simply did not have the money to pay for the stone required to do the necessary walling. As a result many a small farmer found himself working as a farm labourer for the local landowner. As enclosure spread across the dales thousands said goodbye to the land to work in the lead mines, in the textile mills or overseas. Enclosure, there is no doubt, led to more productive farming methods but brought little or no benefit to the vast majority of the population of the countryside. The flight from the land into the great cities did, however, drive forward the Industrial Revolution.

The first Parliamentary Enclosure Act was passed in 1604 and related to land in Dorset. It can be said to have provided the impetus to divide up the land across the country. Following limited enclosure in the first half of the eighteenth century there was an explosion of enclosure activity in the century following 1750. By the time the last Act was passed in 1914 the face of the English countryside had had what might be described as a make over. In a period of over two hundred years between 1700 and 1914 some 5,400 Acts of Enclosure were passed by Parliament affecting some seven million acres of common land.

It was this rush to enclose in the eighteenth and nineteenth centuries that led to the building of the many walls that criss-cross the dales. Let us take for example the amount of walling involved in the enclosure of land in High Abbotside township (into which parts of Lunds Fell, Great Shunner Fell and Lovely Seat all fall) following the passing of the 1824 Act. Under the Act a 930 acre pasture and two rough grazing areas of 4,280 and 5,316 acres were divided up. As Christine Hallas has written the total amount of walling required for this enclosure was 4,717.5 chains (one chain equals 22 yards).[4] In the early nineteenth century the local rate for walling was 3s.3d. (16p) per rood (seven yards). On this basis the total bill for walling the above enclosures would have been £2,409. This breaks down to £1.4s. (£1.20) per acre for the pasture which was divided into small fields and 3s. (15p) per acre for the rough grazing areas. Taking £15 per annum as the average wage for a labourer this walling, on High Abbotside, would have generated a year's work for 160 wallers. Hallas has calculated that, if these walling estimates for High Abbotside are projected to all of Wensleydale affected by enclosure, the total wage bill for walling would have been £26,927. Taking the same annual wage of £15 this would have provided work for 1,795 men for one year.

I now turn my attention to an examination of wall building as a craft. The first stage in building a dry stone wall is to fix a line on the ground. Following this the turf and topsoil are removed to provide a trench some four feet wide for the level foundations of the wall. A dales dry stone wall is actually two parallel walls in one made of large, square stones which angle slightly inwards. No large gaps should be left between the squared stones which make up the wall. The two walls stand adjacent to one another bound together by large stones called 'throughs.' The gap between the two walls is filled up with small stones and general rubble including chippings from stones shaped prior to being fixed in the wall. A standard wall needs a number of good throughs usually three rows of them jutting out on either side. There are often 21 throughs to every seven yards of wall.

Walls which are often five to six feet high narrow in width with height. At its base a wall is two and a half to three feet wide narrowing to between twelve and sixteen inches at the base of the top stones. All walls slant upwards and inwards; this is known as the 'batter.' This inward slope of a wall, providing it is built on firm foundations, increases its strength. To increase the strength of the wall as it grows in height the stones of each row should lie across the joints of the row below. To accommodate the wall's top stones there needs to be a good level surface. The top stones usually form a single row and are often fixed in place with lime mortar to prevent them being dislodged by the climbing activities of both sheep and walkers. Such top stones or capstones as they are sometimes called are usually flat and overhang the wall a little on each side. Occasionally these top stones are stood vertically on their end.

With all the enclosure momentum there was an urgent need to build the walls which had been drawn up on paper by surveyors. The walls were

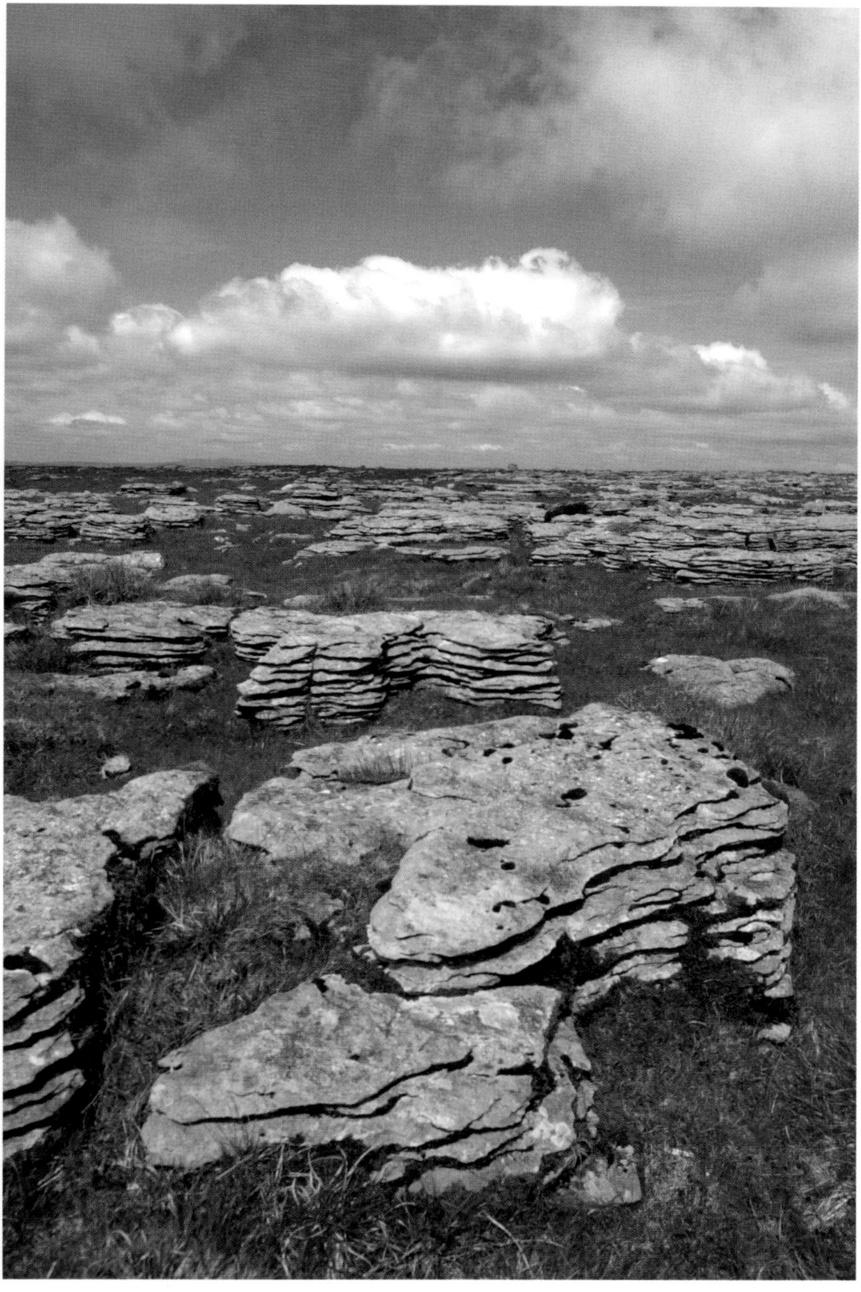

*Limestone pavement alongside the Cam High Road between Beggarman's Road and Kidhow Gate.*

*Above, lonely Kidhow Gate on the south west slopes of Dodd Fell. Here, at 1877 feet above sea level, the Cam High Road meets the Pennine Way.*

*Below, view from Wether Fell of the Ten End ridge on the left with Lunds Fell on the far right.*

*Looking down Dentdale from the slopes of Great Knoutberry Hill.*

*Above, looking towards Lunds Fell, far left, from Garsdale Station on the Settle-Carlisle line.*

*Below, The Green Dragon public house near Hardraw Force.*

built by men prepared to work long hours for 2s 6d (12.5p) per seven yards which was regarded as the amount of walling a man could complete in a day. Walling was not a particularly difficult job for a man with strong hands and a good eye for the appropriate stone. Although some walling techniques had developed in earlier centuries it was the enclosure movement of the eighteenth and nineteenth centuries which greatly enhanced walling skills. Men in a variety of occupations - farmers, labourers, local masons and dykers - took up walling. While building a wall the experienced waller could instantly work out the shape and dimensions of the next stone he needed for the row he was working on. He could even identify the required stone lying on the ground before specifically placing it in the wall.

Today, most dales farmers have a degree of walling skill sufficient at least to repair gaps in their boundary walls. Equally they are happy to employ professional wallers to ensure quality workmanship when they require significant repair work doing or need a lengthy stretch of new wall. In recent years there has been an explosion of demand in the dales for walls and wallers.

Good wallers still abound throughout the dales, their skills often seen at agricultural shows. A waller must have the energy to manhandle his raw material, have a keen eye for the most appropriate stones and the skill to lay them to produce a good, strong, upright wall. A waller's tools include string used in the wall's alignment, the simple wooden template to test the wall's cross section, spades and picks for digging trenches and a mason's hammer for shaping the stones. When building a wall two wallers will tend to work either side of it. A single waller on the other hand will move from one side of the wall to the other as the work requires it or will work from one side and lean over the other where the height of the wall will allow him.

In the Yorkshire Dales stone is abundant giving wallers plenty of material to choose from. For example they can re-use fallen stones or select their stones from the nearest rocky outcrop, a local quarry, or even from the edges of fields and pastures. Wallers will use stones smoothed by water action as well as gritstones with more defined edges. Stone, although strong, can be split and shaped to the form required. Costs involved in moving heavy, bulky, unwieldy stone are not a problem due to the ubiquitous nature of the material.

In the southern half of the national park limestone has been extensively used in wall building whereas further north it has been sandstone. In upper Wensleydale where these rocks are part of the Yoredale Series both have been used. Sandstone is probably easier to work with than limestone which does not split as easily and is less uniform in terms of the shape and size of its stones. Of the sandstones, gritstones are the strongest but can be easily hammered into shape to produce good strong walls of close fitting stones.

A good wall will probably last a century or more. So what uses do walls have? What is their purpose? Firstly, dry stone walls act as boundaries between farms. On the farm walls parcel the land out into meadows, pastures and moorland. They prevent stock trampling down the hay crop. Later in the season such stock can be kept in walled fields to feed on the late summer and early autumn grass. When there is severe weather on the tops the lambing ewes can be safely penned close to the farm where they can be nourished until lambing is over. Sheep, standing in the lee of walls, are protected from the rain and keep relatively dry. Dry stone walls protect sheep from the bitterly cold winds of winter whilst allowing light draughts to blow through their chinks to dry out their fleeces. Birds such as the wheatear often perch on walls whilst the pied wagtail uses a wall for a nesting site. A rabbit may use a wall both as its home and as a place of refuge.

Walls also act as boundaries along Yorkshire Dales country roads and walls have been preferred to the hedgerows of lowland areas due to their greater usefulness in enclosing stock and giving protection from the weather. In order to facilitate mixed grazing of stock, walls were given creep holes to allow sheep to move between pastures. Usually specifications, as to the size of walls and how they should be built, were clearly laid down in the enclosure awards such as where there should be gates, step stiles, squeeze stiles and creep holes.

Walls come in a whole variety of shapes and sizes - from low to tall, from straight to irregular, from good condition to a tumble down state. Even the most carefully crafted walls need attention to repair damage done by the elements particularly frost and high winds. Gales are a perennial problem in exposed places such as fellsides where a sudden gust may be strong enough to blast a gap in a wall. Ramblers climbing walls can bring about their collapse as can sheep. In recent years many old walls have been demolished or allowed to fall into disrepair to create larger pastures. To maintain the walls on his land in good condition can take up a considerable amount of a farmer's time and money.

Walls are often moss and lichen-covered and give the appearance of being very old which in many cases they are. New gritstone walls take on the colour of honey whilst the limestone walls are silvery white. Whilst walls today are thought of as a vital part of the Yorkshire Dales scenery this was not always the case. Initially what we see as their aesthetic contribution to the landscape was unappreciated and often heavily criticised. For example during the great period of wall-building spanning Georgian, Regency and Victorian times some folk expressed their dismay at the disappearance of the huge expanses of open fields and criticised the visual impact of the straight lines of walls in bright, freshly quarried stone. Walls are, today, a major feature of the upper Wensleydale landscape. The problem is that whilst we look on them as an essential part of the picturesque scenery we may often take them, along with field barns and lime kilns, just a little for granted as they blend into the surrounding rocks. However it is no exaggeration to say that dry stone walls are now a part of our Yorkshire Dales heritage be they weathered, mellowed or covered in mosses and lichens.

# 6
# GREAT SHUNNER FELL

In this chapter I consider the effects of the Ice Ages on upper Wensleydale before turning to the topography of Great Shunner Fell with particular reference to its huge bulk and extensive summit area, its often severe weather and the coal once mined on its flanks. I then follow the tracks and pathways to its summit to admire the impressive views before travelling through the dramatic Buttertubs pass to look at the famous potholes. I also marvel at the dramatic nature of Hardraw Force and its gorge before tracing the history of its brass band contests.

## *Monarch of the dale*

IT was Scandinavian settlers who gave many of the fells in the Yorkshire Dales their names. Great Shunner Fell probably acquired its name from the Old Norse words 'sjon' and 'fjall' which translates as Sjonar's mountain or lookout hill, highly appropriate given its greater height relative to its neighbours.[1]

Before turning to a consideration of the topography of Great Shunner Fell I examine the effects of the Ice Ages on upper Wensleydale. At least three distinct Ice Ages have occurred across the north of the British Isles during the last 500,000 years as the ice advanced and withdrew. The last major one occurred between 25,000 and 15,000 years ago with the ice reaching its greatest extent and depth in the middle of that period. A mini Ice Age occurred about 11,000 years ago but this only lasted the best part of a millennium, a relatively short period in geological timescales. During these Ice Ages the Pennines were exposed to the snow-bearing winds off the Atlantic which had the effect of turning Great Shunner Fell and its neighbours into the epicentre of a zone of accumulation known as the Dales Ice Centre. As more and more snow gathered on the high Pennines, particularly the western windward slopes, less and less melted. The fell country of the Yorkshire Dales was buried beneath an ice sheet covering the whole of Scotland and the north of England. I will examine the impact this huge consolidation of ice and snow on Great Shunner Fell and its neighbours had on the surrounding landscape of hill and dale.

Most of the ice in the Yorkshire Dales National Park flowed out from the north west corner before fanning out to the east and south. The main dales were buried by a huge depth of ice with only the highest peaks remaining above it. The valleys, radiating out from the Dales Ice Centre, contained glaciers and consequently acquired definitive glaciated profiles. Glaciers, carrying rocks and gravel, ground down each dale eroding the sides and leaving behind glacial moraines and drumlins. No grass, soil or rocks would have been visible.

The Wensleydale glacier eroded the valley sides thereby creating the dale's trade mark appearance of terraced, stepped fellsides. The surface limestones and shales were removed and long rounded hills called drumlins were formed under the ice. Drumlins can lead to the divergence of a beck as in the case of Fossdale Beck at Hardraw. Glacial moraines are comprised of boulder clay (a mixture of clay, sand and rocks) and are formed at the sides of a glacier or at its snout. A good example of a terminal moraine is to be found at Brown Moor just below Hawes. This acted like a dam causing a short-lived shallow lake to form which is now the Ure's flood plain around Hawes.

Yorkshire Dales valleys are what we call glaciated troughs with surprisingly less than half their depth being due to glacial action. The main dales, although covered by the ice, had already been carved out by the erosive power of pre-glacial rivers over millions of years. Pre-Ice Age Wensleydale was shallower and probably a little more winding than it is today. Melt water following the end of the Ice Ages helped also in the shaping of the dale's landscape but the effect was minimal compared with pre-glacial activity. Today, that most common of glacial deposits, boulder clay, covers large tracts of the dales to a depth of about five yards providing rich grass land such as that found in Wensleydale. As the ice receded new plants and wild flowers flourished in the new glacial soils with the landscape slowly coming to resemble what we see today.

~ ~ ~ ~ ~ ~ ~ ~ ~ ~ ~ ~ ~

Situated in the far north west corner of the Yorkshire Dales National Park at the heart of the North Pennines, Great Shunner Fell, a real titan of a hill, makes its presence felt, not so much through its height at an impressive 2,349 feet above sea level, but through its massive bulk. Everything about Great Shunner Fell is on the grand scale as, apart from its own size, it is completely surrounded by high rolling moorland and encircled by high fells. It overlooks the wide and verdant Wensleydale and narrow, winding Swaledale, with its huge eastern flank effectively sealing the latter in to the west. Given its height and location it is surprising to find that it is not on the Pennine watershed which runs a few miles to the west of the fell. It is close to the watershed that the River Ure flowing east and the River Eden flowing north then west have their sources. By contrast all Great Shunner Fell's becks ultimately drain eastwards into the North Sea.

Great Shunner Fell is a great, sprawling fell with a girth of some twenty square miles. It is liberally endowed with peat hags and a number of buttresses which radiate out to enclose minor dales such as Cotterdale, Fossdale and Great Sleddale which have interesting, dramatic and picturesque features in their own right. Let us take Cotterdale for example. Not in as dramatic a setting as that of Hardraw, but still a very attractive feature, is secluded Cotter Force. It is to be found on Cotterdale Beck which flows along the western flank of Great Shunner Fell. The waterfall, a little haven of tranquillity and repose, lies a short distance from the A684 just to the west of Appersett. Its wooded limestone ravine is full of larch and mountain ash, wild ferns and mosses. Like many of the area's waterfalls it can best be seen in winter and early spring when the absence of foliage enables the small cascades to be clearly seen tumbling down from ledge to ledge. There are two or three low falls of about ten feet falling into a deepish pool. When Cotter Force is lightly frozen it is particularly beautiful especially when the sun sparkles on the ice crystals and the trees surrounding it are covered in frost. In spring wild flowers such as saxifrage and primrose grow on the walls of the gorge. Following the beck upstream from the waterfall you pass small fosses before the trees are left behind and you emerge onto the moors.

Great Shunner Fell's position places it at the centre of a ring of high fells which lie in upper Wensleydale, upper Swaledale and Mallerstang. As the highest point on the ridge linking Wensleydale with Swaledale it overlooks both and can be said to belong to one dale as much as the other. Whilst Great Shunner Fell's looming presence, above its neighbours, can be seen from many points in Swaledale one is not drawn to its height in quite the same way when travelling up Wensleydale. True it keeps a watchful eye over upper Wensleydale but its great height does not give it a prominence or a dominance, that one might be led to expect, compared to some of the lower but more shapely fells. This is largely due to the fact that not only is it set back from the main valley but also to the fact

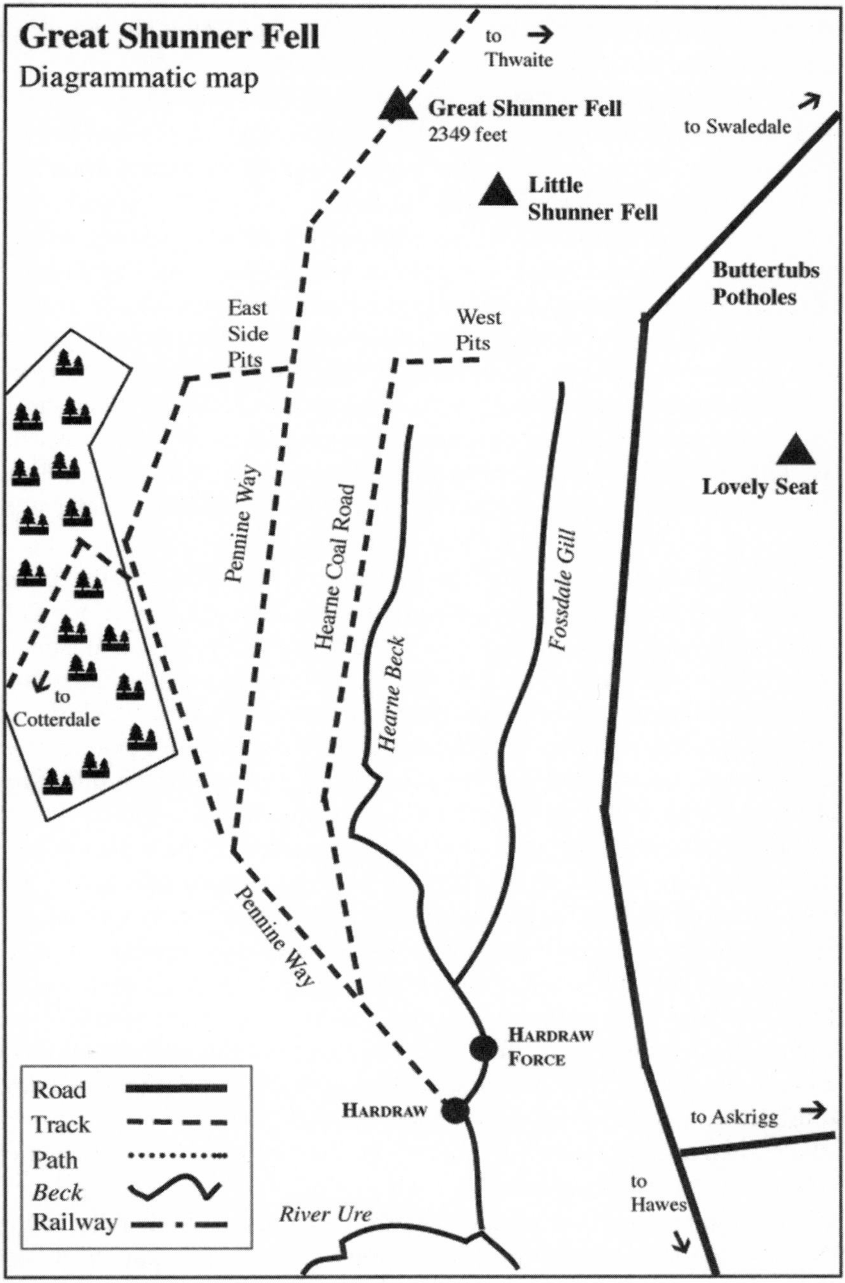
Great Shunner Fell
Diagrammatic map
to Thwaite
Great Shunner Fell
2349 feet
to Swaledale
Little Shunner Fell
Buttertubs Potholes
East Side Pits
West Pits
Lovely Seat
Pennine Way
Hearne Coal Road
Hearne Beck
Fossdale Gill
to Cotterdale
Pennine Way
HARDRAW FORCE
HARDRAW
to Askrigg
to Hawes
River Ure
Road
Track
Path
Beck
Railway

that its summit lacks its own individual profile being merely the highest point on a vast moorland ridge. As to its shape one writer has described it as being like a barbed arrow pointing north west.[2]

Whilst Great Shunner Fell might not show off its height to the best effect in Wensleydale you should not lose sight of the fact that it has the distinction of being not only the highest fell in both that dale and Swaledale but the third highest in Yorkshire after Whernside and Ingleborough. Until boundary changes, in 1974, it was also the second highest fell in the old North Riding after Mickle Fell. As Phil Clayton has pointed out, not only is it the highest point on the Pennine Way in Yorkshire, but the highest point reached on this long distance path in over 100 miles tramping north from Edale. It also has the longest continuous southerly ascent of any fell along the whole of the Pennine Way and is the highest point on its line of latitude between the west and east coasts. The climb out of Hardraw village to the summit is some five miles - somewhat tedious in bad weather, exhilarating and uplifting under blue skies.

Clayton also points to the fact that, of all Yorkshire's fells, Great Shunner has the most extensive summit area above 2,000 feet. This huge, sprawling, isolated fell top, covers approximately five square miles. It consists of a mass of millstone grit, peat hags, moss and heather, in the midst of which stands the summit wind shelter and Ordnance Survey column. Largely due to the thousands of Pennine wayfarers trekking across the fell, erosion has taken its toll of the fell's surface of peat bogs and groughs. To combat this problem the Yorkshire Dales National Park has, in recent years, replaced the duck boards with traditional, long-lasting stone flags. These have been laid across the worst areas of erosion on the summit and the higher slopes on both the Wensleydale and Swaledale sides. Because of the number of flags required and the difficulty of access they were first stockpiled on the Buttertubs pass from where they were flown by helicopter to the fell. No doubt the intrusiveness of these flags will offend the purists but most walkers will accept them as a practical necessity in the fight against erosion. Having walked them a number of times myself it is possible to believe that, as they blend into the terrain, they will become just another feature of the natural landscape.

Great Shunner Fell, in common with a number of high fells in the Pennines, is located at the heart of an area of very heavy rainfall. Local flooding in its neighbouring valleys often occurs as its becks, swollen by the summit rainfall, roar down the fell emptying themselves into the Swale and the Ure. Some storms on the fell are apocalyptic in their violence sending huge torrents down the various water courses. One such is Thwaite Beck on the northern slopes of the fell where one violent cloudburst did a great deal of damage to the landscape as it roared down Stockdale. In winter the precipitation often falls as snow which accumulates, in many places on the fell, to considerable depths. In the gullies and behind the walls, on the higher north facing slopes of the fell, it is not uncommon to find snow lingering until April and after severe winters much later than that.

One of the most severe snowfalls to blanket Great Shunner Fell occurred in January 1895. It blocked the Buttertubs pass between Wensleydale and Swaledale until about the middle of March. Stone walls and fences were buried in three to four foot drifts. Walls of snow, some ten to fifteen feet high, lined the sides of the road. Every attempt by road gangs to cut a way through was frustrated by the wind blowing the snow back on to the road again or by fresh falls. Isolated farms and cottages were faced with severe food shortages. In early March some Swaledale folk reached Hawes using sledges only to find that there had been no market there for weeks.

Travelling on the fells in such winter conditions was undoubtedly fraught with difficulty and danger. One vicar of the parish of Hardraw, who knew the area well having been the incumbent for over 40 years, often had to walk along the tops of walls to avoid floods or deep drifts. It was either that or make long circuitous detours bringing with them the danger of exposure to the elements. On one occasion when making a journey of over five miles to the hamlet of Lunds, where he was also a vicar, he missed the stone slab over a snow filled gully and fell into ten feet of snow only extricating himself after a long tiring struggle.

~ ~ ~ ~ ~ ~ ~ ~ ~ ~ ~ ~

Coal mining is a very old industry in the dales being documented, in Arkengarthdale, from as early as the thirteenth century. Along the fells, between Wensleydale and Swaledale, there are several isolated collieries which supplied the farms and lime kilns during the eighteenth and nineteenth centuries. Coal has played a prominent role as an extractive industry on Great Shunner Fell as its southern slopes, dotted with evidence of old pits from Cotterdale across to Fossdale, testify. For instance the Pennine Way, as it crosses the fell heading north, passes many bell pits between Black Hill Moss and Bleak Haw.

The Pen Lane track out of Hardraw, which forms part of the Pennine Way across Great Shunner Fell, was laid out to provide an access road to the fell's coal mines. At just about the mile point above Hardraw a rough track branches off to the right. Known as the Hearne Coal Road it follows Hearne Beck along the side of a somewhat desolate ravine to West Pits. Here near Pickersett Edge on Fossdale Moss, only a few hundred feet below Great Shunner's summit, were to be found some of the largest coal pits in the area. Unfortunately West Pits, which supplied a large area with domestic coal, closed down just before the First World War. However to offset the shortage of coal during the General Strike it re-opened briefly.

Back on the main Pennine Way, just after the last wall before the open moor, a track bears to the left. After a mile or so it splits into two, the left hand track descending through a large conifer plantation to Cotterdale village, the right hand track continuing along the fellside to the coal pits on East Side. Here the Cotterdale pits were worked from a big level supplying a large area with domestic coal until well into the twentieth century. These pits provided some two dozen or more 'livings', or livelihoods, in Cotterdale making it relatively prosperous.

Coal seams are not intruded into the rocks like minerals but are a normal part of the strata deposited in and around the ancient seas. The Yoredale rocks formed in a shallow sea which periodically became so shallow as to form extensive estuarine swamps where forests could grow. Following subsidence the debris of the forests, which had accumulated as peat, was submerged and covered with limestone or shale muds to produce coal. Within the Yorkshire Dales National Park there are thin coal seams in the Yoredales, a consequence of which is that numerous small pits were to be found where the coal outcrops on the high fells. For example pits were located on the outcrops of the Tan Hill coal seam which lay between the Yoredale series of rocks and the millstone grits.

Coal was mined by tunnels straight into the hillside or by bell pits where a vertical shaft was sunk to the coal seam perhaps only fifty feet below the surface. A coal seam, usually about two feet thick, was mined in all directions until it became unsafe following which another pit was started. At West Pits the coal was mined by penetrating the fellside with a gallery or passage for about one third of a mile. Beyond this gallery the miners grafted and sweated in a tunnel the same size as the seam which was approximately two and a half feet wide by three feet high. The miners loaded the coal on to bogies which they pulled along the tunnels by slings and chains. Later the coal was transferred to larger wagons waiting in the gallery. West Pits at the peak of its production produced nearly 400 tons of coal per annum.

The coal seams across Great Shunner Fell were variable in thickness and quality. For example some coal contained a lot of ash and sulphur making it unsuitable for domestic use but good enough for lime burning. Many small pits mined this ash and sulphur coal over much of the lower hill slopes in Wensleydale with much of it being used in lime kilns. Great Shunner Fell coal was not the best quality being described as ' burnable shale.' However even poor quality coal was valuable if it was in relatively close proximity to its users. There was always a demand for local coal as it was preferable to peat particularly for the smelting of lead and burning in lime kilns.

To get access to Great Shunner coal, farmers with their carts, came from all over the area. Many were anxious to get to the head of the queue at the moorland mines in order to collect a load of the ready mined coal. Some men even waited all night to ensure that they obtained an early load the following morning. Others returned home leaving their carts overnight before returning the next day. It is reported that a coal carting business was started up with the price for carriage being whatever the price of the coal was. Although coal cost only 2s 8d (10.6p) for eight hundredweights it did have to be collected which took the best part of a day.

It was the growth of modern transport, particularly the railway, which brought in cheap coal from the major coal fields and led to the decline of the Great Shunner Fell pits. Great Shunner Fell coal was never exported on any great scale and was always in demand before the railway came. The only evidence of a coal industry today on Great Shunner Fell are tracks across the moors and a few crumbling buildings. Old workings can be recognised by small spoil heaps of black shale often grassed over such as those above Cotterdale and on Fossdale Moss.

~ ~ ~ ~ ~ ~ ~ ~ ~ ~ ~ ~ ~ ~

In the desolate valley of Great Sleddale, on the northern slopes of Great Shunner Fell, lie the remains of a copper mine. Local tradition speaks of large untapped veins but another story is probably nearer the truth. A Reeth speculator employed two men to work the site during which they struck a vein. Whilst one stayed to work it the other went to Reeth on foot, a mere fourteen miles, to report to the proprietor on the lucky strike. By the time the two men returned in a horse and cart the vein had been worked out.[3]

On the way down to Thwaite, from Great Shunner's summit, the spoil heaps of Trial Level, the former lead mine, can be seen a little distance off to the side of the walled lane. Some lead mine ruins, of which there are many in Swaledale, can be dated back to the reign of Henry VIII. All of them ceased to be economical and the industry closed at the end of the nineteenth century. I will turn my attention more fully to the lead mining industry when I examine Lovely Seat.

Possibly one of the greatest views to be had in the Yorkshire Dales is that from the summit of Great Shunner Fell. In the section which follows, after noting the various routes to the summit, I opt for the Pennine Way following it out of Hardraw noting the cairns and beacons along the route. From the summit all the main fells ringing Great Shunner Fell - to the east, west, north and south - are identified.

### *You can see all t'world from t'top o' Shunner*

The Pennine Way, the inspiration of Tom Stephenson and others, became Britain's first long distance footpath with the completion of all its stages in 1965. To begin its ascent of Great Shunner Fell the Pennine Way climbs out of Hardraw via Pen Lane, by the side of the old school building, to emerge on the open fell. One of the more disconcerting aspects of this southerly approach to the summit is the way in which the various shoulders of the fell deceive the walker into believing that the summit is close; in fact it is concealed until you are virtually on it. Whilst it is true that Great Shunner's summit does not have a very dramatic profile when approached from the south, on a fine day this gradual ascent can be very rewarding with its sense of space and freedom complemented by the outstanding views back over Wensleydale and Hawes. Although it is a long trudge of five miles from Hardraw to the summit it is a relatively easy ascent with height being gained almost imperceptibly in the absence of steep gradients.

After crossing Bluebell Hill the Pennine Way passes, after the last wall before the open moor, the westward track leading to Cotterdale. It then continues northwards crossing open country marked by cairns, beacons, old coal pits, rocky outcrops, shake holes and the ubiquitous sheep. The prospect is one of wild rolling moorlands stretching far into the distance. As altitude is gained the terrain changes from limestone to gritstone and from grassy slopes to extensive peat bogs. Fortunately the latter are now crossed by stone flags laid down in the last few years. Eventually the elusive summit that you think you will never reach is arrived at. On the summit there is a stone windbreak in the shape of a cross with seats all around it. It is as a view point that Great Shunner Fell summit excels with the panorama being extensive in all directions.

Many walkers reach Great Shunner's summit in all seasons but mainly in the summer. To walk the Pennine Way across this huge fell clear visibility is essential. On a summer's day with a gentle puff of breeze and the birds singing the ascent can be glorious, a real lifting of the spirits. By contrast in mist and rain it will seem tedious not to mention endless. Jessica Lofthouse recalls walking over Great Shunner from Cotterdale.[4] All she could remember of the crossing was the icy coldness of the clinging mist, the squelching peat bogs and an urgent desire to abandon the fell with all possible haste.

Other routes to the summit of Great Shunner Fell include two from Cotterdale. The first follows a zigzag path from Cotterdale village through a conifer plantation, to the east of the village, up on to East Side. It then goes past the site of the disused coal pit to join the Pennine Way below Jiglemea Crag from where the track is followed to the summit. The second route is a rather long and arduous one. On leaving Cotterdale village it goes up through a conifer plantation, to the west of the village, onto the open fell from where it follows a northerly line over Tarn Hill, Bubble Hill and Sails before heading north east towards Knoutberry Currack and Great Shunner's summit.

A third northerly route to the summit leaves Hardraw to follow the Pennine Way for about a mile before turning right along a track known as the Hearne Beck Road. This track ends at West Pits from where one strikes out in a north west direction for the summit.

A quiet and peaceful route from the top of the Buttertubs pass goes across some two miles of grass and peat before going over Little Shunner Fell to reach the summit. The summit of Great Shunner Fell can also be reached by following the Pennine Way south from the village of Thwaite in Swaledale. From the village the route follows the Keld road before taking the track up Stockdale. This leads onto the north facing slopes of the fell from where it heads westwards before turning south. This route, three miles to the summit compared with five from Hardraw, is also marked by cairns and stone flags placed across the peat hags.

Finally there are two pathless, virtually unused routes to the summit. The first goes south across the moors from the tiny hamlet of Angram on the road between Thwaite and Keld; the second from the valley of Great Sled Dale which lies on the north western side of the fell.

Great Shunner Fell is liberally endowed with what the Ordnance Survey describes on its maps as beacons, cairns, or piles of stones. The Welsh word currack, which means stones, is also sometimes used. The fell is dotted with so many cairns that it is believed to have more than any other fell in Yorkshire. Many cairns lie on the route of the Pennine Way offering useful guidance when the weather is misty which, on Great Shunner Fell, is often the case. On such a vast fell a cairned track is a fairly safe option in poor conditions. Some cairns are actually on the track or close to it whilst others can be seen at a distance.

On the way from Hardraw to the summit you pass cairns and beacons that stand out for their height, structure or prominent position. Just past the turn off for Cotterdale sits Hume Sett Beacon overlooking the latter dale. Further on, just to the left of the Pennine Way, the cairn on Jingle Mea Crag stands ten feet high and measures some six feet across at its base. Almost opposite the latter, to the right of the track, is a tall, well built beacon at Crag End which many a weary walker has mistaken for the summit. The finest group of cairns consists of a dozen or more, south east of the summit, on Stony Edge near to three small tarns. Some of this group stand at around six feet high. From the summit down to Thwaite the Pennine Way route is marked, at regular intervals, by modest sized cairns.

Many of Great Shunner's cairns are extremely well constructed, with some being tall enough to be seen from many neighbouring fells. It is generally believed that many of them were built by shepherds and miners as aids to navigation particularly in hill fog. Another view is that they were built during the period of the Scottish raids to imitate armed soldiers ready to defend the area. This may well be the reason why locally such cairns are often called 'stone men'. It is also possible that the cairns had something to do with Great Shunner Fell acting as a look out post, perhaps involving a signalling system, through the lighting of bonfires where the cairns stood. Cairn builders have been active over many centuries with Great Shunner Fell being just one of many fells to benefit from their efforts. The proliferation of cairns on the fell has prompted some purists to complain that the fell is over-cairned. Despite their complaints I am sure that many thousands of Pennine Way walkers have been more than glad of the company of the cairns, in their trudge to the summit, when Great Shunner Fell has been swathed in mist.

~ ~ ~ ~ ~ ~ ~ ~ ~ ~ ~ ~ ~ ~

From the stone triangulation point on the summit the view is such that, as Ella Pontefract and Marie Hartley comment, one can easily identify with the shepherd reported to have said, 'You can see all t'world from t' top o'Shunner.' The view from the top is extensive with many square miles of high moorland rolling away, wave like in all directions, towards the encircling high Pennine fells. Walkers undertaking the strenuous climb to the summit will be handsomely rewarded for their effort, providing the weather is clear, with panoramic vistas in all directions. In some detail what will they see? What follows is a guide to the mainly, but not exclusively, natural features to be seen from Great Shunner's summit with particular reference to the surrounding fells and valleys.

Starting in the north west and proceeding in a clockwise direction you see on the skyline Cross Fell, at 2,930 feet the highest peak in the Pennines, famous for its Helm wind which rushes down its western slopes with great force. Cross Fell is the most prominent summit in a range of high fells which includes Knock Fell at 2,780 feet, Great Dun Fell at 2,782 feet and at 2,271 feet Dufton Fell. A few miles to the south east of Cross Fell and almost due north of Great Shunner Fell lies Mickle Fell. At 2,591 feet it is easily recognisable with its flat top. South of Mickle Fell the A66 can be seen crossing the high moorland of Stainmore, a road notorious for being closed regularly to high sided vehicles due to its often severe cross winds. South of the A66 lies Nine Standards Rigg at 2,171 feet. It is separated from Great Shunner by Birkdale Common and Angram Common with the silver streak of Birkdale Tarn glimpsed in the middle of the former.

If you now turn to the north east you will see, across the valley of the Swale, Rogan's Seat at 2,203 feet rising high above the villages of Muker and Gunnerside. Just off to the north west of this fell the keen observer will see the white building of Tan Hill which is England's highest pub. To the east, at the foot of Great Shunner Fell, lies the village of Thwaite above which stands at 1,636 feet attractive Kisdon Hill carrying the Pennine Way on its eastern flank. Although not a particularly high fell it is an unusual one in the fact that it is an 'island' cut off from the surrounding fells by the River Swale and Thwaite Beck.

Looking east there is an exceptionally fine view down Swaledale with its hills enclosing it tightly and its meadows clearly distinguishable from its fellside pastures. Beyond the scars of Fremington Edge, above Reeth, Roseberry Topping can be picked out on the horizon with, despite its modest height of 1,051 feet above sea level, its mountain peak profile. Now comes a surprise for it is claimed that, on the evening of Her Majesty's Jubilee in 1887, not only was the beacon on Roseberry Topping seen from the summit of Great Shunner Fell but the sea beyond. Given the increasing level of pollution since late Victorian times the right atmospheric conditions for this sighting to occur today must be rare indeed. Broadly east of Great Shunner Fell and separated from it by Little Shunner Fell, Thwaite Common and the Buttertubs pass lies Lovely Seat at 2,215 feet, one of Wensleydale's 2,000 footers. To the east of the Buttertubs pass you can seen Lovely Seat's western escarpment towering above Cliff Beck. Muker Common, the northern flank of Lovely Seat, slopes down to the village of Muker a mile down the dale from Thwaite. The southern slopes of Lovely Seat are part of the great Abbotside Common with Stags Fell, its prominent southern escarpment, overlooking Wensleydale.

From the summit of Great Shunner Fell the view to the south is magnificent. Directly facing you across the valley are three more of Wensleydale's 2,000 foot fells. The most easterly of them is Wether Fell with its highest point, the relatively flat plateau of Drumaldrace, at 2,014 feet towering above its lower peak of Yorburgh. To the west of Wether Fell lies Dodd Fell with its rounded summit. At 2,192 feet Dodd Fell is the highest point on a long ridge which has a lower summit called Ten End at 1,910 feet. West of Dodd Fell lies Great Knoutberry which, at 2,205 feet, is the highest elevation on the long ridge of Widdale Fell. Behind these three Wensleydale giants lie, from left to right, Buckden Pike at 2,303 feet, Fountains Fell at 2,192 feet and the famous Three Peaks of Penyghent, Ingleborough and Whernside at 2,277, 2,372 and

2,415 feet respectively. If the weather is exceptionally clear the sea may be glimpsed at Morecambe Bay, to the west of Ingleborough, through a gap in the fells. For the walker who reaches the summit of Great Shunner Fell this magnificent array of fells to the south is not easily erased from the memory.

Finally let us turn our gaze to the west. Immediately you see another of Great Shunner Fell's neighbours, Sails, and the last of Wensleydale's 2,000 foot fells in this clockwise panorama. To the north west are two more prominent fells, Hugh Seat at 2,260 feet and High Seat at 2,326 feet, which lie on the same ridge as Sails. This ridge runs for many miles in a north-south direction with Mallerstang Edge as its western escarpment. The most southerly of these, Hugh Seat, is named after Sir Hugh de Morville who, as mentioned earlier, took part in the murder of Thomas Becket. Further west, beyond Great Shunner's close neighbours, lies Wild Boar Fell at 2,324 feet which, when viewed from the east, west and south, has a distinctive flat top but when viewed from the north takes on the appearance of an alpine peak due to the angle of the rocky escarpment called the Nab. Between Mallerstang Edge and Wild Boar Fell the valley of Mallerstang broadens out to the north west into the Eden Valley which leads to Carlisle and the Solway Firth. To the south of Wild Boar Fell is Swarth Fell whose westerly neighbour is Baugh Fell with its summit of Knoutberry Haw at 2,217 feet topping off its huge bulk. On the far western horizon the Lake District fells are prominent with Skiddaw and Helvellyn particularly striking.

I have now completed my detailed description of what can be seen from the summit of Great Shunner Fell. It is inevitable that people will have their own opinions as to which direction provides the most impressive view. Personally I favour the southern view but that is primarily influenced by my feelings for Wensleydale. Those whose favourite dale is Swaledale will probably favour the view to the east. Surprisingly some people find Great Shunner Fell uninteresting claiming that it has an undistinguished top with few features worthy of attention. It has even been suggested that it is not worth the trouble to climb. It seems to me that such an opinion fails to capture the spirit of what this fell has to offer. Great Shunner Fell, apart from its exceptionally fine views in all directions, typifies the wildness of the high Pennines. It offers a limitless landscape under a broad sky, a great sense of the outdoors with the added bonus that, on many days of the year, there is a good chance you will have it to yourself.

From Hardraw, in addition to the Pennine Way taking walkers to the summit of Great Shunner Fell, there is a motor road which climbs high onto the fell's eastern flank passing the famous Buttertubs potholes on the drive to Swaledale. In the section below I examine the formation and appearance of these potholes before considering the folk tales associated with them. After the potholes I explore the features of the high moorland terrain to be seen from the Buttertubs pass which include views of Wensleydale and Swaledale. The section concludes with stories of travellers who, over the years, made the journey over this famous road.

## *The Buttertubs*

IT has been the practice over the years to attach imaginative names to the many potholes found in the Yorkshire Dales - names such as Gaping Gill, Churn Milk Hole, Bull Pot, Crackpot and Cowpot spring to mind. Hence the intriguing name of 'Buttertubs', given to a cluster of five potholes lying, either side of the Wensleydale to Swaledale road, just a short way down from the summit of the Buttertubs pass on the Swaledale side.

So why the name Buttertubs? There are a number of explanations all associated with butter. One is that they resemble a collection of butter churns. This view is supported by the fact that the first local maps named them Butterpots. Their circular shape and fluted sides gave them (using a degree of imagination) a certain similarity to the slatted tubs once used by local farmers to make butter. Another story has it that farmers returning from Hawes market in Wensleydale, having failed to sell all their butter, lowered their unsold stock into the cool depths of the shafts to keep it fresh until the next market day. It is also believed that, when prices fell to as low as 6d (2.5p) a pound, farmers used the Buttertubs as a convenient dump for their unsold, unwanted butter. It has also been suggested that, as Wensleydale was a prime producer of butter, the name Buttertubs may have assuaged any fear associated with deep potholes that local folk might have had.

In topographical terms the Buttertubs are a collection of potholes, the products of countless centuries of running water eroding the limestone. Heavy rain falling on and then draining off Great Shunner Fell has eroded downwards to form deep shafts. The streams, flowing across the different bands of rock (limestone, shale and sandstone) of the Yoredale Series, came to a layer of limestone and dissolved shafts in it.

How can we best describe the main features of the Buttertubs? First and foremost they are deep circular pits or potholes in the limestone. They are often described as being yawning chasms or deep clefts in the ground. They have been likened to deep chimneys connected at the surface by limestone bridges. Looking into them one sees rising from their floor what appears to be broken columns or pillars of rock differing in height and displaying unusual shapes. These tall columns of rock look like elevated blocks of basalt similar to those found on the Giant's Causeway in Northern Ireland. They also bear a certain resemblance to the stalagmites which are commonly found in cave systems. These ancient temple size columns and the sides of the shafts have been worn by water action into displaying ridges and hollows to produce a fluted, groove-like effect. It would appear that this fluting is a consequence of erosion in the vertical fissures in the limestone.

The depths of the Buttertubs are such that a local man once described them, with tongue firmly in cheek, as bottomless with some deeper than that. In actual fact they are about 65 feet deep with one reportedly reaching a depth of 100 feet. Descending them can only be managed with the aid of ropes. At the bottom of the shafts rocks and pebbles cover the floor. Much of this debris is caused by natural rock falls and those thrown down by visitors attempting to assess their depths. At the bottom of the deepest shafts layers of dead vegetation and ice have been found following the winter frosts.

Streams from the bogs on Great Shunner Fell flow into some of the Buttertubs on a virtually permanent basis. After heavy rain on the fellsides these swollen streams, if there is a high wind, throw up a good deal of spray, as they plunge over the lips of the shafts. The water from the streams, after falling to the floor of the shafts, seeps away through deep fissures in the limestone. It then follows a short underground course before exiting the system on the fellside above Cliff Beck some 300 feet lower down the ravine. It has been said that water can sometimes be heard deep down within the Buttertubs but more usually the only sound to be heard is that of a trickling stream falling gently into the depths of a shaft.

With the shafts receiving moisture, in the form of run off from the surrounding moors, vegetation has managed to establish a hold on the walls of the shafts and around their rims. This moisture is retained due to the mosses which cover the sides of the potholes. As a result of the virtually permanent dampness a great variety of vegetation has been able to colonise the fluted, ledged sides of the shafts such as ferns, golden rod, juniper, butterwort, wild raspberry, bird cherry, wild rose, foxglove, rowan and alder. Even at the bottom of the shafts it is not uncommon to find ferns growing. It is refreshing, on a hot day, to look down the deepest shaft at the moisture laden walls and plants and hear the sound of falling water splashing into the depths.

Although it is generally acknowledged that the water, falling into these shafts, exits near Cliff Beck there has been speculation that, given the way the limestone stratum is arranged in this area, water from the Buttertubs might find its way to vast unexplored cave systems beneath Stags Fell, the southern flank of Lovely Seat. Others speculate that these shafts are not merely shallow rents in the surface of the fell but the openings to an immense, vast, subterranean cavern complex. To date no such underground cave systems have been discovered in this area.

Before the age of motorised transport the Buttertubs were, for most people, remote and isolated. Today, although they are still relatively remote from the major centres of population, they are easily accessible by car and on foot from both upper Wensleydale and upper Swaledale. For many people they are an interesting feature to visit, particularly on a fine day, and can be safely approached if the normal precautions are observed. Like any potholes they are perilous for unwary visitors who do not take precautions when going close to the edge of the shafts to peer into the depths. In early times they constituted a danger to wayfarers travelling after dark, or in fog, if they strayed off the road. Their depth was a concern for early travellers for even if a person survived the fall rescue would not be quick and simple. To facilitate access to the viewing areas steps now lead down to them from the road. Despite the fact that some of the holes are railed off, such barriers are insufficient to deter those determined to stand on the edge of the shafts. Happily there does not seem to be any record of any person having ever fallen down any of the holes. Not so in the case of sheep which have been known to occasionally fall down them to be subsequently rescued by farmers lowered down by ropes. There is the story of Christopher Metcalfe who, when a boy, was often lowered down them to retrieve a fallen sheep; popular belief has it that he would only permit his father to take charge of the rope.

In days gone by some country folk felt the Buttertubs to be sinister and that they were the work of a giant. Legends tell of Swaledale folk who, on their way over the pass from Wensleydale at night, ran as fast as they could to get past the spot. Irrespective of the potential danger posed by the shafts themselves the area is not a place to be caught out alone, especially after dark, as the weather on Great Shunner Fell at this altitude can be truly appalling with severe storms producing torrential rains and high winds. Even sunny days do not totally lessen the fearsome appearance of the shafts. Inevitably the presence of deep potholes on a high, lonely moorland pass is the natural backdrop for grim and in some cases macabre tales. As Jessica Lofthouse has recorded Halliwell Sutcliffe the writer, in his romantic stories set in the Yorkshire Dales, had the Buttertubs potholes in mind when he talked of 'a fox with a pack of hounds in full cry have more than once been lost therein.'

The Buttertubs pass, linking Wensleydale with Swaledale, is a high level road running along the flanks of Great Shunner Fell with Lovely Seat, like a towering sentinel, opposite. At 1,726 feet above sea level it is one of the highest and steepest mountain passes in England. From Hardraw it climbs all of nine hundred feet and descends eight hundred feet to enter Swaledale at Thwaite. From Hawes it is six miles over the pass to Thwaite the road going between the two Buttertubs potholes on the east and the three on the west.

The Buttertubs pass is an ancient road between the two dales. Prior to the Norman Conquest it was a pedestrian path before later becoming a cart road for wheeled vehicles. Today it is considered to be the finest of the four metalled roads which cross the huge wedge of high ground between Wensleydale and Swaledale. This was not always the case as in the early part of the twentieth century it had a narrow, very rough, stony surface. It was looked on as something of a challenge by the first motorists and motor cyclists. Later, with the dawn of the motoring age, it acquired a better surface to meet the increase in the number of vehicles using it.

On leaving Thwaite the walled road, here known as Cliff Gate Road, rises steeply to follow a terrace along the side of Great Shunner Fell. As it rises higher the ravine of Cliff Side appears on the left, at the bottom of which Cliff Beck flows. Although there is a strong cable barrier now between the road and the ravine there was a time when the road was unfenced. On such an unfenced highway motorists were advised to drive in the middle of the road to minimise the chance of the wheels going over the edge. The motorist driving down to Thwaite has many tricky bends to negotiate one such being nicknamed 'suicide corner.' Today buses and coaches literally crawl over the pass.

Apart from the bends and the precipitous ravine there are other hazards to be overcome such as torrential rain, snow, ice, mist, high winds, wandering sheep and landslips. It is not uncommon for motorists to feel their vehicles slip badly when there is a light covering of ice, snow or slush. It has even been known for drivers to feel fearful, even in some cases 'freeze', at the thought of negotiating such a narrow road with such a precipitous drop on one side and a steeply rising fellside on the other. The early traveller probably dreaded a stumble on the rocky road which might catapult him into the abyss where he might never be found. Clouds often smother the pass creating extremely poor visibility necessitating drivers to be extra vigilant in negotiating the road. Caution is the watchword, when travelling over the Buttertubs pass, for both pedestrians and motorists but especially the latter.

At the bottom of the deep ravine Cliff Beck is fed by numerous foaming streams which leap down the rocky, scree-strewn slopes of Lovely Seat after heavy rain. Cliff Beck flows north to join Straw Beck and eventually the Swale. In days gone by one could see haymakers at work in the tiny fields at the bottom of the ravine where once there was a lead mine. The northern slopes of Lovely Seat, dropping down to Muker, are criss-crossed with dry stone walls in great profusion. Whilst the summit of Great Shunner Fell lies some way off towards the north west, across not particularly well-drained moorland, the lofty heights of Lovely Seat, above Cliff Beck, are much closer and seem to be guarding the pass.

The Buttertubs road crosses wild, desolate, unfenced, boggy moorland once the walled sections are left behind. In the past it was a gated road with one above Thwaite and another just above Simonstone giving access to the open moor. To walk or drive over the Buttertubs is not to be missed. You can enjoy the mountain air, appreciate the views of the moors and those of the encircling fells and experience the savage grandeur of the pass itself. There is no human habitation up here. Between the village of Thwaite and the hamlet of Simonstone, a distance of five miles of the most demanding terrain, there is only a solitary gamekeeper's dwelling close to the latter.

The Buttertubs pass lies in the region of the heaviest rainfall in Yorkshire with an average of seventy inches per annum. Days of rain and mist are often the norm on the pass. A heavy storm cloud hanging over Great Shunner Fell can turn a delightful summer's day into something closely resembling darkness. In the fury of a storm, with high winds and driving rain, it is not the place to be caught out on foot as there is a complete absence of shelter. Winter can be very severe on the pass as Edmund Bogg recalls.[5] He once made one very slow crossing in a raging snowstorm in which he was battered by particles of ice and snow and in which he could not distinguish between the white fells all around him and the sky. Today, when snowbound, the road can only be identified by a line of snow posts.

The pass can also have the effect of creating certain moods such as a feeling of desolation, of great solitude but equally one of awe at the scale of the landscape. When there is little traffic on the pass the silence is broken only by the wind and the occasional cry of a moorland bird. Although the road passes through a wild environment there is a sublime beauty about the moors and fells when sunlight floods across them.

It is interesting to reflect on the variety of people who must have trekked over the pass throughout the centuries. Soldiers, peddlers, packmen, shepherds, lead miners, farmers, hosiers, cheese and butter merchants would all have made the journey either on foot, on horseback, or by horse and cart. This tide of humanity flowing over the Buttertubs increased dramatically in the nineteenth century as people, from all walks of life, were attracted to the market and annual fairs in the rapidly expanding town of Hawes. How many travellers making these journeys must have been overtaken by darkness in this desolate spot? Many must be the number of tales, some of them of unusual misdeeds committed, told over the years about this sometimes eerie, sometimes threatening place, particularly in winter. Most travellers would have preferred a fine summer's day for their journey. Even Lovely Seat seems to detract from the pleasure of its name when it throws its dark shadow over the pass.

One difficult journey over the pass, in dreadful winter conditions, was that made by the Broderick family. One of the family wished to be buried on the fells behind the Swaledale family home of Spring End, fells which he loved and had roamed over as a youth. In 1886, the year of his death in Hawes, his funeral procession set out in icy cold weather to cross the pass. A blizzard blew up dumping deep snow on Great Shunner Fell blanketing the whole district. It was therefore with great difficulty that the funeral procession arrived at Muker. There are no doubt scores of other harrowing journeys across this wild landscape. Today the pass is busy, not only with local people and farmers visiting Hawes market, but with tourists particularly in the summer.

Every journey over the Buttertubs pass, providing the visibility is good, is rewarded with one of the most extensive panoramas seen from a motor road in the Pennines. The views are similar to those seen from the summit of Great Shunner Fell without being quite so extensive owing to the summit of the pass being some six hundred feet lower. However, whereas Buttertubs can be accessed by car, Great Shunner summit can only be reached on foot. Travelling from Muker to Hawes the view south, over Wensleydale, is one of the great Pennine views. One range of hills rises behind another along the length of the dale. The spurs of Great Shunner Fell fall away to allow a richly rewarding view of Ingleborough, the most striking of the Three Peaks, projecting its flat top into the southern sky. You can see Dodd Fell's dome-like summit, the long ridge of Widdale Fell and, on a very clear day, Morecambe Bay. Straight in front is, as Bogg has described it, the lion couchant bulk of Wether Fell with Drumaldrace the lion's head and Yorburgh its tail.

The view to the north, over Swaledale, as you descend the pass into Thwaite is also a splendid one. Away to the north east is the wonderful vista of the vast hill country which was identified in the view from the summit of Great Shunner Fell in an earlier section. Directly in front is shapely Kisdon Hill with Rogan's Seat behind. Due east you look down the winding length of Swaledale itself with virtually every pasture identified by its own barn.

The views from the pass in winter can be very beautiful. Bogg, travelling south over it in deep snow, looked down on Hawes and saw it glistening with an iridescence under the rays of the sun. Away to the west he says it was impossible to pick out where snow-capped summits stopped and where the sky began.

After the exhilaration of the high Buttertubs pass and the intriguing potholes I now return to the valley to visit Hardraw Force. First of all I will take a look at the dramatic features of the waterfall itself, including the source of its parent stream, before turning to its formation and the impressive gorge in which it is set.

### *The waterfall and gorge at Hardraw*

HARDRAW Force lies on Fossdale Gill in the valley of Fossdale. To appreciate the dramatic natural beauty of this magnificent waterfall and its environment you follow the gill from its source, across the pastures and meadows and through the gorge at Hardraw to its confluence with the river Ure. I will begin however with a look at the valley of Fossdale. An alternative spelling of its name is Forsdale which locally is always pronounced 'Forzdel.' The valley of Fossdale cuts into the lower slopes of Great Shunner Fell just below the high moors of Abottside. Less harsh than its neighbour, the valley of Hearne Beck, Fossdale consists of relatively level, productive meadows.

An interesting aspect of Fossdale's history is the suggestion that it was here, not at Dale Grange near Askrigg, that the true site of Fors Abbey was to be found before it eventually moved to Jervaulx. Evidence for this, as set out in Ella Pontefract and Marie Hartley's book on Wensleydale,[6] rests on a number of factors. For instance 'Fors' means waterfall of which there are a number on Fossdale Gill including Hardraw Force; equally however there are waterfalls close to Askrigg. The case for Fossdale was bolstered by legends suggesting that a meadow alongside Fossdale Gill was a cemetery and that sanctuary was gained once the bridge to Fossdale farm had been crossed. More tangible evidence for the abbey site being in Fossdale was the finding of a 'jagger' bell like those once used by monks on their packhorses. In addition to the *vaccary* (dairy farm) associated with the abbey, it is likely that there were some additional buildings, the foundations of which could be the mounds to be seen in a meadow close to the gill. Pontefract and Hartley also cite the old legend that, early in Henry VIII's reign, Jervaulx monks had a small chantry at Hardraw whose brethren lived in Fossdale. Colin Speakman appears to be in no doubt that Fossdale was the original site of the abbey.[7] He cites as evidence for this the discovery there, over a century ago, of a monk's grave and the fact that Jervaulx monks once managed a large sheep grange in Fossdale.

Fossdale Gill rises high on the eastern slopes of Great Shunner Fell not far from Wofell Scar. It initially flows through a gorge, negotiates a number of small waterfalls in Clough Wood before merging with Hearne Beck. It then crosses a stretch of pastureland before entering the attractive strip of sylvan woodland called Shaw Gill Wood. (A path follows the beck through this wood from High Shaw before joining the

Buttertubs road.) The gill then runs along a narrowing channel before falling almost 100 feet over the cliff at Hardraw. It then races cheerfully through the gorge below the falls before flowing peacefully across meadowland as Hardraw Beck to quietly expire in the waters of the River Ure.

In the early seventeenth century Hardraw was spelt with an e - Hardrawe. The name derives from the Old English words 'herde' and 'raw' which together mean a row of shepherds' cottages.[8] Dr Whittaker believes that, as Hardere is a common Saxon name, Hardraw is derived from Hardere - aw meaning the water of Hardere its Saxon owner.[9] Another interpretation has it derived from the Celtic words 'ard' meaning high and 'dwr' meaning water .

Hardraw Force, plunging 96 feet, is the highest single drop waterfall in England above ground. Some underground waterfalls, such as Fell Beck in Gaping Gill pothole on the slopes of Ingleborough, are higher. The water at Hardraw tumbles, without any obstruction, all the way down to the pool at its foot. This was probably not always the case as, way back in its geological past, it probably fell from ledge to ledge thus being more of a cascade than a waterfall. Even as a cascade it would still be an attractive feature but perhaps not so grand as its present day impressive sight. After making its leap the gill leaves the slopes of Great Shunner Fell for the last time to descend to the level of the River Ure. A Chinese visitor to Hardraw, comparing the location with that of waterfalls in China, was amazed to find it located so close to a village, without precipices or lofty mountains towering above it and with a motor road giving easy access.[10] There seems to have been little in the way of fatalities at Hardraw Force over the years but at the beginning of the nineteenth century stories were circulating about unfortunates who were killed by falling over the cliffs.

As Fossdale Gill reaches the centre of the cliff at Hardraw it hurls itself in one unbroken leap into the pool known as The Dub which awaits it almost a hundred feet below. This arch-like column of water, falling with such power, is relentless. After heavy rain it is a compelling, awesome sight with the column of water doubling or even trebling in width as it makes its precipitous descent. As the water recklessly careers over the cliff it preserves a columnar shape for much of its descent, albeit not a uniform one, before widening at its base and disintegrating into The Dub. Great sheets of vapour are given of as it falls. The Dub, which receives

*Above, view from above Sedbusk on the slopes of Lovely Seat of, from left to right, Wether Fell, Dodd Fell and Ten End.*

*Below, looking along the Cam High Road (Roman Road) on Wether Fell from its junction with Beggarman's Road, on the left.*

*Above Ten End rising above the valley of Sleddale from above the village of Gayle.*

*Another view of the potholes near the Buttertubs pass.*

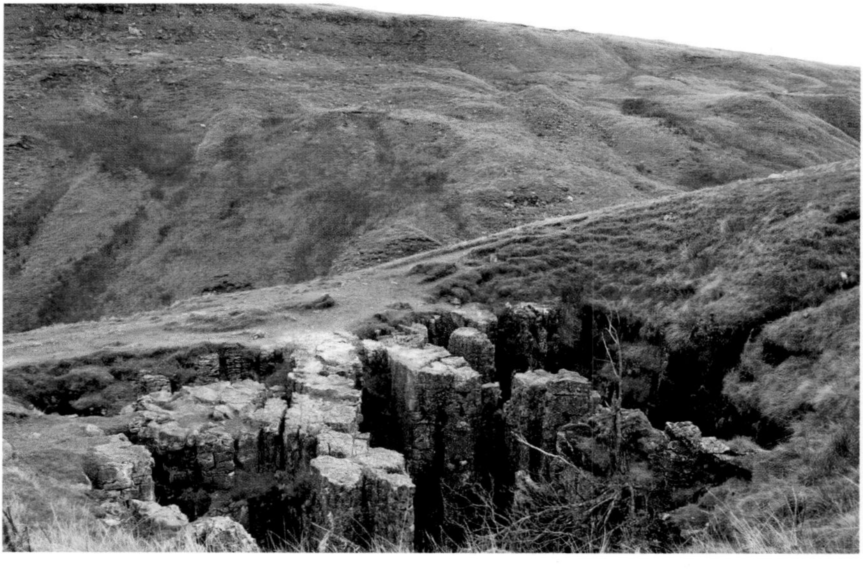

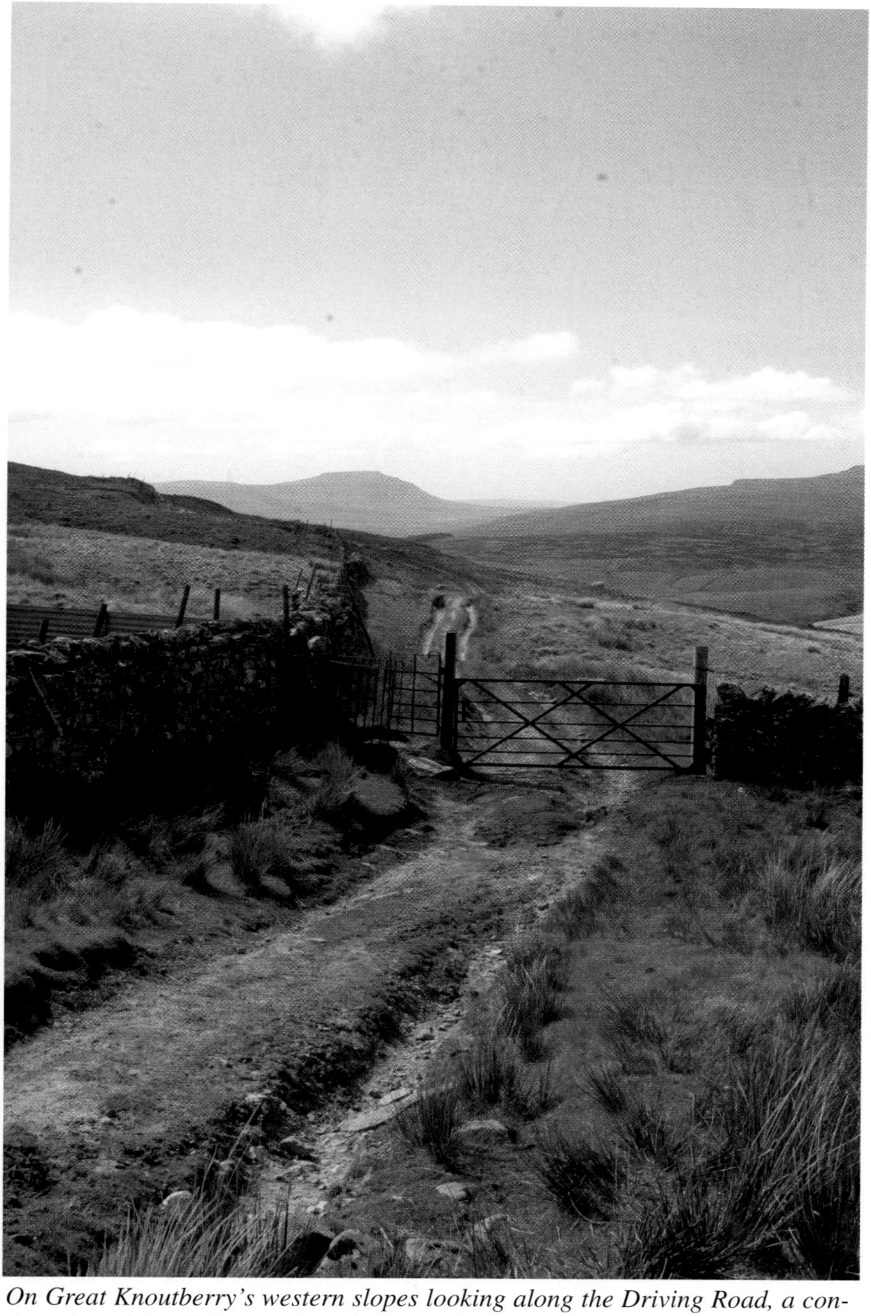

*On Great Knoutberry's western slopes looking along the Driving Road, a continuation of the Galloway Gate drove road, with Ingleborough on the skyline.*

*Looking north along a section of the drove road known as the Driving Road.*

this huge quantity of water, is a deep pool lying amongst boulders strewn at the base of the cliff. It was formed by the erosion of the shales at the foot of the waterfall. After heavy rain The Dub becomes a maelstrom of turbulent water dangerous to the unwary.

Owing to the projection of the gill away from the cliff, by some ten yards or so, a space has been created which allows people easy access to walk safely behind the falls. Once there you can peer up at the giant, overhanging cornice or lip of limestone. Due to the space to be found on the ledge behind the falls it is possible to remain fairly dry when walking along the path there. Care should be taken though as, lying as it does on the shales, the path is often slippery due to drips from the rocks and spray from the water falling into The Dub. The path, behind Hardraw Force, can almost be considered a cave such is the width of space between the falling water and the cliff face. As they fall the tiny droplets of water can take on the appearance of beads. To stand behind the waterfall on the ledge under the lip, the visitor cannot fail to be impressed by the view of the gorge as seen through the falling water. The ledge or shallow cave, particularly in spells of dry weather, is home to various birds who nest in it. On a hot day to take a walk behind the falls is a pleasantly cool activity. There is a legendary story of a dog which having supposedly disappeared into this cave emerged in another cave above Cotterdale having lost all its hair.

The lip, over which Hardraw Force falls, is the edge of a huge, hard, resistant limestone block which projects out, some five yards from the cliff face, causing the water to shoot out over the lip in one great uninterrupted fall. The reason why the limestone projects out from the cliff face some fifteen feet is due to the fact that the layers of sandstones and softer shales below it are more easily eroded by spray from the falling water. This process has been going on throughout geological time with the lip having collapsed many times. Each time this process occurs the gorge is extended as the cliff face is pushed further and further back. The fine grained, dark stone at the top of the waterfall is called Hardraw Scar Limestone one of the rock types which comprise the Yoredale Series of rocks. These rocks can be clearly seen behind the falls with Hardraw Scar Limestone on top, sandstones and shales below. The Yoredale Series lies below the young rocks of the millstone grits and above those of the older Carboniferous period.

During the 1850s concern was expressed at the way Fossdale Gill was eroding the projecting limestone rim of the waterfall. Consequently the eroded area, near the edge of the waterfall, was filled in with solid blocks causing the rim's height to be raised slightly in the process. More serious damage occurred, following the great storm of 1890, when exceptionally severe floods in the area destroyed the lip of the waterfall and the repairs that had been carried out in the 1850s. The loss of the lip turned the magnificent 96 foot single drop waterfall into a series of cascades. Lord Wharncliffe, on whose land Hardraw Force was situated, was aware that the falls were a very special feature of the landscape and immediately ordered his work force to put into effect his plan for restoring the lip to its original shape. Today, when you gaze at the water pouring over the reconstructed lip and walk behind the falls, it is good to reflect on the fact that we owe a huge debt to Lord Wharncliffe and his policy of restoration.

The winter of 1739-40 was a famously cold one. The frosts were so severe that many waterfalls in Wensleydale, including Hardraw, froze. It was even cold enough for Londoners to hold a fair on the iced-over Thames. As ice at the bottom of the waterfall met with that at the top a hollow tube of ice, the height of the cliff, was formed. The water from Fossdale Gill continued to fall through this column of ice which eye witnesses described as looking like glass. Such a sight was not easily forgotten by people who came from far afield to view it. Local residents were so captivated by it that they reportedly danced and capered around it. The next time the waterfall froze completely was in January 1881 when it was photographed with the water flowing through a column of ice just as in 1739-40. In the legendary winter of 1947 the column of water formed into a single, elongated icicle. In the most recent of severe winters, that of 1963, the ice formed a most beautiful stalagmite.

Hardraw Force came into existence when Fossdale Gill met the cliff or, to give it its correct geological name, rock step, on its way into Wensleydale. The waterfall owes its great height to the slight eastwards deflection of Fossdale Gill to avoid the glacial debris which now forms Smithy Hill. Had it not been for this obstruction the beck would have found a lower, more direct course for its journey to the Ure. The waterfall at Hardraw is thus a product of the Ice Age.

The gorge was formed by the continual cutting back of the cliff over which Fossdale Gill falls. The erosion of the soft shales of the cliff left the harder limestone at the top without support thus precipitating its eventual collapse, a process repeated over and over again. The waterfall has been eroded backwards upstream since the last Ice Age, to form what geologists call a recession gorge some 250 yards long. Fossdale Gill, in its current state, could not have carried out such a massive erosive feat of creating such a gorge. What happened was that, in the first 1,000 years of its life, it was supplemented by huge torrents of melting ice with massive erosive power. It is known that Hardraw Force was created some 14,000 to 15,000 years ago when the ice melted and sent Fossdale Gill on its detour to the Ure. On that basis it has been calculated that the waterfall has retreated up the gorge by approximately just short of one inch per annum. It is interesting to reflect on what an amazing sight, at the end of the last Ice Age, the then young River Aire would have presented as it plunged over the lip of Malham Cove before it disappeared into the limestone upstream of the cove in later years.[11]

Hardraw Force lies in a secluded, dramatic, yet beautiful gorge encircled on three sides by high cliffs. Fossdale Gill, after its spectacular leap, flows amongst rocks and slopes covered in wild flowers. When one stands near the falls, at the head of the gorge, there is a feeling of being in awe of such grand, lofty surroundings. The gorge, some 600 feet long, 200 feet wide and 90 feet deep, is narrow, winding and wooded. The gill has carved out this picturesque gorge over a long period of geological time. What makes the gorge so attractive is the fact that the falls are hidden to the visitor until after rounding the last bend. The gorge is open on its southern side from which Fossdale Gill makes its escape to the Ure.

Whilst the waterfall undoubtedly creates an environment of awesome grandeur the gorge, too, has been considered by some to be a wild, savage place, particularly after heavy rain, when the mighty roar of the waterfall carries through it. For example a south westerly storm, blowing up the gorge, is both wild and impressive as the rain and wind are funnelled up it towards the waterfall where the water is tossed into the air in clouds of spray. It is when the gill is in full spate, following days of rain on Great Shunner Fell, that Hardraw Force and Fossdale Gill are at their most spectacular. In these conditions the water is often discoloured brown from the peat on the moors. Despite this rather wild impression of the gorge held by some people, others have felt that the bird song and the gentle, babbling sound of the gill in its more gentle moods, flowing between the tree lined cliffs and flower strewn slopes make it an altogether charming bower.

The cliffs at Hardraw produce a variety of colours from the pale limestone to the black, brown and grey of the shales. The gorge also treats us to a colourful display of wild flowers such as the golden saxifrage, red campion, anemone, primrose, wood violet, bluebell, forget-me-not and snowdrop. The sides of the gorge are covered with trees, bushes and wild plants whilst on the cliff face, over which the waterfall plunges, there is often a colourful display of mosses, ferns and lichens which grow in and adapt to the fissures. The splendour of the russets and browns, throughout the gorge in the autumn, is not to be missed. Likewise in winter the trees and foliage thickly overlain with frost and silvery icicles create a scene of great beauty. On sunny days there is a nice contrast with one side of the gorge lit by brilliant sunshine whilst the other side lies in shadow. On overcast days the gorge can be a somewhat gloomy place but spirits are soon lifted by the commanding sight of the waterfall, the water dancing along, the greenery of the trees and bushes and the colours of the wild flowers.

Occasionally a rainbow-like effect of colours is created over the waterfall by the afternoon sun over Wether Fell shining on the spray rising from the surface of The Dub. Sometimes in bright sunshine the waterfall displays a spectrum of changing colours when viewed from different vantage points in the gorge. The spray from has often been likened to delicate glass or white lace cloth. Stories tell of how our ancestors associated nymphs and fairies with the waterfall.[12]

I will end my portrait of Great Shunner Fell on an art and music theme. First I consider the Romantic poets and painters such as Wordsworth, Ruskin and Turner who were inspired by Hardraw and its environment. I then visit Victorian times to explore the origins of the brass band contests at Hardraw which, despite long periods in the twentieth century when they were not held, still survive today.

## *Poets, painters and brass bands*

THE dramatic nature of the waterfall at Hardraw and the impressive gorge within which it lies, first became known to the wider public through the works of poets, painters and writers of the Romantic Age between 1780-1840. Amongst those who visited Hardraw Force during this period were Wordsworth, Turner and Ruskin. It is probably true to say that the artist Turner exercised what might be described as artistic licence in his depictions of Hardraw Force and its environment. This was probably due to his desire to conform to the fashion of the times namely the 'picturesque' gothic cult. As Mike Harding has commented visitors to the waterfall must have been surprised, to say the least, to find a narrow, tree covered valley rather than a wide one virtually bereft of trees as Turner had portrayed it.[13] Visitors would also find a waterfall splendidly impressive in its own right, which didn't need Turner's exaggerated scale.

Wordsworth visited Hardraw with his sister Dorothy in the winter of 1799. He was enchanted by the water, shooting directly over their heads as they stood behind the waterfall, describing it as, 'a scene so exquisitely beautiful.' The day was cold for their visit with icicles hanging from the rocks. Wordsworth was also captivated by the colours around him, the soothing murmur of the continuously falling water and the quiet solitude of the gorge. Today Hardraw Force and its gorge is a relatively quiet environment but not so unfrequented as in Wordsworth's day.

~ ~ ~ ~ ~ ~ ~ ~ ~ ~ ~ ~ ~

In the nineteenth century Hardraw was a major tourist attraction for the Victorians not only for the waterfall but also for a musical event. Due to its excellent acoustics a brass band contest and choir competition were inaugurated there of which the former, despite two world wars and a number of other setbacks, has survived into the twenty-first century. Crowds of many thousands came to listen to both the bands and the choirs. The slopes of the gorge were often covered with brass band enthusiasts and ordinary spectators who had come to enjoy a musical day out and a picnic on the grass. In these early days crowds of up to 18,000 were not uncommon. One can picture the scene - people strolling around the gorge, others sitting on the grass, the ladies in full skirts carrying their sunshades. Paths wound up the hillsides protected, where they were dangerous, by railings. Some enthusiastic visitors no doubt courageously walked or, more likely, scrambled behind the waterfall. For many folk the setting, the open air competition and the large crowds were a novelty. In short it was an occasion.

Contest days were good natured, friendly affairs for the most part. Although extra police were drafted in to keep the peace such days usually passed off fairly quietly. The majority of visitors were there for the music or just a good day out in beautiful surroundings and were not there to cause trouble. For many people the contests were their only holiday.

From all over the north of England they came particularly from Yorkshire, Lancashire and Durham. They came for more than just the music enjoyable though that was. For instance many who came were those who earlier had left the dale (or their descendants had) and who were anxious to visit family, friends and familiar haunts. Once the railway reached Hawes in 1878 thousands of visitors, in subsequent years, poured in on excursion trains on band contest days. It is reported that the number of excursion trains reached as many as 26 per day with one arriving every ten minutes in order to get people there in time for the concerts. They had to be parked in sidings down the dale until the railway authorities eventually brought in controls on the number of excursions able to use the line.

In the early days of the contests people paid sixpence (2.5p) to take a wagonette ride from Hawes to Hardraw. Before they were conveyed by wagonette to Hardraw the bands often played and paraded through Hawes before being judged at the Fountains Inn for smartness of turnout. As the twentieth century unfolded bands and their supporters came by bus, coach and car, bringing with them all the inevitable problems of parking and congestion. Behind the Green Dragon refreshments were provided in tents; often there was little or nothing left to eat by the end of the day. In 1883, to add to the fun of the contests, the famous tightrope walker Blondin performed a variety of stunts. One of these involved performing the feat of crossing the gorge on his rope whilst cooking an omelette at the same time.

It was a committee of public spirited people in the musical life of Hawes and its surroundings who, in 1881, first organised the Hardraw Brass Band and Choral Contest. They offered substantial prizes to the best brass bands and choral societies who competed. The contest proved so successful that it became an annual event. The land was lent by Lord Wharncliffe who owned the shooting lodge Simonstone Hall (his seat was at Wharncliffe Hall near Sheffield) and whose estate included part of Fossdale in which Hardraw Force and the Green Dragon Inn lay. Bands came to compete against one another not just from Yorkshire but from other parts of the country. Bands such as Besses o' th' Barn enhanced their already glowing reputations in brass band circles and beyond as a result of winning first prize at Hardraw. Besses scored a hat trick of contest wins in 1897, 1898 and 1899 for which they won the 50 guinea Hardraw Scar Challenge Cup. Along with the introduction of the band contest a choir contest was introduced with neither, fortunately, drowning out the music of the other. The choir contest was held in the area upstream of the waterfall on the banks of Fossdale Gill.

The brass band concerts were held in the wooded gorge between Hardraw Force and the village of Hardraw where there were superb acoustics. The grassy slopes could accommodate large audiences with 7,000 attending in 1889. Bands and choirs performed on level areas of grass at the bottom and top of the scar respectively. Those visitors wishing to just visit the waterfall were directed along the west path to take them clear of the musicians' playing area. As the contests continued Hardraw became a household name in the world of brass bands. After the First World War a circular stone bandstand with wooden seats was built for the competing bands to perform in. A 1925 photograph shows the bandstand in full use. Prior to its construction the musicians performed on a temporary wooden stage, erected on the lower slopes of the gorge, where the 'terraced' seating is now. The audience sat by the gill and looked northwards towards the musicians. Ed Blythe bought the grounds in 1920 and put a huge amount of enthusiastic effort into making the Hardraw Force and its environs safe for both contestants and the expected large crowds. He built the bandstand near to the little bridge which spanned the beck. Blythe's work in building the bandstand was part of a post World War One effort to revive the renowned brass band and choral contests of the late nineteenth century. Sadly, despite a few contests held in the 1920s, his effort, time and money to make the revival a success were disappointed due to the advent of radio and through it more easily accessible music.

The Brass Band and Choral Contests were usually held in June and, as we have seen, were initially well supported by folk from all over the north of England. The contests peaked in the mid 1890s (24 entries in 1892) but continued annually until 1902 when only three bands entered. After this date it is not clear whether the contests were held annually up to the First World War. In 1925 only five bands entered the contest and in 1927 only two. It is believed that the 1929 contest was the last until 1976. In 1925 a programme cost 3d (1.25p) and in 1926 2d (0.8p). In 1900 people came to hear the fifteen choirs which attended but the number of choirs entering the contest had dropped by 1925 to four and in 1926 and 1929 to five.

In 1900 the *Darlington & Stockton Times* reported that the initial popularity of the band contests had waned. One likely reason for this was the withdrawal of concessionary fares by the railway companies which had previously been given to bands attending the contests. Despite this Hawes was very busy and lively with trippers brought in on the special band contest excursion trains put on by the North East Railway Company and the Midland and Lancashire Companies. The low number of bands entering the contests was a further pointer to the decline in the popularity of the brass band contests which had peaked in the mid 1890s. For example in contrast to the fifteen choirs who turned up in June 1900 for the choir contest, only three bands out of an entry of six turned up.

One notable absentee from the 1900 contest was Besses o' th' Barn which in 1899 had completed three successive wins at Hardraw. It is not clear whether they absented themselves by choice or were in fact excluded from entry by virtue of the hat trick of wins. The position is unclear because at the National Brass Band Contest held at Belle Vue, Manchester, the rules decreed any band winning three times in succession should be barred from entry to the contest for one year. Previously hat trick winners had faced a penalty of being barred for two years. Did these national rules apply at Hardraw to deprive Besses of an appearance? Another view is that Besses was content to sit on its laurels and give other bands a chance of winning thereby suggesting the band chose to be absent.

The following year, 1901, a large crowd gathered under grey skies to hear a mere five bands compete out of an entry of fourteen. Other factors contributing to the demise of the Hardraw Brass Band Contest were the outbreak of war in 1939, the closure of the Wensleydale Railway in 1954 and competition from other brass band contests. For example the biggest one in the country at Crystal Palace, because of its larger prizes, was an inducement for the top bands in the north of England to travel south.

Following the 1929 contest, which was the last one prior to the Second World War, no other attempt to revive the Hardraw contests occurred until 1976. Although 5,000 folk attended in that year the profit was barely adequate from that year's contest to provide for poor seasons which, sad to say, would, given the dales' unpredictable weather, inevitably occur. For the centenary concert in 1981 fourteen bands attended whilst the 1983 contest is remembered for its snow. In 1985 for organisational reasons the contest was held in Hawes Auction Mart car park. The 1986 contest was cancelled because it was thought the entry of only ten bands was not viable.

During the intervening years of 1987 and 1988, when no contests were held, preparations were made for the revival of the contest at Hardraw by the Yorkshire and Humberside Brass Band Association (YHBBA). All the contests since their revival in 1989, right through to 2002, have been held on a Sunday in September with the exception of the year 2000. Once again the stirring sound of brass bands filled the gorge at Hardraw and carried beyond.

September dates were chosen to ensure the contests would be clear of the holiday period thus enabling bands to enter. It was also designed to extend the tourist season for local businesses. The September Sunday contest also came, rather conveniently, the day after the British Open Brass Band Championships held annually at that time in Manchester. The exception to the September Sunday tradition occurred in the year 2000 when it was moved to June. This move was due to the fact that, during the years of the revival, there were many requests to the YHBBA for a change of date from the one in early September. Unfortunately the band entry in 2000, the year of the move, was only ten, well down on the fifteen entries in 1999. In competitions like Hardraw, where the standard was so close, it was common practice for all the bands to be recalled to the bandstand to play again. However at Hardraw in 2000 it is believed that, because of the low turn out, the bands present were recalled to spin out the music-making for the benefit of the audience. Also in the year 2000 on the 17th June, the day before that year's contest, Besses gave the Millennium concert which also commemorated their hat trick of wins one hundred and one years earlier. No contest was planned for 2001 due to the previous year having been poor financially. As it turned out it would, in all likelihood, have been cancelled anyway due to foot and mouth disease.

Financial problems bedevilled the Hardraw Brass Band Contests throughout the years of their revival with the YHBBA having to support them financially to maintain their continuation. The association is not helped by the fact that it is precluded from obtaining lottery awards due to the contest being a musical competition. Equally although the contests have been held, albeit intermittently since 1881, they do not qualify for a grant under the Heritage Awards Scheme.

# 7
# LOVELY SEAT

Lovely Seat acts as a sentinel guarding the Buttertubs pass. After describing its topography, with particular reference to the quarrying of stone on Stags Fell and the huge sheep farming area of Abbotside Common, I examine the rocks beneath my feet in the context of the geology of the Yorkshire Dales as a whole. As a spin-off from the geology of the area I look at the lead mining industry focussing on the Sargill Lead Mine on the south eastern slopes of the fell. Finally I turn my attention to the wildlife to be encountered on Wensleydale's high fells.

## *Guarding the pass*

THE word 'lovely' today means attractive or beautiful but this should not lead us to believe that the fell's name originally meant this. In fact the name 'lovely' is likely to be a corruption of the Scandinavian word *luin* meaning a sound or an alarm. The other half of the fell's name, 'seat', is likely to be a corruption of the word *saetr* meaning high summer pasture. The name seems to have been passed down to us as 'Lunasit' or 'Lunnersett' which, in terms of its local pronunciation, gives Lovely Seat as the nearest approximation to its original name. Another interpretation is that the name Lovely Seat is derived from the Norse words meaning Lorn's summer pasture.

It is also possible that Lovely Seat was part of a signalling system, involving its neighbour Great Shunner Fell, set up to warn the settlers in Thwaite in Swaledale of impending dangers. Harry Speight suggests that *luin*, meaning sound the alarm, may have involved a trumpet call but then questions its necessity.[1] He points out that, as Lovely Seat's summit is some two miles from Thwaite, it is not certain that any trumpet signal would be heard well enough to act as a warning to the old Norse settlers down in the village even if a warning were required. However he does acknowledge that the situation was a dangerous one with Thwaite being at the junction of routes from Wensleydale, Keld and Swaledale. He thinks the dangers were most acute in winter time when packs of wolves coming from the forested hills were attracted to the farmsteads.

It is probably the case, as Phil Clayton points out, that when the Ordnance Survey compiled the map for upper Wensleydale and upper Swaledale a century and a half ago, the surveyors misheard the name 'Lunasit' or 'Lunnersett' (possibly due to dialect difficulties) and called it what they thought they heard - Lovely Seat.[2]

~ ~ ~ ~ ~ ~ ~ ~ ~ ~ ~ ~ ~ ~

After Great Shunner Fell, Lovely Seat, at 2,215 feet, is the second highest of the six Wensleydale 2,000 foot fells. It is the highest point on the great wedge of land which stretches between the Askrigg to Muker road over the Oxnop Common in the east and the Buttertubs pass in the west; and in a north-south direction between Straw Beck in Swaledale and the River Ure in Wensleydale. The fell has a very steep western face rising out of narrow, secluded and lonely Cliff Side which lies below the terrace carrying the road over the Buttertubs pass. To the west, across the pass, lies the great sprawling mass of Great Shunner Fell. Lovely Seat's southern flank slopes gently down towards Stags Fell (stag being a local name for a young horse) with its steep, distinctive, geologically interesting escarpments of High and Low Clints which overlook Hawes. The whole eroded summit of Lovely Seat is covered with vertical islands of peat in areas of sand and thin, sparse grass. In addition many drainage channels criss-cross the fell's slopes. From near the summit a number of becks drain south east such as Coal Gill. Lovely Seat, like Great Shunner Fell, once had several coal pits around the 1,500 foot contour.

The summit cairn is large and squat and is made out of local flags quarried on the southern edge of the fell. There are four cairns on the summit edge, four or five more higher up and a splendid ten footer on the top. Cairns and beacons are also to be found in profusion on the south west corner of the fell such as on Pike Hill for example. With the Buttertubs road reaching over 1,600 feet ascent of Lovely Seat is relatively easy. From the Buttertubs pass it is about a mile or so to the summit.

From the western edge of the summit there is a good view south of Wensleydale and the green valley of Widdale with distant Ingleborough rising sphinx-like beyond. To the west the view takes in the sprawling southern flanks of Great Shunner Fell. The route up Shutts Lane from Sedbusk to the top of the moor and North Rakes Hill provides good views of upper Wensleydale. From High Clint there are excellent views to be had of Wether Fell, Dodd Fell and the long ridge of Widdale Fell, all cradling Hawes. From this point the River Ure is also in full view as it threads its way through Wensleydale's meadows.

Between the village of Sedbusk and the hamlet of Litherskew on the slopes of Stags Fell is to be found, in rough pasture, the entrance to underground passages known as the Maze Hole Caverns. The passages are natural sink holes with access via a vertical pit or pothole. The chambers are 29 feet deep and extend laterally for about 150 feet. They are famous for stalactites and encrustations of different hues. Here, according to Bogg, the locals believed that the fairies liked to meet annually to make merry.[3] A variation of this tale is that the water kelpie, a water spirit in the form of a horse, was said to haunt the district between the Ure and High Abbotside neighing and snorting by the path leading to Sedbusk.

As I explored the stone industry in some detail earlier, when I considered the Burtersett stone quarries, I will deal here only with those aspects of the industry specific to Stags Fell. Across upper Wensleydale's hillsides spoil heaps provide clear evidence of the amount of quarrying and mining of the Yoredale sandstones which occurred. For example on the southern slopes of Stags Fell there are numerous spoil heaps, now grassed over, providing clear evidence of what was once a flourishing industry. The village of Sedbusk, on the lower slopes of the fell, was once virtually surrounded by numerous stone quarries which have, now happily, been blended back into the landscape.

Beds of good quality sandstone which lay underneath Stags Fell were comprehensively mined and quarried in the nineteenth century for use in the building industry. The sandstone was cut from the fell in large blocks before being split into flagstones. Stone taken from Stags Fell was used for roofing, walls, houses and barns. For roofing purposes the strong sandstone splits easily into thin slates and is widely used in Wensleydale. By contrast thicker slabs were used for flooring and paving. Of the stone used further afield it is said that Victoria Station in Manchester was built from it.

Rather than sinking shafts it was considered easier to mine into the hillside for two reasons. Firstly, large quantities of earth did not have to be excavated before the stone could be extracted. Secondly, in the latter part of the nineteenth century, there was a plentiful supply of labour owing to the decline of the lead industry and the consequent closure of many lead mines. Many lead miners were equipped with the knowledge and techniques

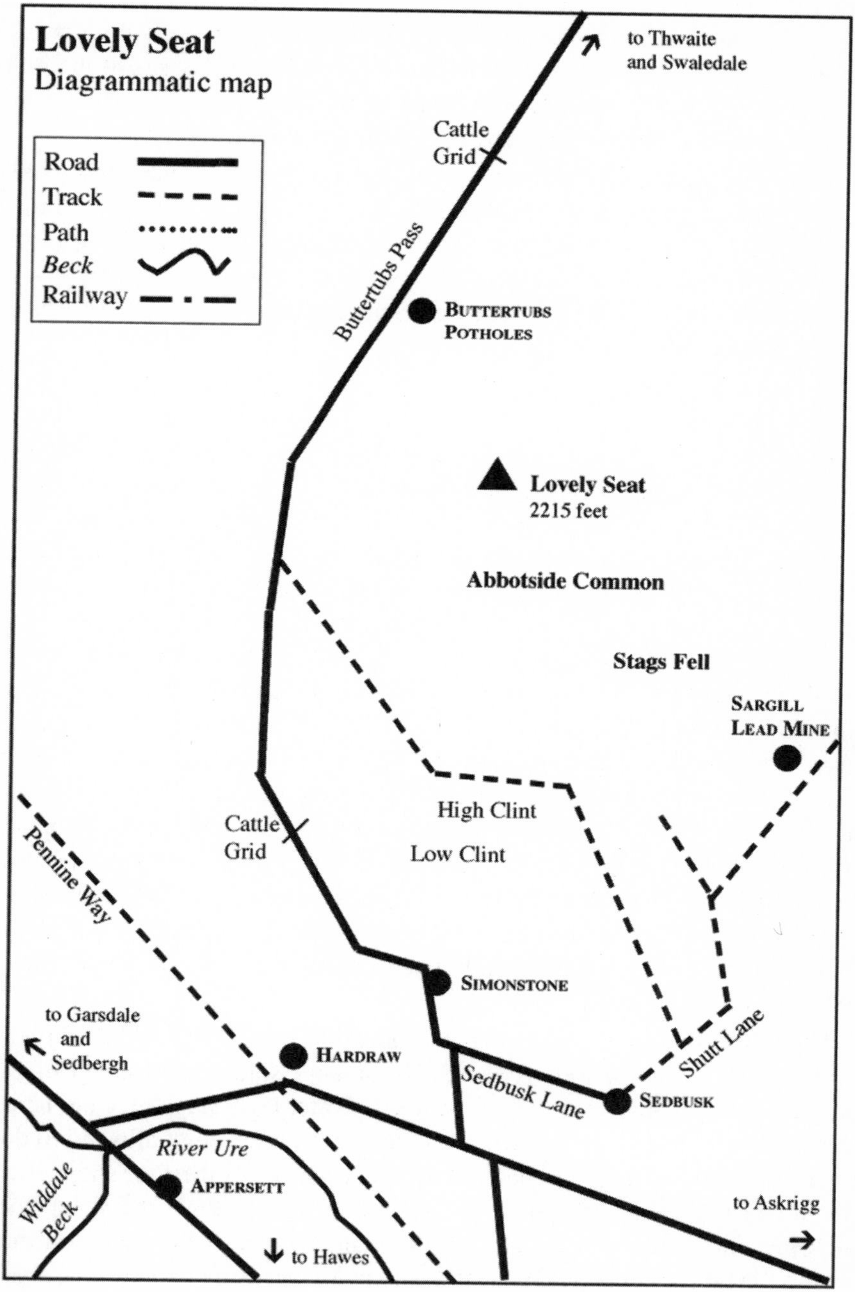
Lovely Seat
Diagrammatic map
Road
Track
Path
Beck
Railway
to Thwaite
and Swaledale
Cattle
Grid
Buttertubs Pass
BUTTERTUBS
POTHOLES
Lovely Seat
2215 feet
Abbotside Common
Stags Fell
SARGILL
LEAD MINE
High Clint
Low Clint
Cattle
Grid
Pennine Way
SIMONSTONE
to Garsdale
and
Sedbergh
HARDRAW
Shutt Lane
Sedbusk Lane
SEDBUSK
River Ure
APPERSETT
Widdale
Beck
to Hawes
to Askrigg

required for the job of digging out the stone from an underground face. Tunnels, the remains of whose entrances can still be seen, were driven into Stags Fell. The workings ran west to east along the slopes of the hill following the horizontal outcrop of the bed. The quarrymen worked in damp, dark levels to get the valuable roofing and building stone out.

Whilst strong shire horses hauled the larger slabs of stone down the fell side, ponies brought down smaller weights of stone. It was, apparently, not unknown for some heavy slabs to accidentally career down on their own. At the end of the nineteenth century a very large tonnage of stone was shipped by rail every month from Hawes station to East Lancashire and Manchester.

~ ~ ~ ~ ~ ~ ~ ~ ~ ~ ~ ~ ~

Consisting of some 10,000 acres Abbotside Common, in upper Wensleydale, stretches along the north side of the Ure from Hell Gill, near the Cumbria-North Yorkshire border, to Skellgill near Askrigg. By virtue of its size it encompasses the southern slopes of three of the fells in this narrative - Lovely Seat with which we are currently concerned plus Great Shunner Fell and Lunds Fell. Its name comes from the fact that the land belonged to the monks of Jervaulx Abbey, some 30 miles or so down Wensleydale, who used it for raising sheep for their wool. At the Dissolution it was given by Henry VIII to Matthew, Earl of Lennox from whom it descended to James I. He granted it to Ludovick Stewart, Duke of Lennox and Richmond, who had great difficulty in making the tenants accept him. In 1603 he had a survey of Abbotside made because the rents of the farms were too low. From its findings he found he was only receiving £100 when he should have been getting £1,200. Later he sold the estate to three men one of whom was John Coleby. After a number of further changes High Abbotside descended to Lord Wharncliffe who sold it off in 1912.

When the shooting rights to High Abbotside were sold off the number of sheep on the moor were reduced. To manage some 7,000 sheep shepherds were appointed annually for Lunds, Cotterdale, Stags Fell and Low Moor. Under this system farmers on the common were not allowed to do their own shepherding and had to pay a share towards the four shepherds employed. Only at special times, such as bringing down the sheep for dipping, did the farmer assist with the management of the sheep on the moor. When a vacancy for a new shepherd occurred, a new one was elected by a group of landowners called the conservatores. At times there have been up to eighty applicants. The four shepherds lived at Lunds, Cotterdale, Hardraw and Simonstone each one being responsible for upwards of 1,000 sheep. For example those sheep, in the care of the Hardraw shepherd, belonged to nine farmers.

The first 'stinting' occurred in 1837. Sheep are 'heafed' that is bred on the moor and do not stray far from the area in which they graze with their mothers. Shepherds know the moor and are not afraid of hidden gullies and shake holes. What they do dislike on the moor is a bitterly cold wind blowing snow into their faces causing them to fight for their breath. As was noted earlier, when I examined hill farming, farmers today do their own shepherding. The vastness of Abbotside Common can make it a difficult place to be caught out in severe weather. Even in good weather the distance from any habitation can present difficulties in the event of an accident.

From the surface features of Lovely Seat my attention now turns to the rocks below. From the Silurian rocks, through the Carboniferous to the Millstone Grits, I take a detailed look at the various geological periods which have shaped the landscape of not just Lovely Seat and the other 2,000 foot fells of upper Wensleydale but the whole of the Yorkshire Dales.

### *Rocks laid bare*

THE Askrigg Block is the name given to the main geological structure of the Yorkshire Dales. It takes its name from the village in Wensleydale which lies roughly in the middle of the area. It is a deep-seated block of rock, dipping gently to the north east, which has been gradually pushed upwards over millions of years to form the upland heart of the Yorkshire Dales. Along its southern edge three huge splits have created what are known as the Craven Faults, now, reassuringly, stable. What happened was that the land towards the south of the Askrigg Block sheared off from it, slipping down many thousands of feet below the rocks of the block. On the western edge of the block lies the Dent Fault beyond which the ancient Silurian rocks have been lifted to reveal themselves on the surface more than they do on the Askrigg Block itself. The first rocks to be laid down and therefore the oldest were the Silurian. On top of these were laid down those of the Carboniferous Period which included the Great Scar Limestone and the Yoredale Series of rocks, the latter being of particular interest to this study of Wensleydale. Lastly Millstone Grit rocks were laid down on top of the Yoredales.

I will begin with an examination of the most ancient rocks, the Silurian, which form the foundations of the Askrigg Block. These consist of slates, mudstones and gritstones which were the remains of ancient mountain ranges worn down and folded by pressure and heat. On the western side of the Dent Fault, as we saw earlier, these Silurian rocks are visible having been uplifted from the depths of the earth. The rocks of the Howgill Fells and Middleton Fell, some 100 million years older than the Carboniferous rocks of the Yorkshire Dales, are good examples of these ancient rocks.

Within the Yorkshire Dales National Park these ancient rocks are only exposed in a few places such as where the Carboniferous rocks have been completely eroded away in the valley floors. The largest intrusion of ancient rocks into the younger rocks is found in the floors of Ribblesdale and Crummockdale. Here they can be quite clearly identified in the walls of quarries where they display impressive fold structures.

At Thornton Force, near Ingleton, Kingsdale Beck cascades over a lip of Carboniferous limestone before dropping into a pool cut in ancient rocks. The dividing line between the two can be clearly seen halfway down the waterfall with horizontal limestone lying on top of the eroded ends of upright slates. It is worth pointing out that such ancient rocks as the Silurian produce a different landscape to that of the Carboniferous. This is shown to dramatic effect in the Howgill Fells which have more rounded profiles, long steep slopes and deeper ravines than the hills of the Yorkshire Dales further east.

Having examined the oldest rocks, the Silurian, which form the base of the Yorkshire Dales I now turn to those rocks which were laid down on top of them. These rocks of the Carboniferous Period, except for a small area centred on the Howgill Fells in the north west corner, cover the Yorkshire Dales National Park. During this period, some 350-220 million years ago, sedimentary rocks were formed. The name carboniferous is given to them as they contain most of the world's coal seams. The Great Scar Limestone, stretching across the dales, is the major constituent feature of these Carboniferous rocks. In the northern half of the dales it is overlain by layers of Yoredale rocks which in turn are overlain by Millstone Grit rocks. I will look at these two rock types below after first examining the Great Scar Limestone.

The Great Scar Limestone was first deposited some 350 million years ago on to the lower ancient rocks. Within the park it forms a single slab, some 600-800 feet thick, stretching from Wharfedale in the east to beyond Ingleborough in the west. It was given its name because of the dramatic scars associated with it in the south of the park. The first Carboniferous rocks, like the Great Scar Limestone, were formed from millions of shells and skeletons of tiny organisms which lived in the warm, shallow, clear seas which covered the Yorkshire Dales for a large part of the Carboniferous Period. The remains of these life forms accumulated on the seabed, over vast periods of time, eventually forming sedimentary rocks, so named because of their formation by mineral and organic material deposited by water. From these deposits hundreds of feet of limestone evolved.

In the Craven district of the Yorkshire Dales National Park, with the exception of the peaks of Ingleborough and Whernside, the Yoredale rocks laid down on top of the Great Scar Limestone have been completely eroded away over time leaving the latter covering the surface with its prominent white cliffs of Kilnsey Crag, Malham Cove and Gordale Scar. By contrast, with Craven, the Great Scar Limestone is totally buried in Swaledale and is only seen in Wensleydale in scattered outcrops along the valley floor from Appersett to Aysgarth. As a result there is an absence of potholes and underground passages in Wensleydale and the northern part of the dales compared to those to be found around Ingleton, such as Gaping Gill and Ingleborough Cave. The name 'karst' is given to an area displaying the characteristic features of a limestone region to which I now turn.

First I will look at the chemical processes at work in limestone. Limestone is a hard rock but subject to vertical splitting. It contains calcium carbonate and in pure water it is almost insoluble. However, rain water and that from becks can absorb carbon dioxide from the atmosphere to form a weak acid solution which will dissolve limestone and produce calcium bicarbonate. The evaporation of this calcium bicarbonate saturated water causes some of the bicarbonate to revert back into carbonate which, as it is insoluble in water, is then re-deposited.

One of the main agents responsible for the limestone landscape of the dales that we know today is water. With the melting of the ice at the end of the Ice Age fast flowing torrents were able to penetrate into the limestone to create the most impressive underground systems of potholes and caverns - complete with stalagmites and stalactites - in Britain. Another feature of the karst landscape is the sink hole, or swallow hole, a ten to thirty feet deep, funnel-shaped depression in the ground. They are sometimes caused by the sudden collapse of a rock roof over an underground cavern. A more usual cause, however, is the slow erosion of the underlying limestone as aggressive water penetrates down through the cracks and joints causing the soil layer to gradually sink.

Limestone pavements, a common sight in limestone country, are the products of the erosive action of rainwater. What occurs is that the fissures in the limestone are expanded by water solution draining into them to form an area of limestone blocks or clints surrounded by crevices or grikes. Such clints are usually nine to twelve inches wide and about a foot deep. The surface of the clints, whilst generally flat, often carries grooves caused by water running from its top into the grikes. As grikes are damp and sheltered they provide an ideal home for plants. Small patches of limestone pavement are to be found across the dales, such as the one on the southern slopes of Dodd Fell, with by far the most extensive coverage being in the Ingleborough area.

Finally, in my look at the characteristics of limestone country, I turn to the colour of the limestone itself. Usually grey in colour it can range from a cream to almost black. The white of the limestone crags, which is what we associate with the landscape of the Yorkshire Dales, can be attributed to the exposure of the rocks to the atmosphere and rain water. This process leads to the formation of a film or thin patina forming on the surface of the rock similar to the process at work in the green oxidation of bronze and copper.

In the story of the laying down of the rock strata of the Yorkshire Dales I now come to rocks of the Yoredale Series which were lain down on top of the Great Scar Limestone. It was the Yorkshire geologist Phillips who used Yoredale, the old name for Wensleydale, to name a significant series of Pennine rocks some 300 million years old dating back to the Carboniferous Period. Phillips claimed that the Yoredale rocks were best displayed in Wensleydale. Here starting at the bottom were bands of limestone, shale and sandstone, each band about 40 feet thick. Each set of these three bands of rock formed a cycle which is repeated eight times. Each cycle is known by the name of its limestone, for example Hawes and Hardraw. In the north of the park the Great Scar Limestone dips away so that the predominant rocks of Wensleydale and Swaledale are of the Yoredale Series.

Being thin the Yoredale limestones do not display the characteristic features of karst scenery. Despite that the alternating bands of limestones, shales and sandstones of the Yoredales produces a very special landscape, particularly in Wensleydale, with its fells rising to over two thousand feet. As the bands of shale erode easily the harder bands of limestone jut out as scars like horizontal steps on the valley sides, making them a very impressive feature of the dale. For example above Hardraw, on the southern flanks of Lovely Seat, a typical limestone scar has rising above it, on the shales, a gentle terraced pasture above which there is a steep, scree-strewn sandstone slope with yet another limestone scar above. On the upper slopes of the limestone appear numerous sink holes down which water flows to emerge as streams at the foot of the limestone band lower down the fell. On the Yoredales the walker encounters heather moors, peat bogs and sphagnum moss. The base of the summit plinths of the Three Peaks are Yoredale rocks lying above the broad Great Scar Limestone terraces.

Alternate layers of rocks of different types across a river bed can produce waterfalls in which Wensleydale reigns supreme. The Yoredales have produced some of the best limestone-capped waterfalls in the dales along becks, which have worn down deep wooded gorges, of which the most dramatic example is Hardraw Scar.

After the Yoredales were laid down vast mountain ranges were created as the land in northern Britain was uplifted. From these mountains great rivers flowed south bringing down huge quantities of grit which led to extensive deltas being created in the Yoredale seas. Such vast accumulations of grit, through its sheer weight, caused the sea floor to be depressed downwards. Eventually the rocks which formed from the grit on the sea floor emerged from the water. These the highest and therefore the youngest of the Carboniferous rocks to be laid down on top of the Yoredales were the Millstone Grits consisting of gritstones, sandstones and shales. Since its deposition much of this gritstone has been worn away to expose the limestone below. However it still survives in places such as on the summits of the high fells of the Yorkshire Dales including those of upper Wensleydale. Bracken and peat moors usually indicate its presence.

The Millstone Grit shales, grits and sandstones are completely different from the limestones. Gritstone is usually rough in texture, dark, pebbly and pervious to water. Like sandstone it produces sandy, gritty, porous, relatively infertile soils. Millstone Grit got its name due to its toughness and usefulness in the production of millstones. In the dales it lies under great swathes of moorland such as that of Great Shunner Fell and Grassington Moor. Such landscapes are often extensive, dark and brooding, offering a stark contrast to the brightness and greater variety of limestone country. Much gritstone is covered with peat and acid soils which have a marked effect on the vegetation. In deep valleys strong grits stand out from the weaker shales to create scars. After the Millstone Grits were laid down above the Yoredales huge earth movements again lifted the sea bed so that more land masses were formed with swamps creating conditions for forests to flourish which in turn became the major coal fields of northern Britain.

In the section below I turn to a subject directly related to the geology of Lovely Seat, namely lead. After a brief look at the lead industry of the dales as a whole I take a detailed look at the Sargill Lead Mine and Smelt Mill, high on the slopes of the fell, concentrating on its ownership, production, buildings and eventual closure.

### *The Sargill Lead Mine*

LEAD mining, like the textile industry, was a highly important source of wealth in the Yorkshire Dales between the beginning of the seventeenth century and the end of the nineteenth. There is some limited evidence of lead mining in the dales dating back to the late Iron Age and to the Romans. However lead mining was really developed by the great landowners and the monasteries. Later mining companies leased the rights to explore the fells in search of lead. This was particularly the case in the Swaledale-Arkengarthdale area and around Grassington and Pateley Bridge in Upper Wharfedale.

The progressive introduction of new methods and techniques led to a very successful industry with many local mines bringing prosperity to their local village. There was even migration of labour into the dales between 1820-57. Between 1830-50 there were two thousand men in the Yorkshire Dales lead industry. Sadly its success only emphasises the severity of its decline, particularly for families, when the veins gave out and cheap foreign imports from Spain sent domestic prices for lead tumbling. With the decline of the industry lead miners seeking work migrated to the coal fields of Durham, the cotton towns and coal fields of

Lancashire whilst others emigrated to America.

Wensleydale had a few lead mines but nothing on the scale of those to be found in Swaledale. In Wensleydale lead mining was not such a crucial factor in terms of employment as it was in Swaledale. In 1881 less than 400 tons of lead were produced in Wensleydale and by 1893 production had ceased altogether. Most of the generally successful lead mines of the dale were found on the north side of the River Ure with just a few on the south side. The mines on the north side of the valley were to be found in four areas - those close to Sargill Beck on the slopes of Lovely Seat, above Woodhall on Askrigg Common, above Carperby and in Apedale where the largest cluster was to be found.

South of the Ure there were no large mines of any significance towards the head of the dale. Small lead mining trials on the fells above Gayle going up to Fleet Moss were tried unsuccessfully. There are a few around Aysgarth and some in the smaller tributary dales such as Waldendale near West Burton and odd isolated ones in Coverdale. So, although the area covered by upper Wensleydale's two thousand foot fells has only one lead mine of any real significance, the Sargill Mine on Lovely Seat, it is of sufficient importance to merit a general description of the lead mining industry in the area to be followed by a more detailed look at the mine and its smelt mill.

To understand how lead came to be located in upper Wensleydale we need to turn our attention to the geology of the area. As I have noted earlier the Carboniferous rocks of the area belong mainly to the Yoredale Series. This comprises layers of rock, up to1,000 feet thick, in which limestones, shales and sandstones in that order repeatedly follow one another. Lying above them are the Millstone Grit sandstones which form the summits of many of the high fells. Of these rocks the limestones and some of the sandstones are the most significant for the miner. This great thickness of strata has faults running through it in some areas which means the displacement or slippage of great blocks of rock. Along such fault lines various minerals, including lead, have been deposited to form veins. In contrast to coal seams which lie parallel to the strata, mineral veins cut through them vertically.

Millions of years ago there was a major movement of molten rock from the depths of the earth into the lower rocks of the overlying strata. As this magma cooled sulphides and other compounds of lead, copper and zinc were squeezed out of it as liquids to fill up the cracks and fissures as minerals in the overlying Carboniferous rocks. Copper deposits have been found along the Yorkshire border with Westmorland (now Cumbria) and around Dent without much in the way of successful mining operations resulting. A similar story can be told in the case of iron ore where the mining of it has never been more than a small localised operation.

Galena or lead sulphide is the ore from which metallic lead is obtained through smelting. Lead veins in the Pennines are usually found between the one thousand and two thousand foot contour lines. Veins varied in width ranging from a few inches to a few feet. Equally a vein may have stretched from a mere few hundred yards to a number of miles long. Very often the quality of a vein and how far it extended was never known for certain until it was first explored and then worked.

The two methods of reaching a vein are by sinking a shaft or by driving in a level in the hillside. In the seventeenth and eighteenth centuries bell-pits were common. A bell-pit was a narrow vertical shaft sunk down to the vein to a depth of about twenty feet or so. At the bottom of the shaft the exposed vein was then dug out in a tunnel for as far as the miner adjudged it safe particularly with regard to the air he had to breathe. It was called a bell pit because it was bell shaped in cross section. As a bell-pit became unsafe a new one would be dug along the vein. As time passed the side of a bell-pit collapsed leaving a depression in the ground. It is these collapsed bell-pits, each one encircled by a ring of spoil, which you can see on the moors today. A number of bell-pits along the line of a vein have been likened to beads on a string. Apart from bell-pits deeper shafts were sunk to depths of nearly 400 to 500 feet. Levels were then driven off into the vein with the ore dug from the roof of the level creating higher and higher workings.

One method of laying bare a vein was by hushing. This involved damming a beck at the top of a hill to form a small reservoir. When the water was eventually released a torrent poured down the hillside scouring the land surface to expose the underlying rock and reveal a vein of lead. Once a vein had been revealed a level would be punched into the hill side. The first few yards of the level would then be arched with masonry. After the sappers had dug out a shaft they were followed by the pick men who, with the aid of picks, hammers, shovels, drills and later gunpowder, broke up the rock and worked the vein. The sappers and the pick men often worked in small teams by candlelight. The material brought out of the mine by the level mouth or the shaft top was called bouse, a mixture of lead ore and other minerals. Sledges, wheelbarrows or wheeled trucks on light rails were used to move the bouse to the bottom of the shaft for hauling up. The bouse then went to walled bays before being taken to the dressing floors to be crushed and the lead ore separated from other minerals to produce a pure lead ore or galena. As the dressing process used extensive water power so dressing floors were often near streams where waterwheels were used.

From the dressing floors the ore went to the smelt mill where about a ton of lead was smelted on each shift. Here the ore was heated to remove sulphur and other impurities which were burned off as gases. An ore hearth might be four to five feet square with a depth of six to eight feet. Behind the hearth bellows, powered by water, force the air through openings in the hearth. Most smelt mills had short masonry flues to carry away noxious fumes generated by the smelting process. Longer flues, usually pointing up the hill side, replaced these short ones in the late nineteenth century. At the end of the hillside flue there was a terminal chimney.

Until the eighteenth century the lead miner was a part-timer who combined his job in the mine with a farm or a smallholding. Later he would become a full-time wage earner as mining became a highly capitalised industry with many technological improvements. Wages were low in the eighteenth century, reaching an average of 6s (30p) per week but by 1870 they had risen to 12s (60p) a week. Generally conditions in the mines were not good with miners working eight hour shifts from 6am to 2pm, 2pm to 10pm and a night shift of 10pm to 6am. Even before he started work the miner had a long journey across the fell in snow, rain and wind. Often he arrived soaking wet and had to use the miners' shop to change into his work clothes whilst his other clothes were dried. The miners' shop was also somewhere where he could lodge if he did not wish to make the daily journey between his home and the mine. For many years all the miners had for light were candles so the introduction of the acetylene lamp, with its brilliant white light, was a major improvement primarily because it was less easily blown out.

Underground the lead miner had to cope with dust and damp not to mention the fumes from the explosives used and the foul air made worse by poor ventilation. Asthma, bronchitis and pneumoconiosis (a form of silicosis) were common. To improve ventilation mining companies tried to create a draught through the length of the mine. Levels were cramped being only six feet high and four feet wide. Accidents were also common primarily due to roof collapse but timber supports lessened the risk.

Even on the surface conditions could be unpleasant particularly in the early days of the industry when miners, working on the dressing floors, were often exposed to the elements. It was difficult to keep warm and dry, particularly in the case of the latter, as the huge amounts of water used in the dressing process inevitably meant workers were often soaked. Such conditions were later ameliorated as employers provided a shed to house the dressing process and to protect the machinery they had so heavily invested in. Smelt mills, to reduce the danger from fumes, were large, airy places. However, with open arches opposite the hearths, the smelter had heat in his face and cold draughts on his back. Smelt mill fumes were so noxious that they poisoned the vegetation, not to mention the sheep and cattle in the vicinity of the mill.

Having taken a brief, general look at the lead industry across the Yorkshire Dales I now concentrate on the only significant lead mine - Sargill - to have been worked on the six 2,000 foot fells of upper Wensleydale. Most of the lead mines on the north side of the valley are situated on the veins which run in a south easterly direction from Swaledale. One such vein is the Glover Gill Vein, (originally called Lover Gill in the nineteenth century), which runs south east across the watershed, just to the east of Lovely Seat, and is linked to a major east-west fault. On the fell tops the vein was buried in peat and difficult to access but on Stags Fell, the southern slope of Lovely Seat, it was located and worked from a few bell pits on the north side of Sargill Beck in an area called Sargill Side. It was exploited from a level which followed the vein a mile underground.

The small, somewhat remote Sargill Lead Mine lies at an altitude of 1,420 feet above sea level and can be reached via an uphill track from the village of Sedbusk. As previously mentioned, following the Norman Conquest, mining rights passed to the lords of the manors who subsequently leased out mining rights. It would appear that the Glover Gill vein which proved to be rich in places was mined by the Whartons before 1715.

The London Lead Company, a Quaker firm, took out a 21 year lease of the mines of Abbotside from an Edward Wortley in 1734. This lease covered the area from Lovely Seat's slopes to the Askrigg boundary and from the watershed down to the River Ure an area which included the site of the Sargill Lead Mine. Records of 1736 and 1738 show that the Stags Fell Mine, later called Sargill, was by then working. The renewal of the 1734 lease took it up to 1776 the year the London Lead Company began to retrench its Yorkshire mining operations in order to concentrate them further north in Alston Moor and Teesdale. Unfortunately there is no information on these forty odd years of the London Lead Company's management of the Sargill Mine as all the company's records were destroyed when it went into liquidation in 1905.

The next lease we hear about on the Sargill Lead Mine was taken out in 1845. The production figures for the years 1852-63 were very low with the highest annual output for smelted lead barely reaching six tons. Raistrick takes the view that these figures seem to imply that if there had been a rich strike at Sargill it must have been before these poor production figures and probably before the 1845 lease.[4] This fits with the rumours that the mine had been rich in the first few years of the early nineteenth century. By 1866 the then current lease of the mine had expired and Lord Wharncliffe, the land owner, was considering advertising the lease unless the current lessees were keen to renew it and make further improvements to the mine.

Prior to 1750 the ore from the Sargill mine went to the London Lead Company's own smelt mill at Grinton; post 1750 it went to the company's own mill at Marrick. In the first part of the nineteenth century the Sargill Mine was leased by a solicitor and a parson the well-known local Winn brothers. At this time Sargill ore was being transported across the fells to be smelted at Summer Lodge. In 1840, to avoid this inconvenience, the brothers decided to build a smelt mill at Sargill.

During the tenure of the lease the performance of the mine was poor. This, according to Ella Pontefract and Marie Hartley, forced the brothers into accepting a Swaledale miner's offer to take over the mine and search for lead.[5] Apparently it was agreed that, should he be successful in his search he would give the brothers an agreed sum, but if he found none he would not pay them anything. At the miner's request the agreement was documented and signed. The miner then proceeded to dam the beck on which the mine stood. When the water was released its scouring action revealed huge quantities of lead making him very wealthy. The Winn brothers were angry but powerless to do anything about this as the miner merely pointed out that it was just 'minin' proper'.

The Sargill mine had bouse compartments with well-flagged floors and, a little way downhill, a dressing floor. The Sargill smelt mill was located a short distance south east of these mine buildings. It had a direct track to the Cogill Head coal pits and had an abundant supply of peat from Black Bank Hags. The building, 55 feet by 28 feet, had a pit in its western section capable of accommodating a 22 foot diameter water wheel and a single bellows. In the slightly larger eastern half of the building there were two hearths on the side away from the beck. A single flue climbed up the steep hillside to culminate in a massive square chimney.

Each of the mine's smelted pigs of lead bore the name Sargill and weighed thirteen stones. The Sargill mine was, in the mid-nineteenth century, largely exploited by 'hushing' but eventually went into decline and closed in 1870. The size of the spoil heaps, the bouse compartments and the dressing floor all appear to justify the building of the smelt mill despite the poor impression the documents for its last decade might give. Its remoteness probably saved its complex of buildings until relatively recently from much of the destruction suffered by other sites such as Blakethwaite at the head of Gunnerside Gill in Swaledale.

It is probably while you are crossing the fells and moors to such wild and remote spots as the Sargill Lead Mine that you are likely to be aware of upper Wensleydale's birds and mammals. In this the final section of my portraits of Wensleydale's high fells the focus falls on their wildlife. Firstly I identify and describe the great birds of prey, followed by the waders, the grouse and many others. From the birds of the air I turn to the mammals on the ground such as the fox, deer and rabbit.

## *Fauna*

BIRDS are part of the scenery of the Yorkshire Dales. To watch the great birds of prey is one of the pleasures of being amongst the high fells of upper Wensleydale. Of such birds of prey one of the most impressive is the buzzard often seen quartering the hills. It patrols the moors using the rising air currents to soar higher and higher into the sky from where it spirals and glides. It is some 20 inches long, has broad rounded wings and makes a loud mewing cry which sounds like 'peeioo' or 'mee-oo'. The female is some two inches longer. The male's plumage is dark brown whilst its underparts are lighter with brown streaks; its legs and feet are yellow. Its nest consists of sticks, leaves and grass which it builds on low bluffs or on hillsides protected by bushes. The size of the dales population of buzzards is heavily dependent on their food supply which consists of mice, rats, young rabbits, worms, large insects, reptiles and occasionally birds. It seizes its prey on the ground by a sudden pounce as it hunts low over open country. Some ornithologists think it lacks the grace of a kestrel. Although it is capable of out flying other birds, such as crows and seagulls who harry it, it has been known to turn and confront them.

The peregrine falcon is by far the greatest hunter of all the birds of prey. Its numbers declined in the 1960s due to pesticide pollution but have since recovered in the high fell country. Its plumage is dark blue-grey - its crown and the sides of its head almost black. It is between fifteen and nineteen inches long and makes a sound like 'kek-kek-kek-kek'. The female is darker and some three inches longer. The peregrine frequents the moors nesting on rocky ledges or a hole in a cliff using little or no material except for a few sticks. For its food it takes birds on the wing, especially pigeons and mammals up to the size of a rabbit. It shows incredible speed and skill in flight swooping down on its prey or overtaking it at speeds of up to 150 mph. Many of its victims are killed before they know what has hit them.

The peregrine is now a protected bird. In the past they have been faced with the threat of either being taken by falconers or shot by gamekeepers to protect the grouse. During the Second World War the government gave orders for them to be destroyed for fear of the threat they might pose to carrier pigeons. As a result the number of nesting pairs in Britain fell from 700 to less than 100 in just ten years.

Yorkshire's most common bird of prey is the kestrel. It can be seen in the high fells hovering in search of its prey. It is some thirteen to fourteen inches long and has narrow, pointed wings of which the tips vibrate when it hangs suspended in the air. Whilst watching for its prey it keeps its head motionless before swooping down on its victims. The male's head, rump and tail are slate-grey or pale blue whilst its back is a light chestnut brown spotted with black. Its underparts are a deep buff colour streaked with black spots whilst the end of its tail is black with a white tip. The female, which is larger than the male, is reddish-brown, striped and has a barred tail. For its nest the kestrel often makes do with the old one of a crow or other bird in a tree or on a rocky ledge. It feeds chiefly on worms, mice, voles, insects and small birds. It has a short high-pitched cry of 'kee kee kee' or 'kew kew'.

Widely seen across the uplands is the smallest of the falcons - the merlin. Its flight is dashing with quick wing beats interspersed with periods of gliding close to the ground. Whilst the male's general plumage is slate blue underneath it is yellowish with black stripes. Its wing tips are darker and it has a black band at the tip of its tail. The female is more of a brown colour with bars across her tail. The male is between ten and a half and thirteen inches long the female one or two inches bigger. Its nest, for which it uses little material, is usually in a slight hollow in the ground in either grass or heather but may also be on a cliff. For its food it takes voles, insects and small moorland birds. Swift in flight it usually catches its victims, such as a pipit or a lark, on the wing. Its cry is a sort of chattering 'quik-ik-ik-ik'. To be certain of seeing a peregrine or a merlin it helps to know their specific haunts.

The raven too may be seen in upper Wensleydale amongst the crags and scars. Usually a pair are sighted on their own but sometimes a flock may be seen for foraging and roosting purposes. At 25 inches long it is the largest member of the crow family. It is easily distinguished from the carrion crow by its much larger size, stouter bill, and narrower wings. Its nest, built on cliff ledges or rocks, consists of twigs with a lining of grass and wool. The raven lives on carrion, small animals such as rabbits, small birds, eggs, reptiles, insects, worms and grain. It has powerful wing beats and is a very agile flier often performing aerobatics. Like other birds of prey it has suffered persecution. It makes a rather croaky, guttural noise like a grunt, such as a pig would make, which sounds like 'pruk pruk'.

The short-eared owl can be seen over the moors in summer before it migrates to lower ground in the winter. It is fifteen inches long and has very short tufts ('ears') compared with those of the long-eared owl. These tufts are raised when the bird is disturbed. It should be pointed out that, these feathery tufts have nothing to do with the bird's real ears which, like other birds, are concealed by its feathers on the sides of its head. Its plumage and underparts are a buff colour with dark brown stripes and bars. However it often looks quite pale when viewed from a distance. The short-eared owl hunts at dusk but may also be seen hunting by day usually for voles, small birds, beetles and mice. If its nest, which is usually on the ground in heather or sedge, is threatened it utters a barking 'kwowk'. Its song sounds like a low-pitched 'boo-boo-boo-boo'.

Upper Wensleydale benefits from the fact that several wading birds move up to the high moors and fells to breed especially in areas which are likely to be largely undisturbed. One such is the golden plover with its resplendent summer plumage of spotted gold and black with a white border. Its under parts, along with its cheeks and chin, are generally a dusky colour whilst its belly is black. In winter its plumage takes on a less golden appearance. It is eleven inches long and nests on the ground in peat hags and in rough, coarse grass well protected by tussocks. The golden plover feeds on insects, worms, berries, seeds, snails and grasses. Its rather sad, plaintiff, soulful call can be heard from March to September carrying across the moors and sounding like 'too-ee' or 'too-roo, too-roo.' It flies rapidly for short distances on its long narrow wings before alighting on the ground.

The golden plover can be seen on the fell tops although its plumage may make it difficult to spot against the moorland background. Although regarded as rare there are now some several thousand breeding pairs in Yorkshire alone. The golden plover benefits from heather burning in late winter as it likes to nest in such areas where the vegetation is short having been cut back.

Another wader, the dunlin, is seen on the high moors and pastures. One of our most common wading birds its plumage, in winter, is generally grey with white underparts. In summer its plumage is red-brown or chestnut with a large black patch on its lower breast and black streaks on its head and upper parts. It likes to nest on the moor near standing water where it swims as well as wades in search of its food. It is seven inches long, lives on insects, larvae and worms and has a song like a shrill warble.

The largest wader, the curlew, has a five inch long curved bill and distinctive, streaky brown, patterned plumage. It is to be seen over the highest pastures and moors where it nests in a small clump of grass on the ground. It is a fairly large bird measuring some 22-23 inches. It makes its presence known from March to August arriving soon after the peewits. The curved bill is ideal for seeking out its food which consists of worms, frogs, berries and insects. After defining their territories they can be seen making dramatic aerial sweeps almost at ground level. After soaring skywards they level out and float gently back to the ground. During the summer months you can hear it calling mournfully over the moors 'curlwee' or 'crooee, crooee, croee' both by day and by night.

Another familiar wader to the high pastures in the summer is the redshank. It is eleven inches in length and has a long bill and long orange-red legs. It has a white rump with a broad white band along the edge of its wings. Its winter plumage is greyish-brown above and white below. It is a very watchful, alert bird difficult to get close to and is very protective of its chicks. It makes a nest of grass concealed amongst the herbage and makes a sound like 'tu-yu-yu' or 't'keep, t'keep'. It eats insects, worms, spiders, leaves, grasses, birds, seeds and berries.

After deserting the high ground for much of the winter the lapwing, by February, is the first of the waders to return to its breeding grounds in the hills. In the summer, when caught in strong sunlight, the bird's glossy plumage, turns dark green which gives it its alternative name - green plover. It is also known as peewit after its cry. The male, which is twelve inches long, has a longer, spikier head crest than the female. The lapwing haunts the pastures and the lower moorland slopes where it nests in a slight depression in the ground. Sadly, it is often robbed of its eggs by crows, gulls and stoats. It likes boggy areas as feeding grounds for its chicks where it finds lots of insects, worms, spiders and vegetable matter. Because it eats all kinds of harmful insects and their larvae it is considered one of our most useful birds.

The male lapwing in defining its territory and fending off rivals swoops, twists and plunges through the air often pulling out of its dive aerobatically. It beats its wings slowly rolling from side to side as it rises then dives, twisting and turning before landing. If you approach its nest the cock bird beats its broad black-tipped wings to produce a drumming sound. If the eggs have hatched the parents fly with wailing calls and occasionally dive with stiffened wings. It makes the sound 'pee-wit' and has a long whistling note.

The snipe can be heard calling across the moors and high pastures from March to September. It has a patterned plumage of various dark and light brown shades with distinctive stripes on its head and back. Its nest of grass is usually hidden in rushes and it makes a drumming sound with its wings and tail. Between ten and eleven inches long the snipe probes for worms, insects, woodlice and vegetable matter. It spends most of the day resting in the cover of coarse vegetation. The male snipe in protecting its territory makes a sound like 'chip-per, chip-per, chip-per'. In spring when circling high above its nest it dives and produces a sort of bleating sound. One of its flight movements is to zig-zag upwards.

The red grouse, a sub-species of the willow grouse of North America and Scandinavia, is a resident of northern England living on the high heather moorlands. It has a red comb over its eyes whilst its plumage is a shiny, dark, mottled red-brown with blackish wing tips and tail. In winter its stubby legs are covered by white feathers. The male is fifteen inches long, the female smaller and less dark. The red grouse nests on the ground amongst the heather and feeds on heather, bilberry, crowberry, caterpillars and other insects. It has a short very powerful bill which enables it to pluck the fibrous heather which it digests through its strong gut. It is virtually dependent on heather for food and shelter and only leaves the moors when they are blanketed in deep snow. Its thick plumage provides good protection from the severe cold and wet conditions.

The male grouse hides in the heather for most of the time but in spring it is noisy and demonstrative. It often flies into the air before descending with fast-beating wings and tail widespread onto a clump of heather. Its crowning call sounds like 'kowa, kowa, kowa' and ' gobak, gobak'. In March the cocks fight but in April when the birds are paired and the female is sitting on her eggs a measure of peace occurs. The red grouse, the most individualistic of moorland birds, along with the carrion crow and the wren is virtually the only species of bird on the moors in midwinter. Its call often gives away its position to its main predators the crow and the fox.

The black grouse is also seen on the moors and in the plantations of the Yorkshire Dales. The male is 21 inches long and has a glossy, black plumage with a white bar on its wing and white under its tail. The female is sixteen inches long and has mottled brown plumage. The black grouse nests on the ground amongst the heather and in plantations living off the same food as the red grouse. The ritual of 'lekking' begins in January or February when the males gather on traditional mating sites to await the arrival of the females. The black grouse likes to display its tail feathers when involved in fighting and calling. At the leck the grouse make hissing, cooing, gobbling and babbling sounds.

In addition to the birds of prey, the waders and the grouse, other birds you might see are the ring ouzel, meadow pipit, wheatear, skylark, swift and the swallow. The ring ouzel is fairly common on the hills, moors and mountains when it appears as a summer visitor between April and October. Apart from a white band on the ring ouzel's throat it bears a close resemblance to the blackbird. The female's plumage is a lighter colour with the whitish edging to the feathers giving a dappled appearance. In addition her white throat band has a brown tinge. Its nest is made of grasses and twigs and found usually beneath a clump of heather or grass or in rocks and crevices. It is nine to ten inches long and eats worms, insects, berries, fruit, snails, slugs and grubs. It is known to visit the limestone pavement areas and when seen it is usually gliding silently over the terrain. The ouzel has a high whistle but when it sings its song is short and clear sounding like 'tac-tac-tac' or 'chack-chack-chack' or 'bequick, bequick, bequick'.

The meadow pipit is a small, dainty, little bird whose habitat ranges from the high fells to the lowest pastures. Its is seen around peat bogs, rough grassland and heather moors. It is just over five inches long and has a streaky colour with brown buff stripes. Its neat nest is made of dried grass usually lined with wool and well hidden in the heather or grass at the edge of the moor. It does not hop but has a quick, agile, distinctive run and walk. It eats worms, spiders and seeds but spends much of its time looking for insects on the ground. The male soars steeply making the repetitive sound of 'peep, peep'. As it comes down with its tail up and its stiffened wings spread out it makes a clicking, swishing noise like 'pe-pe-pe-pe-pe-pe'. It also has a more quiet note, when walking along the ground, which sounds like 'pipit'.

The wheatear is an attractive summer visitor to the moors and hillsides. It is only five inches long but is easily distinguished by the sight of its striking white rump as it moves rapidly near the ground. It has pale grey plumage above and cream underneath. Its wings, the tip of its tail and its eye surrounds are virtually black. The female's plumage is more brown in colour but she too has a prominent white rump. For its nest it often chooses an old rabbit hole but is equally happy to nest under a boulder or in a hole in a dry stone wall. It eats chiefly insects, centipedes and spiders and like the lapwing is useful in destroying pests. It makes a noise like 'chack, chack' or 'weet-chack-chack'. It tends to hop from rock to rock or along wall tops.

The skylark returns to all but the higher fells and moors by February. It is seven inches long and its plumage is a striped brown with white on its tail feathers. When it gets excited its brown crest is raised. Its nest is made of dried grass and hidden amongst the tussocks on the moorland edge where it lives mostly on seeds, worms and insects. It has a beautiful and joyful song which can last up to five minutes as it hovers on the wing high in the sky. On the ground it is seen walking or running - it does not hop.

Also seen over the uplands of the Yorkshire Dales between April and October, far from their nesting sites in or around buildings, are the swift and the swallow. The swift's plumage is dark brown but with a light patch on its chin. A small bird, only six and a half inches long, it has long, narrow, curved wings. Up aloft it twists and glides in easy movements with its wings rigid or with a few rapid beats. It catches insects on the wing and makes a high pitched screaming 'chee-ree- eee'.

The swallow is one of our most loved summer visitors. Its plumage is shiny blue on its back and wings and it has a long forked tail. Forehead and throat are a dark chestnut with the throat also having a dark blue band below it. It is seen gliding low over open country. At seven and a half inches long it nests on beams and ledges and eats mainly flies caught on the wing. As well as making a sound like a 't-weet' it utters a twittering song when in flight. Let us also not forget the starlings who after breeding, flock in large numbers towards the moors.

Other birds to be seen, on upper Wensleydale's hills are those associated with becks, streams, lakes and rocky stretches of rivers, such as the dipper, sandpiper, oyster catcher, kingfisher, heron and black-headed gull. The dipper has a dark brown head, white throat and breast and dark grey plumage on its back. Its belly is a chestnut colour merging into black. Its is seven inches long and eats aquatic insects, beetles, worms, tadpoles and small fish. It is found on becks, lakes and rivers where it builds a nest of moss and leaves in a hole in a rock or riverbank. It bobs up and down on rocks looking for food and even dives and swims under water using its wings. It is even known to walk under water looking for food under stones. It makes a noise like 'zit, zit, zit' - its song is a sweet, rippling warble.

The sandpiper is a small restless wader - a summer visitor between April and October. It breeds in the hills of northern England and is to be seen by trout streams. It is just over seven inches long, has olive brown plumage on its upper parts and breast and is white underneath. It eats insects and some vegetable matter and makes a repeated shrill, high 'peep' or 'twee' sound. When standing it tends to nod its head and move its tail end up and down. Its nest is made of grass and built usually near water and concealed in the vegetation.

The oyster catcher like many other wading birds visits the hills each spring. Its plumage is glossy black on its head, upper breast and back whilst its under parts are white. It has a bar on its wing and across the base of its tail whilst in winter it has a white band across its throat. It has pink legs and a long, orange-red bill which attracts attention. It is seventeen inches long, feeds on worms and insects and nests on the ground. It makes a 'peet, peet' or a 'kleep, kleep' sound and also has a trilling whistle.

Near small tarns on the fells, where it breeds in large numbers, you are likely to see the black-headed gull, the commonest of our gulls on inland waters. In spring and summer it has a dark brown almost black head. Its plumage is light grey but it is easily recognised by its deep red bill and legs together with a its white-edged wings. It is fourteen to fifteen inches long and eats carrion, harmful insects, worms and seeds. Its nest is usually made of sticks and grass in a huge colony near a tarn or in a marshy area. It has a particularly raucous scream which sounds like 'keee-ya'.

The heron is an aesthetically pleasing water bird with its long neck, prominent beak and thin wedged-shaped head. It can often be seen standing quite still on a stone for long periods in becks, rivers and lakes looking for its food which consists of fish, eels, water voles, insects, frogs and young waterfowl. When standing it usually has its head and long neck sunk on its shoulders which it opens out when it stalks fish. It is a large bird, some three feet long, with long grey wings with dark tips which beat unusually slowly and sluggishly. Its nest, made of sticks, is large and built usually in a tree as part of a heronry. It makes a deep resonant 'croak' and a loud 'frank' when in flight. If disturbed it will take flight, drawing in its head and neck and trailing its legs behind as it gains height.

The kingfisher is six and a half inches long and has intense, bright blue upper parts with a greenish sheen on its head and wings. The under parts and around its ears are chestnut-red whilst its chin and a patch on each side of its neck are white. It frequents quiet lakes, rivers and becks nesting in holes in river banks and feeding on water insects, tadpoles and small fish which it dives for. Its usual note is a loud shrill 'chee' or 'chi-kee' repeated two or three times plus a warbling song.

Meadows give way to pastures, the resort of cattle and the ubiquitous sheep. The cattle are predominantly Friesian and the sheep are mainly

Swaledales and Dalesbred. Fallow and roe deer may also be seen on the fell sides but only fleetingly when they have broken from the shelter of their forest cover. Rabbits too are frequently seen on the lower slopes of the fells as is the brown hare. The latter is distinguished from the rabbit by its larger size and the black tips to its long ears. Both rabbits and hares enjoy open farmland and are well camouflaged being able to stay very still. The fox too may be glimpsed on the fell sides searching for carrion although it is rarely seen in daylight unless disturbed. The dog fox barks at night in late January or early February making his presence known during the mating season. Due to its predatory nature the fox population is kept down in upper Wensleydale by foot hounds.

Larger than the weasel a few stoats live on the exposed tops where they feed on meadow pipits and on the few voles which live there. Field voles, on the other hand, tend to thrive more on the grass of the upland pastures whilst finding shelter in burrows hidden in the heather or bilberry tussocks. Moles are common on the meadows and pastures often destroying the grass with their digging. Badgers have their sets in quiet woodland and gills and, when not disturbed by humans, tend to emerge in the last hours of daylight. Spring, when a badger has her cubs in attendance, is a particularly good time to watch them. Badgers tend to have a cleanliness habit which results in them removing old bracken from their setts and replacing it with new. Sadly, today, badgers are mostly seen on the side of moorland roads having been killed by passing vehicles.

The adder lives on the moors but poses little or no threat to humans for the very good reason that you are very unlikely to see one. It is our only poisonous species of snake with a black zig-zag on its back. In a dry spell it emerges from an afforested area to lie on boggy ground. The common lizard may be seen either sunning itself on the dazzling white surface of a clint or moving rapidly into the safety of a gryke. Otters are rare in the Yorkshire Dales but may be seen on certain stretches of the main rivers such as the Ure. Trout and grayling are to be found in the rivers and becks with roach and bream also fairly common.

Amongst the heather and bilberry, in May and June, are to be found colonies of the green harestreak butterfly. The undersides of its wings are a brilliant green which tone in with the foliage. The fairly common meadow brown butterfly is to be seen feeding on various grasses. The skipper butterfly and the ringlet butterfly may be seen fluttering amongst the wild flowers of the pastures. The impressive emperor moth can also be seen on the heather moors flitting above the tussocks. So too can the green-veined white moth which is the most common white butterfly on high ground. The brightly coloured small copper butterfly lives both on the moors and in the valley.

With Lovely Seat I have completed the portraits of the six 2,000 foot fells of upper Wensleydale. For those who feel the urge to walk over them I have added a postscript to the main text setting out the basic details of the route for a walk over each of them. Alternatively for those who wish to drive I have given details of a motor tour through the area. Whether walking or driving I hope the beauty and grandeur of upper Wensleydale will live long in the memory.

# 7
# POSTSCRIPT

To conclude this portrait of upper Wensleydale I have included in this postscript a walk over each of its six 2,000 foot fells. As the information provided gives only a basic outline of the route of each walk it is essential that the walker should use the Ordnance Survey maps 1:25,000 (2.5 inch to 1 mile) of the area for more specific details and to clarify the route.

For the motor tour the route is clearly defined but if drivers require more details they should use a good road atlas of the area.

## *A circuit of Wether Fell*

FROM Burtersett village take the track up Wether Fell to follow it round the fell's northern and western edges to join the Cam High Road. From this junction Drumaldrace, Wether Fell's highest point, can be reached by a short climb up the grassy slope on the left. From the summit return to the Cam High Road and continue downhill in the direction of Bainbridge. Take the third path on the left, opposite Green Scar, to go down the hill back to Burtersett.
Length: approx. five miles.

## *Dodd Fell and the Pennine Way*

FROM the village of Gayle follow the lanes to go via High Bands to join the Cam Road. Turn left to follow this track uphill across the open pastures. Shortly after passing a conifer plantation on the right the track merges with the Pennine Way coming in on the left. The Pennine Way then passes a second plantation to travel along a level terrace, high above Snaizeholmedale, to Kidhow Gate.

On the return from Kidhow Gate the trig point on the summit of Dodd Fell can be reached by climbing the fellside, on the right of the track, at any point in the first mile. After visiting the summit return to the Pennine Way to continue to the junction of the two tracks met on the outward journey. Continue along the right-hand path (the Pennine Way) to go over the slopes of Ten End whose summit is just off to the right. Follow the Pennine Way down into Gayle via Gaudy Lane. Length: approx.ten miles.

### *Around Great Knoutberry Hill*

START the walk a short distance above Dent Station where the green track known as the Driving Road leaves the metalled Galloway Gate. Follow the green track for a short distance to reach a sign and a path on the left. Follow this path to reach the summit of Great Knoutberry Hill. From the summit continue along the same path by the wall down the hill to rejoin the green track. Turn right and follow the track back to its junction with the Galloway Gate.
Length: approx. five miles.

### *Lunds Fell and Lady Anne Clifford's Way*

START the walk west of the village of Appersett at the junction of the road to Cotterdale with the A684. A few yards along the Cotterdale road take the path on the left alongside a wall to go up the hill past a large lime kiln. At the top follow the track known as Lady Anne Clifford's Way as far as High Dike. From here turn right to follow a path across the open moor to where two fences coming up from the south meet to form a point. From here strike north across the pathless moor for about one and a half miles to reach the trig point on Sails, the summit of Lunds Fell. On leaving the summit return to the departure point on the path where the two fences meet to continue eastwards through a large conifer plantation down into Cotterdale village. From there follow the road out of the village back to the start point.
Length: approx.ten miles.

### *Great Shunner Fell and Cotterdale*

FROM Hardraw village follow the Pennine Way to the summit of Great Shunner Fell. On the return take the right-hand path marked Cotterdale to go down the fellside through a large conifer plantation to the village of Cotterdale. From the village follow the gently ascending path on the left-hand side of the beck to eventually rejoin the Pennine Way which is then followed down into Hardraw.
Length: approx. thirteen miles.

### *Lovely Seat*

FROM the village of Sedbusk, just to the north of Hawes, take the track called Shutt Lane up the fellside. Look for a stile on the left from which a sunken track leads uphill. Follow this track around the eastern end of

the cliffs of the escarpment on your left to go across the broad plateau of Stags Fell to join the Buttertubs road. Turn right and follow this road for about three quarters of a mile from where the cairned summit of Lovely Seat can be seen, a short distance from the road, on the right. Strike across the moor to reach the summit. On leaving the summit return to the Buttertubs road to follow it back to Sedbusk via Simonstone. Alternatively after leaving the summit and joining the Buttertubs road look for a cattle grid on the way down. At the latter climb up the fell on the left to walk along High Clints, the highest of Stags Fell's escarpments, overlooking Hawes. Follow the escarpment eastwards curving round with it until you see the outward path going down to Sedbusk. Join it to reach the village.
Length: approx. eight and a half miles.

### *Motor tour*

FROM Hawes take the road towards Hardraw to follow the Buttertubs road to Thwaite in Swaledale. En route look out for the sprawling bulk of Great Shunner Fell, the Buttertubs potholes and Lovely Seat above the deep ravine in which Cliff Beck flows. From Thwaite take the Kirkby Stephen road via Keld to cross the moors to Nateby. Here turn left to go up Mallerstang noting on the left the long ridge on which the rounded hump of Lunds Fell, with its highest point Sails, can be seen.

At the Moorcock Inn turn right along the A684 for a short distance before taking the first left up the Galloway Gate. From this road look out on your left for Garsdale Station, Great Knoutberry Hill, the Driving Road and Dent Station. At Lea Yeat in Dentdale turn left to go past Artengill Viaduct, Dent Head Viaduct and Wold Fell all on the left, to join the Hawes-Ingleton road. Here turn left to go through Widdale to reach Hawes noting on the left the long ridge of Widdale Fell. Just before the centre of Hawes turn right to follow the road to Gayle village. From here take Beggarman's Road to its summit on Fleet Moss where Wether Fell can be seen on the left and Dodd Fell on the right. From the summit of the road take the gated metalled road on the right to reach Kidhow Gate. This is a no through road and marks the end of the tour. Rejoin Beggarman's Road to return to Hawes.
Length: approx. 55 miles.

## Source Notes

Please note that in each chapter a numbered source may cover more than one reference to that particular book.


### *Chapter 1, Wensleydale*

1. Stephenson, Tom, *The Pennine Way*, HMSO/Countryside Commission, 2nd Edition, 1980.

### *Chapter 2, Wether Fell*

1. Clayton, Phil, *On High Yorkshire Hills, Exploring the Two Thousand Footers*, Dalesman, 1993.
2. Bogg, Edmund, *Richmondshire*, Elliot Stock, 1908.
3. Gambles, Robert, *Yorkshire Dales Place-Names*, Dalesman, 1995.
4. Hartley, Marie, & Ingleby, Joan, *Yorkshire Village*, J.M.Dent, 1953.
5. Gunn, Peter, *The Yorkshire Dales, Landscape with Figures*, Century Publishing,1984.

### *Chapter 3, Dodd Fell*

1. Gambles, Robert, *Yorkshire Dales Place-Names*, Dalesman, 1995.
2. Clayton, Phil, *On High Yorkshire Hills, Exploring the Two Thousand Footers*, Dalesman, 1993.
3. Brown, A.J, *Broad Acres*, Country Life, 1948.
4. Raistrick, Arthur, *Old Yorkshire Dales*, Pan, 1967.
5. Stephenson, T, *The Pennine Way*, HMSO/Countryside Commission, 2nd Ed., 1980.
6. Waal, Gerald C. de, *Going Dutch, The Pennine Way*, Gedewe, Holland, 1987.
7. Greaves, Van, *Discovering the Pennines*, Crowood Press, 1991.
8. Speight, Harry, *Romantic Richmondshire*, Elliot Stock, 1897.
9. Anon., *Man in the Moon,* Hawes Weather Lore (poem).

### *Chapter 4, Great Knoutberry Hill*

1. Gambles, Robert, *Yorkshire Dales Place-Names*, Dalesman, 1995.
2. Pontefract, Ella & Hartley, Marie, *Wensleydale,* J.M.Dent, 1936.
3. Bogg, Edmund, *Richmondshire,* Elliot Stock, 1908.
4. Wright, Geoffrey, *Roads and Trackways of The Yorkshire Dales,* Guild Publishing/Moorland Publishing Company Ltd., 1985.
5. Duerden, Norman, *Portrait of the Dales,* Robert Hale Limited, 1978.

6. Mitchell, W. R., *Dent, The Highest Mainline Station in England,* Castleberg, 1995.

7. Hallas, Christine, *The Wensleydale Railway,* Dalesman Books, 1984.

8. Lofthouse, Jessica, *Off to the Dales,* Robert Hale Limited, 1950.

### Chapter 5, Lunds Fell

1. Pontefract, Ella and Hartley, Marie, *Wensleydale,* J. M. Dent & Sons, 1936.

2. Harding, Mike, *Walking The Dales,* Michael Joseph, 1986.

3. Lund, Geoff, Muir, Richard and Colbeck, Maurice, *Yorkshire Dales Stonewaller,* Dalesman Books, 1992.

4. Hallas, Christine, *Rural Responses to Industrialisation. The North Yorkshire Pennines 1790-1914,* Peter Lang, 1999.

### Chapter 6, Great Shunner Fell

1. Gambles, Robert, *Yorkshire Dales Place-Names,* Dalesman, 1995.

2. Clayton, Phil, *On High Yorkshire Hills, Exploring the Two Thousand Footers,* Dalesman, 1993.

3. Pontefract, Ella, & Hartley, Marie, *Swaledale,* 2nd Ed., J. M. Dent, 1944.

4. Lofthouse, Jessica, *Off to the Dales,* Robert Hale Limited, 1950.

5. Bogg, Edmund, *Richmondshire,* Elliot Stock, 1908.

6. Pontefract, Ella, & Hartley, Marie, *Wensleydale,* J. M. Dent, 1936.

7. Speakman, Colin, *Walking in the Yorkshire Dales,* Robert Hale Ltd, 1982.

8. Gambles, Robert, *Yorkshire Dales Place-Names,* Dalesman, 1995.

9. Barker, W. G. M. James, *The Three Days of Wensleydale,* Charles Dolman, 1854.

10. Chiang, Yee, *The Silent Traveller in the Yorkshire Dales,* Methuen, 1941.

11. Waltham, Tony, *Yorkshire Dales National Park,* Webb & Bower (Michael Joseph), 1987.

12. Buckrose, J. E., *Rambles in the North Yorkshire Dales,* Mills & Boon, 1913.

13. Harding, Mike, *Walking the Dales,* Michael Joseph, 1986.

### Chapter 7, Lovely Seat

1. Speight, Harry, *Romantic Richmondshire,* Elliot Stock, 1897.

2. Clayton, Phil, *On High Yorkshire Hills, Exploring the Two Thousand Footers,* Dalesman, 1993.

3. Bogg, Edmund, *Richmondshire,* Elliot Stock, 1908.

4. Raistrick, Arthur, *The Lead Industry of Wensleydale and Swaledale, Volume 2, The Smelting Mills,* Moorland Publishing Company, 1975.

5. Pontefract, Ella, & Hartley, Marie, *Wensleydale,* J. M. Dent, 1936.